Friday Night Warriors

Friday Night Warriors: The Legacy of Ganado Indians Football

Clint Hensley and Chris Doelle

Friday Night Warriors: The Legacy of Ganado Indians Football
1st Edition
Lone Star Gridiron Press
Fresh Media Works
Copyright 2025
ISBN 979-8-9997575-0-0

CONTENTS

FOREWORD

ACKNOWLEDGMENTS

Chapter 1 - **In The Beginning**

Chapter 2 - **The Resurrection of a Program**

Chapter 3 - **The Making of a Champion**

Chapter 4 - **The Glory Years**

Chapter 5 - **Protecting the Tradition**

Chapter 6 - **Rebuilding**

Chapter 7 - **Back to the Playoffs: The Second Run**

Chapter 8 - **Growing Pains**

Chapter 9 - **New Coach, New System, and a New Beginning**

Chapter 10 - **The Playoff Tradition Returns: The Third Run**

Chapter 11 - **Haters Tour: Going Beyond Expectations**

Chapter 12 - **Champions at Last**

AFTERWORD

INDEX

RESOURCES

PHOTOS

AUTHORS PAGE

FOREWORD

There is a unique and powerful atmosphere that surrounds Friday nights in the fall across the state of Texas, especially when it comes to high school football. The excitement, tradition, and community spirit that fill the air are difficult to fully capture in words. Texas high school football is more than just a sport - it is often described as a way of life, almost like a religion. Each summer, fans eagerly await the release of *Dave Campbell's Texas Football Magazine*, often referred to as "the Texas bible," as well as rankings, district predictions, and comprehensive previews of every high school and college football team across the state by sites like *Lone Star Gridiron*, *MaxPreps* and more. On game nights, entire towns come together, seemingly shutting down to support their local team. The energy in the stadium is electric - the high school band plays spirited tunes, cheerleaders keep the crowd energized, and fans passionately cheer from the stands. The football season is long and demanding, beginning in the intense August heat and, for only a select few elite teams, ending in the cold of December. For most teams, the journey is tough and the competition fierce, but the ultimate goal remains the same: to compete for a state championship. Only a few reach this pinnacle, but every team dreams of being among the greats who do.

Long before Friday nights under the lights became Ganado's most cherished ritual, this fertile stretch of land was home to the Karankawa people - skilled navigators, hunters, and fierce protectors of their homelands. A gentle and caring tribe, when their traditions of community, and ceremony were threatened, the Karankawa became fierce warriors in the defense of their territory. This laid the groundwork for a town that today still rallies around its own line of guardians: the Ganado Indians football team. As generations have passed, that same spirit of unity and resilience flows into every Friday-night huddle.

This story centers on that football program in Ganado, Texas - a place where the love and support for their football team runs deep throughout the entire community. To truly understand what Ganado Indian football means, one must experience it firsthand, as the unity and passion from the town are unlike anything else. I (Clint Hensley) have followed the program closely since 1993, beginning at the age of 11, witnessing the transformation of a team with little football history into a respected and successful program. Over the years, I have seen the highs and lows of Ganado football - the victories, the defeats, the rises, the setbacks, and ultimately, the historic triumph of winning the school's first-ever state championship on December 19, 2024.

While not a star athlete, I played some football during school and understood the dedication, effort, and heart that the sport demands. Fueled by a deep love for the game, I have faithfully attended Friday night games and playoff matchups for decades. This story will provide a comprehensive look at Ganado's football history, with particular focus on the seasons since 1995. It is based on personal experience, memories, and a wealth of collected information and resources. The goal is to share and celebrate the journey of the Ganado Indians - from humble beginnings to championship glory - through a detailed and heartfelt narrative.

It was on Friday, September 17, 1993, when I attended my very first Ganado Indians football game - a home opener against the Pettus Eagles, which Ganado won in a close 12-7 contest. That night sparked a lifelong passion for Ganado football. At the time, I was in fifth grade and had not shown much interest in sports before, but that season marked a turning point. It was also a memorable year filled with fond memories of school spirit and influential teachers. My homeroom teacher was the late Mr. Julius Tupa, a beloved figure in the school and community, who also served as my Cub Scout Master. His wife, Lou Ann, had previously taught me in third grade. Another memorable teacher was Mrs. Clara Conner, who played a key role in fostering school pride by teaching students the Alma Mater and Fight Song. Pep rallies were a highlight of the season, often held in the auditorium or gym, and filled with excitement. One especially vivid memory was a pep rally before a game against the St. Joseph Flyers from Victoria, where students were allowed to throw paper airplanes from the bleachers onto the gym floor in a playful act of team spirit. That year, the high school band also boosted morale by marching through the school halls before pep rallies, stopping at various points to play the fight song - one of which was in front of the fifth-grade classrooms, including Mrs. Conner's, where I happened to be. That 1993 season marked the beginning of countless cherished memories for me, who would go on to become a dedicated fan of Ganado football. Over the years, they witnessed many seasons of ups and downs, but none more rewarding than the unforgettable three-overtime victory in 2024 that earned Ganado its first-ever state football championship. These experiences, from humble beginnings to championship glory, remain treasured, and now I am proud to share this story - a journey through the heart of Ganado football.

Chris Doelle's connection with the Ganado Indians goes back more than a decade before and it was through a very different lens. Chris played football in the early 80's for the rival, Industrial Cobras. Through their eyes, a season could end 1-9 and seem to the outside world like a total failure. But, if that one win was against Ganado, all was right in the world. This rivalry was fierce between the two communities across all sports, but football especially. It was only after Texas high school football as a whole became his career, and maturity allowed him to look past those teenage passions, that he began to follow and actively support the Ganado Indians - and in fact, any team that plays with passion, good sportsmanship and an undeniable work ethic.

ACKNOWLEDGMENTS

These are those that are being acknowledged for making this all happen. Thank you for your time as either a coach, teacher, media, supporter, loyal fan or friend.

Monte Althaus, Zachary Andel, Brent Bennett, Bobby Bothe, Andy Bridges, Michael Brooks, Heath Bures, Jaime Bures, Jayme Bures, Joey Bures, Matthew Bures, Ruben Castillo, Liam Carruthers, Jason Chambless, Clara Conner, Josh Ervin, Mike Forman, Clay Green, David Grewe, Noe Guerrero, Clayton Hayden, Craig Hayden, Brian Hicks, B.J. Hicks, Dustin Hicks, Doug Holt, John Hurt, Shelby Hurt, Edmund Kacer, Nathan Kaspar, Henry Keen, Ike Kuehn, Mike Labay, Kara McCain, Father Michael Lyons, Jody Menely, Roland Orsak, Susie Pape, Jose Pena, Mike Rabe, Joey Rosalez, Dr. Jonathan Szymanski, Donnie Tegeler, Trey Thedford, Jimmy Thompson, Jarrett Vick, Keith Wright

This book is also dedicated to all Ganado alumni, fans and Ganado faithful and all of those that have gone before us.

Chapter 1

In The Beginning

The Ganado football program stands on the verge of a major milestone as it approaches its 100th year. Established in 1928, the program had little success in its early decades. Before the 1995 season, Ganado had made only six playoff appearances - in 1939, 1942, 1943, 1959, 1967, and 1982 - with just a single playoff victory, a 12-7 win over Sugar Land in 1942. However, due to World War II, teams of Ganado's size did not advance further after that win. While Ganado recorded 24 winning seasons before 1995, the structure of postseason play was different at that time. Only district champions advanced to the playoffs, unlike the current format where four teams from each district qualify. This often-left Ganado on the outside looking in, even during strong seasons, sometimes as district runner-up or as victims of tough-luck scenarios.

The program began humbly in 1928 under head coach W.B. Connell, with a 1-4 record in its inaugural season. Though the exact opponent of the school's first win is unknown, the team suffered notable losses that year, including defeats to Edna (54-0), Port Lavaca (12-0), and Victoria (33-0). The following years proved just as difficult. In 1929, the Indians finished 0-4, including a lopsided 65-0 loss to Bay City. The 1930 season was particularly harsh, with the team going 0-7 and enduring three of the worst losses in school history: 80-0 to Edna, 79-0 to Victoria, and 73-0 to Port Lavaca - records that still stand. Ganado's struggles continued in 1931 with an 0-8 season under coach Mac McFarland.

The tide began to turn in 1932 under coach J.C. Tomlinson, when the team posted a 1-7-1 record, earning its only win of the season in a 12-0 victory over Port Lavaca - an important moment of redemption. In 1933, under new coach Fred Walker, only one game was recorded - a loss, bringing little clarity to that year. However, the team showed improvement in 1934 with a 2-4-3 record, and in 1935, Ganado finally had a breakthrough season, finishing 8-1 in Walker's final year, though they did not qualify for the playoffs. In 1936, the Indians continued their upward trend with an 8-2 season under John Ledbetter, but once again, the playoff format denied them a postseason berth. These early years were filled with challenges, but they laid the foundation for a program that would steadily evolve. From its difficult beginnings to the cusp of a century of football, Ganado's journey reflects resilience and growth, setting the stage for greater achievements in the decades to come.

One of the earliest and most distinguished alumni from Ganado High School to achieve success at the collegiate and professional levels was the legendary Gil Steinke, who graduated in 1937. Born in 1919 in Brenham, Texas, Steinke went on to attend Texas College of Arts and Industries - later known as Texas A&I University and now Texas A&M University–Kingsville - where he played as a halfback from 1938 to 1941. He led the team in rushing for three consecutive seasons and established himself as a standout athlete. During World War II, Steinke served honorably in the U.S. Navy, attaining the rank of lieutenant. In 1945, he married Mary Anthony Houston, and together they had twin sons, Leslie and Larry, and a daughter, Jan Starnes. Following his military service, Steinke joined the Philadelphia Eagles and played four seasons from 1945 to 1948. He was part of the team that captured the NFL championship in 1948. After sustaining a neck injury, Steinke retired from playing and transitioned into coaching, taking assistant roles at Trinity University, Oklahoma State, and Texas A&M. In 1954, Steinke returned to Texas A&I as the head football coach, a position he held for 23 years. During his remarkable tenure, he compiled a record of 181-62-4, winning six NAIA national championships (1959, 1969, 1970, 1974, 1975, and 1976) and ten Lone Star Conference titles. After retiring from coaching in 1976, Steinke remained at the university as athletic director until 1982. His contributions to the sport were widely recognized; he was inducted into the NAIA Hall of Fame in 1971 and the Texas Sports Hall of Fame in 1976. Steinke later returned to professional football as a coach with the USFL's San Antonio Gunslingers in 1984 and part of the 1985 season, before the league folded in 1986. After a long battle with Alzheimer's disease, Steinke passed away in 1995 at the age of 76 in Austin. His legacy lived on, and in 1996, he was honored as an inaugural inductee into the College Football Hall of Fame. A scholarship fund was established in his name at Texas A&M–Kingsville, and in 2014, a life-size statue of Steinke was dedicated at Javelina Stadium to commemorate his impact on the school and the sport of football.

W.T. Varnell served as the head coach of the Ganado Indians from 1937 to 1941 and played a pivotal role in guiding the football program to its first significant milestone. In 1939, under Varnell's leadership, Ganado captured its first district championship and made its inaugural playoff appearance. That postseason run ended in a 13-13 tie against Schulenburg in the bi-district round, and the Indians concluded the season with an impressive 8-3-1 record. Notable victories that year included a 13-2 win over Refugio, a 30-6 win over East Bernard, and district shutouts against Goliad (28-0) and Port Lavaca (27-0). One of the most remarkable wins in school history came in 1941 when Ganado defeated Vanderbilt 78-0 - a school record for points scored in a single game that stood for 83 years. This occurred before Vanderbilt consolidated with La Ward and Lolita to form Industrial ISD in 1948, with Francitas and Inez joining later that same year.

Following Varnell, Jack Compton took over as head coach and led the team during the 1942 and 1943 seasons, which were both played during the height of World War II. Compton guided Ganado to back-to-back district championships and playoff appearances, a first for the program. In 1942, the Indians finished 7-1-2, highlighted by their first-ever playoff victory - a 12-7 win over Sugar Land. That season also included two games against cross-county rival Edna: a 19-0 win and a scoreless tie. Another key victory came in a 7-0 win over Cuero. In 1943, Ganado made the playoffs again despite a 3-6 record, ultimately falling to Bastrop 31-13 in bi-district play.

C.D. Winstead coached the Indians in 1944 and 1945. While not much information exists about the specific players during these years, it is known that well-regarded community members I.G. Hajovsky and Jerry Williams played under Winstead. Beyond coaching, Winstead became a well-known figure in Ganado for teaching generations of students how to drive. In 1946, A.H. Cheek served a single season as head coach, finishing with a 1-7 record. The team's only victory that year was a 12-0 win over Goliad. Tom Talley then led the Indians from 1947 to 1953, compiling a 30-37 record over seven seasons. Despite some competitive teams during his tenure, Ganado did not reach the playoffs, and Talley's final season in 1953 ended with a winless 0-10 record. Paul Stewart coached for one season in 1954, leading the team to a balanced 4-4-2 record. Following him, Frank Hafernick took over from 1955 to 1958. During his four-year tenure, Hafernick guided the team to an 18-19-3 overall record. While postseason success remained elusive during this stretch, these years helped shape the foundation of Ganado's football identity as the program continued to evolve.

After a 16-year absence from postseason play, the Ganado Indians made their long-awaited return to the playoffs in 1959. Under first-year head coach Leon Chafin, the Indians captured the district championship and finished the season with a 6-3-2 record. In the bi-district round, Ganado faced Katy in Wharton, where Katy emerged victorious with a 38-14 win, ending Ganado's playoff run. One of the most notable achievements of the 1959 season was a 7-0 victory over East Bernard, a team Ganado would not defeat again until 31 years later in 1990. The 1959 team was led by captains: quarterback Dr. Arthur Mumford, Tony Dybala, Danny Jones, and Gene Thomas. Other team members included Russell Pruitt, Roger Barber, Allen Kenroy, Arthur Schomberg, Leonard Otto, Raymond Pagel, Robert Long, Jerry Bryan, John Scheel, Norman Scheel, Eugene Vyvial, Dr. Bruce Bauknight, Bradley Fleniken, Gary Jones, Patrick Venglar, Glen Schoenfeld, Larry Green, James Weaver, Ronald Oswald, Conrad Walch, and Raymond "Bubba" Toman. Wilton Tegeler also contributed to the team, and the coaching staff included Jack Shelton. Team managers were James Webel and Larry Kaspar. The 1959 season marked a significant moment in Ganado football history, ending a lengthy playoff drought and laying the groundwork for future success.

In 1960, the Ganado Indians finished with a 3-7 record in head coach Leon Chafin's second season. As the 1961 school year and football season began, the community faced a major disruption when Hurricane Carla struck on September 11, making landfall near Port O'Connor as a powerful Category 4 storm. The hurricane caused widespread damage throughout Ganado and the surrounding area. Despite the challenging circumstances, the Indians managed to compile an impressive 8-2 record that season, although they did not qualify for the playoffs. The 1961 season would be Chafin's final year as head coach. From 1962 to 1965, Ganado endured several difficult seasons under coaches Gene Smith and Paul Hatem, with no winning records during that period. One notable player from this era was John Kubena, a member of the Class of 1964, who advanced to play college football at Howard Payne University.

Ganado experienced a resurgence from 1966 to 1970, recording five consecutive winning seasons, though only one of those years resulted in a playoff appearance. After a 6-4 season in 1966, Paul Hatem's final year, the program took a significant step forward in 1967 under new head coach Bob Caskey. That year, the Indians overcame a rough 0-2 start - suffering losses to Tidehaven (17-0) and Goliad (38-6) - and went on an eight-game winning streak to claim the district championship. Ganado finished the season 8-3 after falling 28-6 to Sweeny in the bi-district playoff game held at Victoria's Memorial Stadium. Team captains for the 1967 season were James Duncan, Fred Kaspar, and Buddy Konarik. Other contributors included George Hajovsky, Donald Fowler, Robert Bures, Don Hohensee, Jimmy Vesly, Michael Novosad, Alton Tupa, Michael Konarik, Ray Franklin, Ralph Gaskamp, Anthony Fowler, Winstel Miller, Larry Davis, Leonard Sternadel, Carl Schomburg, Jim Gandy, Joe Reyes, Bert Mercer, Tony Rosalez, Robert Supak, Rodney Johnson, David Pagel, Gerald Freeman, Warren "Moose" Johnson, Lance Fowler, and Pat Orsak. Coaches Ray Kelly, Connie Hoffman, and Jerry Hall led the team, and the managers were Danny Keen and Doug Wheadon. Notable wins included a 14-7 victory over Industrial and a 19-8 win over Edna - one of the few victories Ganado ever achieved over its longtime Jackson County rival and the last time they defeated Edna in varsity football. Duncan and Kaspar, both from the Class of 1968, would later play at the collegiate level - Duncan at Southwest Texas State in San Marcos and Kaspar at Texas A&I Kingsville.

The 1968 team had a strong 6-2-2 season but did not advance to the playoffs. In 1969, Ganado finished with an outstanding 9-1 record, earning a share of the district title as tri-champions with Palacios and Needville. The Indians' only loss came in a narrow 14-12 defeat to Palacios. With the three teams tied, a coin flip was used to determine the playoff representative. Needville won the flip, leaving Ganado and Palacios out of postseason play despite excellent seasons. Coach Bob Caskey left the program after the 1969 season, finishing with an impressive 23-6-2 record over his three-year tenure. Standout players Warren "Moose" Johnson and Jim Gandy, both members of the Class of 1970, went on to play college football - Johnson at the University of Texas at Arlington and Gandy at Texas A&I Kingsville. The period from the mid- to late 1960s marked a turning point for Ganado football, as the team reestablished itself as a competitive program and laid the groundwork for future success.

Interestingly, both Fred Kaspar and Jim Gandy, former standout players from Ganado, played key roles on national championship teams at Texas A&I University (now Texas A&M-Kingsville), under legendary head coach and fellow Ganado native Gil Steinke. Kaspar was a member of both the 1969 and 1970 championship squads, while Gandy joined the program as a freshman in 1970 and was part of that year's title team. In 1969, the Texas A&I Javelinas finished with an impressive 11-1 record. Their only loss came midseason against Sul Ross State, but the team rebounded and went on to claim the NAIA national title with a hard-fought 12-7 victory over Concordia College of Minnesota at Javelina Stadium in Kingsville. The following year, in 1970, Texas A&I once again posted an 11-1 record. Their sole defeat that season came at the hands of Angelo State during midseason play. However, they regrouped and delivered a dominant performance in the championship game, defeating Wofford College of South Carolina 38-7 at Sirrine Stadium in Greenville, South Carolina to secure back-to-back national championships. Kaspar and Gandy's contributions to these championship teams not only highlighted their own athletic achievements but also deepened the legacy of Ganado's impact on Texas football through their connection with Coach Steinke.

The Ganado Indians experienced success and winning seasons in the late 1960s, with the 1970 team finishing 7-3 under first-year head coach Jim Allen. However, they did not advance to the playoffs due to three key district losses against Needville, Boling, and Palacios. After this, the Indians struggled for much of the 1970s, posting mostly non-winning records until 1977. One notable player from this era was Brian Hicks, a Ganado graduate from the class of 1972 who lettered all four years and played quarterback from 1968 to 1971. Hicks went on to play at the next level for Texas A&I Kingsville. In 1973, the Indians endured a winless season, finishing 0-8-2. Despite the tough year, their best performances were two scoreless ties: a 0-0 draw against Edna in a non-district game and a 6-6 tie in district play against Boling, the defending 2A state champions from 1972. That year marked the first season for Coach Buddy Keller, who also coached the team in 1974 when Ganado finished with a 3-7 record.

Bill Kyle coached the Ganado Indians from 1975 to 1979 and brought a competitive edge to the football program. Although the team struggled with a 1-9 record in his first season in 1975, they improved to finish 5-5 in 1976. From 1977 through 1984, the Indians maintained winning records every year except 1979, when they ended the season at 5-5. In 1978, Ganado finished as co-district champions with a 6-4 record but lost the district title to Brazos, who advanced to the playoffs while Ganado stayed home.

Rusty Herridge served as head coach in 1980 and 1981. During those seasons, Ganado finished in a three-way tie for second place in the district alongside Industrial and Brookshire Royal, behind district champion Tidehaven. Their records were 6-4 in 1980 and 7-3 in 1981, but they did not qualify for the playoffs.

In 1982, Tom Jones became Ganado's head coach and served through 1987. That same year, the UIL began allowing two playoff teams from each district to advance, including both the district champion and runner-up. Ganado took advantage of this new rule in 1982 by advancing to the playoffs as the runner-up behind district champion East Bernard. The Indians lost a close bi-district game to Shiner, 27-24, in Yoakum. Missing all four extra point attempts in that game made the difference. The team finished the season 7-4. Despite a 41-0 district loss to East Bernard and an 18-7 defeat to Brazos, Ganado rebounded with a key 28-14 victory over undefeated Tidehaven in Week 8. Tidehaven and Brazos both faltered late in the season, allowing Ganado to clinch the runner-up playoff spot. Team captains in 1982 were Troy Oakman, Gerald Bures, Jerrett Sodia, and David Klaus. Other players included Richard Castillo, Roland Orsak, Robert Orzabal, Scott Henning, Danny Sless, Shawn Oakman, Russell Hahn, Jody Meneley, Scott Freeman, Edward Martinez, Greg Wynn, Mike Kacer, Tim Wells, Travis Gregurek, Mark Tupa, Charlie Koudelka, Robbie Kuretsch, Brian Popp, Greg Brown, and Floyd Randle. Coaches Bill Stroman and Randy Ellison and managers Caliztro Vega and Thomas Rivera also contributed to the team. After 1982, Ganado would not return to postseason play for 14 years, finally reaching the playoffs again in 1996.

In 1983, Ganado finished the season with a 7-3 record but was tied with Brazos for the runner-up spot in the district after the two teams played to a 20-20 tie. The playoff spot was decided by a coin flip, which

Brazos won, allowing them to advance to the regional quarterfinals where they lost to district champion East Bernard, while Ganado remained at home. Ganado's last winning season before a long drought came in 1984 when they again finished 7-3, but a 16-0 district loss to Danbury cost them the runner-up playoff position. As a result, both Danbury and district champion East Bernard advanced to the playoffs, and Ganado stayed home.

Between 1977 and 1984, the Ganado district produced two state champions, one state runner-up, and three semifinalist teams. East Bernard won the state championship in 1977, finished as state runner-up in 1982, and reached the semifinals in 1983 and 1984. Tidehaven was co-state champion in 1980 and a semifinalist in 1981. Despite these successes from these district schools, Ganado seemed to be plagued by hard luck during this period, often finishing second best or facing other setbacks that kept them from advancing to the next level. This pattern of near success and disappointment appeared to be the fate of the Indians for years to come.

Chapter 2

The Resurrection of a Program

From 1985 to the end of the decade, the Ganado football program experienced a significant decline. In 1985, the team finished with a 1-8-1 record, with their sole victory coming from a 22-12 district win over Danbury and managing a 28-28 tie against Tidehaven in the season finale. The 1986 season demonstrated the Indians' determination and resilience, as they played several close games. Although the Indians narrowly lost to Bloomington (19-16), Yorktown (20-8), and Tidehaven (21-14), they secured important district victories against Danbury (12-7) and pulled off an upset against playoff favorite Brazos (18-15). However, from 1987 through 1989, the program faced severe struggles, enduring a 27-game losing streak. By 1989, the team had barely enough players to field a full squad, and there was a real risk that the football program might be in jeopardy.

The 27-game losing streak began after a Week 2 victory, a 10-6 win over St. Joseph at Patti Welder Stadium in Victoria on September 11, 1987. The 10 points scored in that game were the most the Indians managed all season, as they scored only 22 points total and were shut out seven times, often in lopsided defeats. After the 1987 season, head coach Jones was replaced by Ralph Diaz, who led the team through the 1988 and 1989 seasons. In 1988, Ganado went 0-9, with a Week 3 game against Bloomington canceled due to the threat of Hurricane Gilbert, which disrupted many games in the area but ultimately made landfall south of Brownsville as a Category 3 storm. That year, Ganado scored just 18 points and was shut out six times. The 1989 season marked the lowest point, as the team finished 0-10… their last winless regular season to date. Ganado scored only 22 points and was shut out seven times, suffering blowout losses in every game. Despite these difficult years, with few players and overwhelming challenges, the players showed remarkable courage and perseverance. Though the program appeared nearly lost, it never disappeared.

In the spring of 1990, Tucker Rackley was hired as the head football coach and athletic director, replacing Ralph Diaz. Rackley brought with him previous coaching experience at Rockport-Fulton and Ingram, where he had successfully turned around a losing program and led the team to three consecutive playoff appearances. His goal at Ganado was to revive the struggling football program by increasing player participation. The 1990 team featured talented senior athletes, including quarterback Clay Green, the De Los Santos twins Edwin and Edward in the backfield, Trent Klaus, and the imposing Clayton Galindo on the line. Ganado finished the season with a balanced 5-5 record, achieving their first non-losing season since 1984. The team ended their 27-game losing streak on September 7 in the season opener against Bay City's junior varsity team, winning 34-12. Although the victory was against a JV squad, Bay City was a 4A program with athletes capable of playing varsity at smaller classifications. The Indians started the season strong, going 3-0 in non-district play with wins over Bay City JV, Louise (16-7), and Weimar (28-12). Their district opener resulted in a close 21-14 loss to Tidehaven.

A highlight of the season came on October 5, when Ganado traveled to East Bernard, a team that had dominated them throughout the 1980s, including a 61-0 blowout the previous year. East Bernard held a narrow 6-0 lead at halftime, but Ganado tied the game in the third quarter on a touchdown by Mark Riojas, followed by a decisive extra point kicked by Chris Tristan that put Ganado ahead 7-6. The game was marked by turnovers, with both teams combining for 14 fumbles and losing 9 of them. The fourth quarter was especially chaotic, with five fumbles and three lost in the final six minutes. In a dramatic finish, East Bernard recovered a Ganado fumble and advanced to the six-yard line with just nine seconds remaining. However, Chris Tristan blocked East Bernard's game-winning field goal attempt, and Ganado recovered the ball as time expired to secure a 7-6 victory. This win marked Ganado's first victory over East Bernard since 1959 and was particularly significant as it occurred on East Bernard's homecoming game - a time when Ganado traditionally played on the homecoming games of other schools. It was also East Bernard's first homecoming loss in many years, making it a memorable and historic triumph for Ganado. The Indians improved to a 4-1 record and appeared poised to make a strong run after the program had seemed lost just a year earlier.

However, what followed was a series of tough breaks. The next week, Ganado jumped out to a 20-0 lead over Van Vleck but allowed 23 unanswered points, ultimately losing 23-20 after Van Vleck scored a touchdown with two minutes remaining. Ganado then lost a close game at Brazos 21-14 and suffered a big home defeat against Industrial, losing 42-6 - the only game that season that was not close. The Indians bounced back with a convincing 34-8 victory over Danbury but fell in a close season finale at Boling, 33-26, finishing the season with a 5-5 record. The district was highly competitive that year, with Tidehaven, Van Vleck, and Boling sharing the tri-district championship, although only Tidehaven and Van Vleck advanced to the playoffs. Ganado played competitively against all three of those teams. While a 5-5 record might be considered average, it represented significant progress for Ganado, signaling that the program was on the rise. This season was a meaningful achievement for the seniors who had endured many struggles in previous years and finally experienced success. Positive developments were evident beyond the varsity team, as both the seventh and eighth grade junior high teams went undefeated in football that year. Overall, Coach Rackley succeeded in restoring respectability to the Ganado football program.

In the 1991 season, Ganado fielded a young team with Billy Benavides taking over the quarterback position from graduated Clay Green. Benavides would lead the Indians as quarterback through his junior and senior years. The offense shifted toward a more passing-oriented attack, featuring two key junior targets: tight end Brad Hurt and receiver Sherman Lee. Although the team had few seniors, some, like running back Clint Matcek and linemen Hank Ledwig, Gregg Fowler, and John Liberda, made important contributions. The Indians faced significant challenges, including a crushing 62-0 loss to Tidehaven in their district opener at El Maton. Tidehaven was ranked third in the state at the time, dominated the season undefeated, and won the district title. Ganado also suffered big defeats with a 52-0 loss at Van Vleck, the district's playoff runner-up, and a 52-10 home loss to Brazos. However, there were some highlights, such as a 20-20 tie against East Bernard, where Ganado led 20-7 at halftime before East Bernard rallied to tie the game. Ganado nearly upset Industrial at Vanderbilt but narrowly lost 15-14 when Industrial blocked a game-winning field goal attempt late in the contest. The season finale was marked by a historic performance from Boling's Cleon Williams, who rushed for 517 yards in a 66-14 victory over Ganado - a record that still stands in the Texas High School Football record book. The Indians ended the season with a 3-6-1 record but were set to return a strong core of players the following year. Additionally, both junior high football teams once again finished the season undefeated, providing further optimism for the program's future.

In 1992, Ganado returned a strong core of seniors, including quarterback Benavides, receiver Lee, and tight end Hurt, along with Ryan Wesselski in the backfield. The team also added three promising freshmen - Douglas Larson, Ben Galindo, and David Marek - who came from back-to-back undefeated junior high teams. Expectations were high for Ganado to compete for a playoff spot. Throughout the season, the Indians remained competitive in most games. In the season opener at home against East Bernard, Ganado trailed 27-22 in the fourth quarter before Chris Alvarez sealed a thrilling 28-27 victory with a 65-yard fumble return. The team started strong with a 4-0 record, securing wins over East Bernard, Louise (28-14), Pettus (20-0), and St. Joseph (2-0). The win against Pettus, Ganado scored all 20 points in the fourth quarter. In the defensive battle against St. Joseph, Ryan Wesselski sacked the opposing quarterback in the end zone for a game-winning safety with just 30 seconds remaining, clinching the victory. The winning streak ended with a hard-fought 13-8 loss at Shiner, which concluded non-district play. Despite the loss, Ganado played competitively against a strong Shiner team, showing promising signs that they could compete with quality opponents.

The following week, in their district opener at Boling, Ganado lost a close, back-and-forth game, surrendering a 28-25 fourth-quarter lead to fall 33-28. Benavides threw for what was possibly a single-game passing record at the time, totaling 348 yards. Lee had a career-best and single-game school record with 270 receiving yards on 11 receptions and three touchdowns. Despite this offensive firepower, Ganado struggled defensively, as Boling's ground game dominated, with three running backs rushing for over 100 yards each.

The next week presented an unusual situation that, to the best of my knowledge, had never occurred before in Ganado football history: one game played across two different days. Ganado traveled to Cobra Field in Vanderbilt, where they had narrowly lost the previous season, ready to compete. However, with 18 seconds remaining in the first quarter and the score tied 0-0, the game was halted due to approaching thunderstorms and lightning. The storm lingered, and after discussions with officials, it was decided that the game would resume the following evening at the same point it had been stopped. On Saturday, Ganado returned to Vanderbilt to continue the game from 18 seconds remaining in the first quarter, still tied at 0-0. Ganado struck first in the second quarter with a short pass from Benavides to Wesselski, taking a 6-0 lead that held until halftime. However, in the second half, Industrial relied heavily on their running game, scoring 21 points and defeating Ganado 21-6.

The Indians rebounded the following week with a 28-14 victory over Danbury on their homecoming game, which would be their final win of the season. Ganado closed out the year with blowout losses to Tidehaven (53-0) and Van Vleck (52-26), finishing the season at 5-5, matching their record from 1990. Boling emerged as district champions, while Industrial, led by first-year head coach Mike Treybig, upset Tidehaven in the final week to secure the runner-up spot and advance to the playoffs. Overall, Ganado had a competitive season and played hard throughout the year, but close losses - similar to those in 1990 - proved costly. Two major accomplishments stood out: Billy Benavides ended the season with 1,569 passing yards, which was possibly both a single-season and career passing record at the time. Sherman Lee led the area with 900 receiving yards on 50 receptions and 11 touchdowns, setting a single-season receiving school record that would stand until 2021.

Ganado entered the 1993 season as a very young team, with only five seniors on the roster: Michael Sulak, Travis Kaspar, Brian Thomas, Ronnie Simicek, and Nick Metzger, a foreign exchange student from New Zealand. The team had just four juniors - Richard Perez, Garrett Conner, Nathan Chanek, and Ryan Konarik - but a large sophomore class of sixteen players who received significant playing time and some were even starters. This sophomore group had gone undefeated in junior high football and was also strong athletically in other sports. The classes below the sophomores also showed promise, with successful junior high programs indicating a bright future for Ganado athletics. Coach Rackley adapted the team's offense to a more option-based scheme to fit the personnel, especially since the previous passing quarterback and receivers had graduated. Sulak stepped in as the starting quarterback, while sophomore Jamie Bures also took snaps and contributed playing time. Sophomore Douglas Larson became a key running back in the backfield alongside Kaspar and Conner. Despite having talented athletes, the team faced challenges competing mostly against teams with more experienced upperclassmen.

During the season, some of the challenges the Indians faced, including being shut out four times. The team opened the season with a 28-0 loss at East Bernard but rebounded to win three consecutive games against Louise (42-20), Pettus (12-7), and St. Joseph (27-13), reaching a 3-1 record. However, the momentum shifted as Ganado suffered a mid-season slump, losing three straight home games to Shiner (47-0), Boling (39-0), and Industrial (48-14). In the Shiner game, the Indians struggled offensively, gaining only 27 total yards and two first downs. After this difficult stretch, Ganado rallied to overcome a 14-12 halftime deficit at Danbury, ultimately winning 28-14. This victory earned them the Victoria Newscenter 25 Team of the Week honors.

In their final home game of the season, which was also homecoming, Ganado started strong against a very good Tidehaven team. The Indians even scored first in the opening quarter, but the touchdown was nullified by a penalty, and Tidehaven quickly took control, scoring 26 points in the second quarter and eventually routing Ganado 59-6. The season finale against Van Vleck marked a potential turning point for the program. Van Vleck was one of the largest schools in Class 2A and would move to Class 3A in the 1994 realignment, while Ganado was among the smallest 2A schools. Despite the apparent mismatch and Van Vleck's history of dominance over Ganado, the Indians played one of their best games of the season. The score was tied 0-0 in the final minutes, and although Van Vleck missed a field goal, an offside penalty on Ganado gave them a second chance, which they converted to win 3-0. This close game demonstrated that Ganado could compete with top teams, and with a roster loaded with sophomores gaining valuable experience, it served as a stepping stone for future success. The Indians finished the season with a 4-6 record.

Expectations were much higher for Ganado in 1994, as most of the team was returning from the previous season. However, there were only four seniors on the roster: Garrett Conner, Richard Perez, Nathan Chanek, and Ryan Konarik, all of whom were key contributors and held starting positions. The majority of the team consisted of underclassmen, including a large junior class with a year of experience and several sophomores who had been successful in junior high. This combination of talent and experience led to expectations that Ganado would challenge for a playoff spot. Additionally, the school welcomed a new principal, Jack Turner, whose son Dennis was a junior athlete. Dennis transferred from Class 1A Burkeville and was expected to contribute significantly. Jamie Bures would lead the offense as quarterback, with Turner playing both quarterback and running back, while Douglas Larson returned as a key player in the backfield.

Ganado opened the season at home against #8 ranked East Bernard, which featured Shane Lechler, an all-around athlete who played quarterback, safety, placekicker, and punter, never leaving the field. Lechler would later have a stellar career as a punter at Texas A&M and in the NFL with the Oakland Raiders and Houston Texans. Facing a quality opponent in East Bernard, Ganado learned a lot about themselves as a team. Despite playing hard, Ganado lost a close game 14-6. The Indians rebounded with three straight wins over Louise (50-0), St. Joseph (7-0), and Van Vleck (28-14). The victory against Van Vleck was a significant step forward, as Van Vleck was a Class 3A school and had previously dominated Ganado in district play. With a 3-1 record, it appeared the program was making positive progress, especially as the defense was also performing well.

Ganado's final non-district game was against undefeated 4-0 Flatonia, a perennial power in Class 1A that had been realigned to Class 2A that season. Flatonia featured a standout running back named Joe Williams, who was one of the leading rushers in the area. Although Ganado gained more first downs and total yards by the end of the game, they fell short on the scoreboard with a 39-30 loss. The Indians struggled to stop Williams, who dominated the running game with 244 rushing yards. Despite the defeat, Ganado once again demonstrated determination and played competitively against a strong program.

Ganado finished the non-district portion of the season with a 3-2 record but opened district play with two losses, putting the team in a difficult position to compete for a playoff berth. The Indians narrowly lost their district opener at home to Industrial by a score of 20-13. This was followed by a big 41-6 defeat at the hands of Tidehaven in El Maton, the only team to beat Ganado by more than two scores that season. Tidehaven went undefeated in the regular season and secured the district title. Ganado then rebounded with a convincing 36-7 victory over Danbury, positioning themselves to compete for a playoff spot if they could win their final two games against Bloomington and Boling.

However, the game against Bloomington was a major disappointment. Bloomington entered with a 1-7 record and had just suffered a 47-6 loss to Industrial, a team Ganado had played closely. Despite this, Bloomington defeated Ganado 41-30 in a game that Ganado was expected to win. This loss was devastating because a win would have kept playoff hopes alive heading into the final game against Boling. With playoffs now out of reach, the Boling game became a battle for pride. Ganado once again played hard but narrowly lost 25-20, finishing the season with a 4-6 record for the second consecutive year.

While Ganado was more competitive in 1994 thanks to the added experience on the team, the duplicate 4-6 record fell short of expectations. The many close games and narrow losses left the team and fans wanting more. The athletes were present, and Ganado was determined to turn those close games into wins moving forward.

Chapter 3

The Making of a Champion

1995

In the spring of 1995, Ganado Independent School District did not renew Coach Rackley's contract, prompting the search for a new head football coach and athletic director. With only four seniors graduating and a large, experienced group of returning lettermen, expectations for the upcoming football season were high. This transition marked the beginning of a new and successful era for the Ganado program. On April 17, Monte Dean Althaus was hired as the new athletic director and head football coach. Althaus had previously served for six years as the defensive coordinator at Class 2A Eldorado under Coach Doug Kuhlman. Notably, Steven Saldivar, a fellow Eldorado native who had joined the Ganado staff a year earlier, coached the offensive line and defensive tackles. Coach Althaus brought a renewed energy and competitive spirit to Ganado athletics, aiming to elevate performance across all sports. He inherited a team with 21 returning lettermen, including multiple two- and three-year varsity players with significant experience and a strong desire to win. During the final six weeks of the school year, he used his time to become familiar with the athletes and introduce his systems and goals, ensuring a smoother transition by the time two-a-day practices began in August. One of Althaus's primary goals was to increase competitiveness in every football game, particularly in district play, where Ganado had previously struggled, posting a 6-22-1 record from 1990 to 1994 under Coach Rackley. His offensive philosophy centered on a split-back, run-focused attack with occasional passing, while his defensive approach emphasized a "bend but don't break" split 6 scheme. He strongly advocated for preventing big plays and forcing opposing teams to sustain long drives, believing that extended drives increased the chances of mistakes and minimized scoring opportunities. To further bolster the program, Althaus hired Andy Bridges, formerly of Jourdanton and San Angelo Lakeview, as offensive coordinator. Bridges had previously coached alongside Althaus, bringing valuable continuity and shared vision to the new coaching staff.

On August 9, the Ganado Indians officially began their 1995 football season with the first practice on a hot and humid morning at "The Hill," the nickname for the Ganado practice field and athletic facilities located at Ganado Stadium. The team entered the season with a wealth of returning talent and high expectations. At quarterback, Jamie Bures, an all-district selection, returned after passing for 819 yards and totaling 1,262 yards in the previous season. In the backfield, Douglas "Junior" Larson and Doug Holt also returned, bringing strong experience and production. Larson, also an all-district honoree, was the team's leading rusher for the second consecutive year with 557 yards, while Holt contributed 451 yards from the tailback position. The receiving corps was led by all-district wide receiver Casey Sulak, who returned after gaining 258 receiving yards the year before. Tight ends Doug Bubela and Jason Chambless also returned to provide depth and strength. The offensive line featured returning all-district center David Marek and tackle Brock Larson, though both began the season sidelined due to injuries. Marek returned relatively quickly, but Brock, who injured his knee on the first day of after-school practice, did not return until district play began. During Brock's absence, his brother Douglas Larson shifted from running back to offensive tackle to fill the gap. Guards Nathan Kaspar and Sammy Cardenas, along with tackle Clayton Webernick, rounded out the rest of the offensive line. Defensively, the team was anchored by standout returning players. Defensive back Dennis Turner and four-year starter Ben Galindo, both first-team all-district selections, returned at safety and defensive end, respectively. Ben's brother, Anthony "Bully" Galindo, teamed up with Fabien Benavides at the defensive tackle positions, while Chambless returned to the other defensive end spot as another all-district player. Douglas Larson and Holt led the linebacker unit, bringing both physicality and experience. The secondary included Turner, along with Tim Alvarez and Bubela at the halfback positions, while Bures and Kaspar contributed at cornerback. Special teams were also solidified by the return of Joe Rodriguez, the all-district punter, who had averaged 39.8 yards per punt the previous year. A significant and promising addition to the team was junior Greg Lee, a talented athlete who had previously clashed with Coach Rackley and stepped away from the program. Coach Althaus, however, encouraged Lee to return, recognizing his exceptional athletic ability and the positive impact he could have on the team's success.

After working through two-a-days and preseason scrimmages, the Ganado Indians entered their 1995 season opener against East Bernard prepared and focused. The matchup was a significant opportunity for Ganado to prove itself, as East Bernard had gone 12-2 the previous season and reached the state quarterfinals, losing to eventual state finalist Schulenburg. Although East Bernard was fielding a much younger team this year, having graduated a large, athletic senior class that included standout Shane Lechler and had captured back-to-back baseball state titles, the challenge remained daunting due to the program's strong tradition. Their primary returning weapon was running back Roddy Blunston, who had rushed for nearly 2,000 yards the year before. Ganado, on the other hand, had the edge in experience and depth. However, the game was played in East Bernard, making it a true test of resilience. The first half was a defensive battle, with Ganado holding a slim 3-0 lead at halftime thanks to a 28-yard field goal by Dennis Turner. The game's turning point came early when East Bernard marched down to Ganado's goal line on their opening drive. Defensive tackle Anthony Galindo delivered a key hit that jarred the ball loose, and Timmy Alvarez recovered the fumble and returned it upfield, halting the scoring threat. This play perfectly exemplified Coach Althaus' defensive philosophy: bend but don't break, prevent big plays, and capitalize on opponents' mistakes. East Bernard was kept out of the end zone for the entire game and didn't threaten again until their final possession, which ended in an interception. The Indian defense was especially effective in containing Blunston, limiting him to just 45 yards rushing. In the second half, Ganado's offense came alive, gaining 200 yards after managing only 70 in the first half. Quarterback Jamie Bures led the way with three rushing touchdowns, helping the Indians secure an impressive 23-0 shutout victory on the road. The win marked a strong and memorable start to the season and the beginning of Coach Althaus' tenure at Ganado with a 1-0 record.

Ganado continued their strong start to the 1995 season with a dominant performance in their home opener against Louise. The game began with an explosive play as Doug Bubela returned the opening kickoff 80 yards for a touchdown, setting the tone early. Bures threw for 113 yards and connected twice with Greg Lee for touchdowns, with Lee finishing the game with 96 receiving yards. Doug Holt added two rushing touchdowns, and Ganado overwhelmed Louise in all aspects of the game, securing a commanding 60-0 victory. The following week,

Ganado traveled to Patti Welder Stadium in Victoria to face St. Joseph and delivered their most complete performance of the season up to that point. The Indians dominated all three phases of the game - offense, defense, and special teams. Bures threw for 201 yards, including a 55-yard touchdown to Lee, who continued his strong season with 128 receiving yards. Holt contributed 95 rushing yards and two touchdowns. The defense once again stood tall, earning their third consecutive shutout with a 36-0 win. Returning home to face Van Vleck, the Indians showed no signs of slowing down, racking up 446 total offensive yards. Bures passed for 133 yards and two touchdowns to Bubela and Jason Chambless. In a creative play, Lee threw an 80-yard touchdown pass to Bubela on a reverse, with Bubela ending the game with 105 receiving yards. Although the defense allowed its first touchdown of the season, Ganado still cruised to a dominant 47-6 win, improving their record to 4-0.

Despite their impressive early-season success, there was still some uncertainty about just how good the team truly was, as their four victories had come against opponents with losing records. This lingering question would soon be answered as the schedule grew tougher. Next on the schedule for Ganado was a much-anticipated matchup against the undefeated Flatonia Bulldogs, who also entered the game with a 4-0 record. This game marked the beginning of a tough three-week stretch for Ganado, and while it wasn't a must-win in terms of playoff implications, a victory against a quality opponent would serve as a significant confidence boost heading into district play. Flatonia returned standout running back Joe Williams, the area's leading rusher at the time, and the contest also coincided with Ganado's homecoming festivities. Unlike the high-scoring shootout from the previous season, which Flatonia won 39-30, this year's game turned into a defensive slugfest, with both teams struggling to gain field position and scoring opportunities. Ganado had two chances to score in the first half, but a 24-yard field goal attempt by Turner sailed wide right, and a halfback pass from Turner to Bures resulted in a 16-yard loss, stalling another drive. Flatonia, meanwhile, failed to capitalize on their own chances, losing two fumbles and throwing an interception to end the first half, which concluded in a 0-0 tie. Late in the third quarter, Flatonia appeared poised to break the stalemate when they began driving deep into Ganado territory. However, Bubela made a critical interception at the five-yard line to halt their momentum. Just two plays later, Bures connected with Lee for an electrifying 81-yard touchdown pass. The play was initially designed to go to tight end Chambless on a drag route, but Bures quickly adjusted when he noticed Flatonia defensive back Sylvester Estrada had slipped in coverage, leaving Lee wide open. Bures launched a deep pass to Lee, who completed the long score. Turner added the extra point, giving Ganado a 7-0 lead with just 59 seconds remaining in the third quarter. The game remained tight, and Flatonia mounted a final push late in the fourth quarter. Williams intercepted Bures at the Ganado 37-yard line and led a determined drive, carrying the ball on five of the next eight plays and eventually scoring on a three-yard run with 1:58 left in the game. Rather than settling for a tie, Flatonia opted for a two-point conversion, lining up in a swinging gate formation to confuse the Indians. However, Ganado's defense held firm. Chambless read the play perfectly, broke through the line, and sacked quarterback Howard Kutac to deny the conversion and preserve a hard-fought 7-6 victory. This win was a milestone for Ganado, pushing their record to 5-0 and providing proof that the team could not only compete with but also beat strong programs. Perhaps most importantly, it marked the first time in recent memory that the Indians had come out on top in a close game against a high-caliber opponent, signaling a turning point in the program's culture and confidence.

With a 5-0 record, Ganado entered district play in a highly anticipated matchup against their longtime Jackson County rivals, the Industrial Cobras, who were also undefeated at 5-0. Industrial had won the last ten meetings dating back to 1985, and this game presented Ganado with the perfect opportunity to end the losing streak and assert itself in the playoff race. Both teams were playing excellent football, and the rivalry carried more weight than it had in years. Played on Friday, October 13, at Cobra Field in Vanderbilt, the game drew a massive crowd, with much of Jackson County in attendance. With another undefeated team, Tidehaven, waiting the following week, the stakes were high, and it was clear a very good team from this district might miss the playoffs. Ganado came into the game as much as a 19-point favorite, but whether it was the pressure, the big-game atmosphere, or the mystique of Friday the 13th, things did not go as expected. Industrial fumbled on their second offensive play, giving Ganado prime field position, but the Indians' promising drive ended with Casey Wells intercepting Bures in the end zone. Later in the second quarter, Ganado reached the Cobra 4-yard line but again failed to score. Meanwhile, Industrial had two first-half touchdowns nullified by penalties, and the half ended in a scoreless tie, 0-0. In the third quarter, Industrial finally broke through. After recovering a Ganado fumble, quarterback Ashley Jalufka led a drive that included a key 25-yard pass to Bart Vanlandingham. John Schaar capped the drive with an 11-yard touchdown run, and Eric Woodring's extra point gave the Cobras a 7-0 lead. Ganado responded with another drive deep into Industrial territory, but Wells again picked off Bures at the 12-yard line. The Indians had one final chance with 1:15 left in the game, but a fourth-and-six pass fell incomplete. Industrial then sealed the game when Matt Bain scored from seven yards out with just 13 seconds left, handing Ganado a 14-0 loss. Despite Bures throwing for 189 yards and the Indians moving the ball consistently between the 20s, turnovers and red zone inefficiency proved costly. The loss dropped Ganado to 5-1 overall and 0-1 in district, putting them in a hole if they hoped to make the playoffs.

Next came the even greater challenge of facing the 6-0 Tidehaven Tigers, who entered Ganado on an 18-game regular-season winning streak dating back to 1993. Ganado had not defeated Tidehaven since 1984 - the same year they had last beaten Industrial - and recent matchups had been one-sided defeats. Tidehaven's roster was filled with speed and power, led by explosive backs Jeffery Williams, C.J. Babik, and Peter Quinn. They were anchored by 6-foot-4, 310-pound lineman Josh Lovelady, who would go on to play for the University of Houston, and senior all-district linebacker David Lucio, now Tidehaven's current head coach and athletic director. Despite the odds, the loss to Industrial appeared to galvanize the Indians. They responded with one of their best weeks of practice under Coach Althaus, and it showed on game night. The matchup turned into a thrilling back-and-forth contest with five lead changes. Ganado led 13-8 at halftime and, after falling behind 14-13 in the third quarter, regained the lead at 21-14 late in the third and never gave it up. Bures had a strong performance, passing for 126 yards and a touchdown to Bubela, and also led the team in rushing with 88 yards. A critical component of the offense was the return of Douglas Larson to the backfield. He rushed for 57 yards and scored two touchdowns, with his brother Brock Larson delivering key blocks, including one on Tidehaven's massive Lovelady. One of Douglas's biggest runs came as Ganado was backed up deep in their own territory, helping shift field position. The defense stepped up as well, limiting Tidehaven's leading rusher, Williams, to just 47 yards. The 21-14 win was a monumental moment for Ganado football. Not only did it snap a long losing streak against Tidehaven, but it also revitalized their playoff hopes. Now 6-1 overall and 1-1 in district, the Indians were back in the hunt. To keep their postseason dreams alive, they would need to win their final three games against Danbury, Bloomington, and Boling - and hope for a little help from other teams.

By the time Ganado reached the final stretch of the season, they were playing at their peak, sitting at 6-1 and dominating their last three opponents in convincing fashion. At Danbury, Ganado quickly seized control of the game. Joe Rodriguez set the tone by returning the opening kickoff 94 yards for a touchdown, sparking a first-half onslaught that ended with a commanding 34-0 lead at halftime. Bures threw for 165 yards and two touchdowns, both to Lee, who recorded 110 receiving yards. The Indians never looked back and cruised to a 48-0 shutout victory. The following week, in their final road game of the season at Bloomington, the dominance continued. Ganado exploded for 21 points in the first quarter alone. Bures led the offense once again, passing for 181 yards and a touchdown to Lee while also rushing for four touchdowns himself. The defense held strong, earning their fifth shutout of the season in a 42-0 rout. In the regular season finale at home against Boling, the Indians capped off their campaign with a 38-12 win, breaking a nine-game losing streak against Boling that dated back to 1986. The victory marked Ganado's ninth win of the season and seemed to secure what should have been a well-earned playoff berth.

However, Ganado's postseason fate was not determined on the field that night, but a week earlier in Vanderbilt, where a pivotal district matchup between Tidehaven and Industrial would shape the final standings. Tidehaven's 13-0 win over Industrial on November 3 created a three-way tie for the district championship, as all three teams - Ganado, Tidehaven, and Industrial - finished district play with identical 4-1 records and identical 9-1 overall records. With the district title and playoff spots now hinging on a positive point system (based on point differential in games played among the tied teams), Ganado unfortunately came out on the losing end. Despite their 21-14 win over Tidehaven, Ganado held just +7 points. Industrial, thanks to their 14-0 victory over Ganado, led with +14, while Tidehaven had +13 from their

13-0 win over Industrial. As a result, Industrial was awarded the district championship and #1 playoff seed, Tidehaven secured the runner-up spot, and Ganado, by the slimmest of margins, was left out of the playoffs. It was a heartbreaking end to an otherwise exceptional season, with Ganado finishing 9-1 - matching the records of the two playoff qualifiers - yet missing the postseason due to a technicality in the tiebreaker system.

By the end of the 1995 season, Ganado had accomplished nearly every goal that Coach Althaus had set when he took over the program that spring. The only thing missing was a playoff appearance - a painful omission that became a driving force for the returning lettermen as they entered the offseason determined to end the program's playoff drought, which had stretched all the way back to 1982. Despite the heartbreak, the team had plenty to be proud of. They had made tremendous progress, changed the culture, and left a lasting mark on Ganado football. The 14 seniors on the team were the heart of this transformation. Although they never got the chance to play in a playoff game, their impact was undeniable. They were true winners - on the field and in life - and many went on to become successful men and fathers. Among them, Dennis Turner attended the Air Force Academy and later graduated from the University of Texas. Nathan Kaspar joined the Navy and eventually walked on as a special teams player at UT through the ROTC program. These seniors laid the foundation for future success, and there was a shared belief that had the team reached the postseason, they were talented and motivated enough to make a deep playoff run - possibly three or four rounds. Statistically and defensively, the 1995 Indians were dominant. Quarterback Jamie Bures had a standout season, finishing as the area's leading passer with 1,577 yards and 13 touchdowns. He also became Ganado's all-time career passing leader with 2,575 yards and 21 touchdowns. The team recorded five shutouts and allowed just 52 total points all season, demonstrating one of the program's strongest defensive efforts ever. Signs of growth extended beyond varsity football. The Ganado junior varsity team went undefeated at 10-0, with many of those players set to move up to the varsity squad in 1996, continuing the upward momentum. The entire 1995–1996 school year turned out to be a landmark period for Ganado athletics. The boys' basketball team won the district championship over Industrial and made a deep playoff run, eventually falling to their rivals in the regional finals - just one step away from the state tournament, where Industrial went on to lose to East Chambers in the semifinals. The baseball team also made the playoffs for the first time since the program had been reinstated in 1990, after a 25-year absence dating back to 1965. The 1995–1996 school year was filled with firsts, milestones, and momentum, setting the stage for what was to come. As the long offseason came to an end, anticipation for the 1996 football season began to build. With talent, determination, and unfinished business driving them forward, Ganado was ready - and history was about to be made.

Chapter 4

The Glory Years

1996

The historic football season for Ganado began on August 7 during the intense summer heat of two-a-day practices at "the hill." The team returned 14 lettermen and welcomed a talented group of athletes, including standout receiver Greg Lee, who led the area the previous year with a 30.1-yard average per catch, totaling 842 receiving yards and 10 touchdowns in 1995. Bryan Hurt, who had led the junior varsity team, stepped in as the new quarterback to replace the graduated Jamie Bures. At fullback, seniors Doug Holt and Justin Hoskins returned, while sophomore Sterling Watson, who had rushed for over 1,000 yards as a freshman on an undefeated JV team, took over at tailback. The offensive line featured returning talent such as Brock Larson, who had recovered from a knee injury, and all-district players Fabian Benavides, Clayton Webernick, and Chad Green, with juniors Donald Kovar at center and Caleb McCain and Adam Galindo rotating in at guard. Defensively, the team aimed to build on a dominant season in which they allowed only 52 points. The line was anchored by Benavides and Anthony "Bully" Galindo at tackle and Webernick and Jarrett Lambert at end, making the defensive front one of the team's greatest strengths. Holt returned at linebacker alongside new starter Tommy Tristan, while the secondary featured seniors Timmy Alvarez and Kyle Pair, with sophomores Heath Bures and Michael Tristan also taking on key roles. Although Ganado was picked to finish fifth in the competitive District 28-2A by *Dave Campbell's Texas Football Magazine*, they were determined to prove themselves and earn respect. Many players played both offense and defense, demonstrating an exceptional work ethic and dedication to winning and reaching the playoffs. By December, the team had undoubtedly earned the respect they sought at the season's outset.

Ganado opened the 1996 football season in dominant fashion with a 55-0 home victory over Yorktown. The Indians showcased a powerful ground attack, racking up 342 rushing yards. Sophomore Sterling

Watson made an impressive varsity debut, rushing for 176 yards and scoring two touchdowns. Fullbacks Doug Holt and Justin Hoskins also contributed with two touchdowns each, while quarterback Bryan Hurt added 102 passing yards. The defense was equally dominant, limiting Yorktown to just 108 total yards and forcing four turnovers. The following week, Ganado secured a landmark win on the road against Shiner, a program honoring its 1986 state championship team. Despite missing key starters Holt (due to disciplinary action) and Greg Lee (recovering from a minor ankle injury), Ganado led just 6-0 at halftime before exploding for 30 points in the third quarter. This 36-0 victory marked Ganado's first-ever win over Shiner and stood in stark contrast to the 47-0 defeat they suffered against them in 1993. Watson delivered a breakout performance, scoring four touchdowns and rushing for 242 yards - 173 of those yards coming in the third quarter alone. The Indians closed out non-district play with a 14-0 win at Flatonia, where both Holt and Watson rushed for over 100 yards and one touchdown each. With a 3-0 record, all shutout wins, Ganado entered district play with strong momentum and confidence. Their district opener against Boling was set to coincide with homecoming night, raising anticipation even higher.

As Ganado entered District 28-2A play, the team knew the path to the playoffs would require consistent, high-level performance over the next seven weeks. The district was regarded as one of the most competitive in Class 2A across the state, with Ganado, Industrial, Tidehaven, and East Bernard all entering district play undefeated. Although Boling had been considered a playoff contender in the preseason, they suffered a major setback when a key running back was lost to a season-ending knee injury in their opener. Despite this, Boling played Ganado tough in the district opener. The game was closely contested, with both teams nearly equal in total statistics. However, Ganado gained the upper hand by winning the turnover battle, recovering four Boling fumbles. Boling became the first team to score against Ganado all season, tying the game at 7-7 in the second quarter. Just before halftime, Hurt connected with Lee for a 40-yard touchdown, giving Ganado a 14-7 lead. In the fourth quarter, Hurt threw another touchdown pass, this time to Holt from six yards out, sealing a 20-7 victory. The win pushed Ganado's record to 4-0 overall and, more importantly, 1-0 in district play. The following week, Ganado traveled to Van Vleck and spoiled their homecoming celebrations, which included honoring alumnus Charles

Austin, who had won a gold medal in the high jump at the 1996 Atlanta Olympics. The Indians dominated the game with a 33-6 victory, outgaining Van Vleck 354 to 132 in total yards. Watson rushed for 130 yards and a touchdown, while Holt added 127 yards and two scores. Van Vleck's speedy running back, Demetrick Monroe - who had competed at the state track meet - was mostly contained, although he did break free for a touchdown just before halftime. With the win, Ganado improved to 5-0 overall and 2-0 in district, setting up a crucial matchup at home against a strong East Bernard team. East Bernard had just delivered an impressive 24-0 win over preseason district favorite Industrial, signaling that they were a serious contender and providing Ganado with their biggest test yet.

East Bernard entered the much-anticipated district showdown with an explosive three-headed rushing attack led by sophomore quarterback Marlon Blunston and junior running backs Lee Davis and Lenter Thomas. Their offense, though simple in design, was highly effective, executing the option, sweep, and cutback plays with precision, supported by a strong offensive line and a tough, aggressive defense. Having physically dominated preseason district favorite Industrial the week before, East Bernard posed Ganado's toughest challenge yet. For Ganado's defense, the key to victory would be discipline - staying in lanes and avoiding big plays. The first half was a tight battle, with both teams moving the ball and trading turnovers. Ganado struck first with just 28 seconds left in the half when Hurt connected with Lee for a 29-yard touchdown. However, the extra point was missed, and the Indians took a 6-0 lead into halftime. East Bernard responded immediately after the break, driving 74 yards in 12 plays and scoring on a 4-yard run by Lenter Thomas. The extra point that would have given them the lead was blocked by Tommy Tristan, keeping the game tied at 6-6 - a pivotal moment in the game. In the fourth quarter, Ganado leaned on its T-formation offense, grinding out yards and controlling the clock. The Indians appeared poised to score the game-winning touchdown after reaching the red zone, but a mishandled pitch pushed them back and ultimately stalled the drive. East Bernard mounted a final offensive push behind Blunston, but Lee intercepted a pass to halt the threat, sending the game to overtime tied 6-6. This was the first year the UIL adopted college-style overtime for high school football, and it would be the first overtime game for both programs. Ganado got the ball first in overtime and returned to its T-formation.

Holt powered in a touchdown from the one-yard line, and Jarrett Lambert's extra point made it 13-6. East Bernard's possession saw Blunston drive them to the one-yard line in three plays. On what appeared to be a scoring play, Blunston was ruled down just short. On the next play, a pitch to Thomas bounced off his chest, and Lambert recovered the fumble, sealing the dramatic victory for Ganado. The stadium erupted in celebration as players, coaches, and fans reveled in the hard-fought win.

The Indians were now 6-0 overall and 3-0 in district play, tied with Tidehaven for first place. East Bernard and Industrial each had one loss, and with four games remaining, Ganado was on the verge of snapping a 14-year playoff drought. A key stat from the game was that Ganado committed no penalties, highlighting their discipline. Holt led the ground attack with 104 rushing yards, while Hurt threw for 125 yards. Ganado continued its dominant run by defeating Brazos 47-0 the following week. Greg Lee caught two touchdown passes - one from Hurt and one from Heath Bures - and also returned an interception for a score. Watson rushed for 94 yards and two touchdowns as the Indians totaled 234 rushing yards and 200 passing yards in another well-rounded performance. The Indians returned home and overwhelmed Danbury 66-20, racking up 441 rushing yards and scoring 53 points in the first half alone. Hurt was perfect through the air, going 2-for-2, both completions resulting in touchdowns. Watson and Holt each scored three touchdowns, with Watson rushing for 174 yards and Holt adding 165 yards. Lee added two touchdown receptions and a spectacular 95-yard kickoff return for another score. With an 8-0 record and a perfect 5-0 mark in district play, Ganado was now set to face Industrial and Tidehaven - the two teams that had gone to the playoffs the previous year while Ganado watched from home. A win over either would all but guarantee a playoff spot, thanks to the Indians' undefeated standing and their tiebreaker advantage over East Bernard.

November 1, All Saints' Day, became a historic and unforgettable moment for the Ganado Indians football program. It marked the long-awaited rematch against Industrial at Cobra Field in Vanderbilt - the very field where Ganado's playoff hopes were dashed a year earlier in a 14-0 loss. This time, the stakes were high, and the mission was clear: end the 11-year losing streak to the Cobras, reverse the heartbreak of the past, and clinch a playoff berth. A cold norther swept in that afternoon, and Ganado battled a stiff wind throughout the game. Industrial struck first with a 49-yard touchdown pass from quarterback Ashley Jalufka, handing Ganado its first deficit of the entire season. However, the Indians remained composed and answered in the second half when Hurt connected with Lee on a 47-yard touchdown strike. Although the two-point conversion attempt failed, the Indians trailed only 7-6. On their next possession, Ganado mounted a defining 80-yard, 16-play drive that consumed over six minutes. Heath Bures capped it off with a 7-yard touchdown run, and Hurt again found Lee for a successful two-point conversion, giving Ganado a 14-7 lead. A crucial moment came when Industrial recovered a pooched kickoff into the wind, setting up at the Ganado 34. They reached a fourth-and-14, and Jalufka found Derek Moreland wide open in the end zone, but the pass was ruled incomplete, shifting momentum back to Ganado. The Indians dominated time of possession in the second half, with Holt grinding out 132 yards on 32 carries. Hurt added 97 passing yards, and Watson crossed the 1,000-yard mark for the season. Industrial managed only eight offensive snaps in the entire fourth quarter. Lee ended a Cobra drive with an interception, and Jalufka's final fourth-down pass fell incomplete with 1:14 remaining - sealing the emotional and long-awaited victory. With the 14-7 win, Ganado snapped the 11-year losing streak to Industrial, and more importantly, secured its first playoff berth since 1982, ending a 14-year postseason drought. The Indians also clinched the district's number one seed, while preseason favorite Industrial was eliminated. It was a remarkable moment for a team that had been picked to finish fifth in the preseason rankings. The significance of the victory drew major attention: the following week, former KHOU Channel 11 sports anchor Gifford Nielsen landed on Ganado's practice field in a helicopter to present the team and Coach Althaus with the "Team of the Week" plaque for the Houston viewing area. Still, Althaus emphasized that the job wasn't finished - beating Tidehaven was essential to claiming the district title outright. The Indians had shared the title the previous season, and they were determined not to do so again. Riding their peak momentum, Ganado delivered a dominant performance in the regular season finale, steamrolling Tidehaven with a 35-0 halftime lead and cruising to a 42-14 victory. It was a complete team effort, with five different players scoring. Watson rushed for two touchdowns, Holt led the team with 169 rushing yards and one touchdown, Lee electrified the crowd with an 80-yard punt return for a score, Hurt connected with Bures for a touchdown pass and also rushed for another himself. With the win, Ganado closed out a perfect 10-0 regular season - its first undefeated campaign in school history - and claimed the outright District 28-2A championship. The Indians were not just back in the playoffs - they were doing it in record-setting, unforgettable fashion.

The next chapter of the Indians football season was filled with unforgettable memories and unprecedented accomplishments as the team embarked on a historic playoff run. After securing their first playoff berth in 14 years, the Indians were not content to merely participate - they were determined to make a deep push toward a state championship. Despite lacking postseason experience, Ganado's preparation, driven by the leadership of Coach Althaus and his staff, was second to none. With overwhelming support from the community, packed pep rallies, and massive playoff crowds, the team embraced the moment and rose to the occasion. Ganado's playoff journey began in the bi-district round against a strong Weimar team at Victoria's Memorial Stadium. Weimar, coming off a heartbreaking 20-19 loss to powerhouse Schulenburg, featured a dangerous offense and a stout defense. Ganado struck first with a one-yard touchdown run by Holt on the last play of the first quarter. Weimar tied it up 7-7 after capitalizing on a Ganado fumble, but the Indians responded forcefully. Lee returned an interception 40 yards for a touchdown, and Bures blocked a punt that set up a 15-yard scoring run by Watson, giving Ganado a 21-7 halftime lead. The Indians stumbled out of the gate in the second half, managing only six offensive plays in the third quarter. Weimar scored quickly on a 35-yard run by L.J. Johnson, then followed up with a grueling 18-play, 79-yard drive capped by a two-yard touchdown. However, a game-saving stop by Michael and Tommy Tristan on the two-point conversion attempt preserved Ganado's 21-19 lead. Holt would seal the win with two late touchdowns, finishing with 197 rushing yards, as Ganado earned a 34-19 victory - their first playoff win since 1942, ending a 54-year drought and marking only the second in school history. Now 11-0, Ganado was building momentum with every snap.

In the area round, Ganado faced 6-5 Rogers at Brenham's Cub Stadium. Though Rogers had started the season 0-5, they rebounded with five straight wins and featured a modern shotgun spread offense that was rare at the time. Ganado's defense adapted quickly and dominated, holding Rogers to just 11 rushing yards (much of which came off sacks) and intercepting four passes. Holt rushed for 196 yards, but Lee stole the show with three electrifying touchdowns - a 15-yard fumble return, an 85-yard punt return, and a 35-yard touchdown reception from Hurt. Lee totaled 237 all-purpose yards on just nine touches, powering Ganado to a convincing 35-7 win and a 12-0 record. For the first time in school history, the Indians were playing football over the Thanksgiving holiday. The regional round brought perennial South Texas playoff contender Freer to the schedule, with the game played on Black Friday at Buccaneer Stadium in Corpus Christi. Heavy rains turned the field into a muddy mess, but Ganado embraced the conditions. Freer took an early 3-0 lead on a field goal, but Ganado responded when Lee intercepted a pass and returned it 27 yards for a touchdown, giving the Indians a 6-3 lead. After a defensive stop at their own four-yard line, Ganado nearly scored again before halftime but settled for the narrow lead. In the second half, the Indians dominated both sides of the ball. They opened with a 76-yard touchdown drive capped by a 35-yard Hurt-to-Dunlap strike, followed by a successful Holt two-point conversion. Later, Watson scored from four yards out to finish a nearly 10-minute drive that sealed the 21-3 win. Ganado's defense was suffocating, allowing just seven offensive plays and five total yards to Freer in the second half, while collecting three interceptions. Holt continued to lead the ground attack with 141 yards on 30 carries, and Hurt added 108 passing yards. The victory pushed Ganado to 13-0 and made them the first team in school history to play football into December. Awaiting them in the quarterfinals for the Region IV championship was none other than traditional state powerhouse Refugio - setting the stage for another monumental showdown in a season already filled with history.

On Friday, December 6, the Indians delivered one of the most historic and emotional victories in school history by defeating state powerhouse Refugio 6-0 in the regional final, advancing to the state semifinals for the first time ever. Leading up to the game, Refugio was widely favored to win the region and was averaging an astounding 53 points per game, fresh off a dominant 28-0 victory over East Bernard - a team Ganado had narrowly beaten 13-6 in overtime. It was clear this would be Ganado's toughest test yet. The day began on a somber note for the Ganado community with the tragic loss of Larry Conner, a well-known and respected businessman and devoted supporter of Ganado football, in an early morning accident. Though the town mourned his passing, the Indians pressed forward with heavy hearts into the biggest football game in school history at that time. A near-capacity crowd of over 10,000 fans filled Victoria's Memorial Stadium to witness the showdown. Statistically, Refugio appeared to control the game: they held a significant edge in first downs (17 to 6), total yardage (237 to 157), time of possession (over 34 minutes to just 13 for Ganado), and offensive plays (67 to 29). Their running backs Bill Bisby and Reggie Hollins effectively moved the ball, rushing for 111 and 66 yards, respectively. Despite these numbers, Ganado's defense came up huge time and again. Refugio's downfall came in missed opportunities and turnovers. They entered Ganado territory five times and came away with nothing - missing two field goals, fumbling twice deep in Indian territory (once at the 14-yard line and again at the 1), and throwing a game-sealing interception at the goal line with 1:19 left, picked off by Lee. Ganado, by contrast, played a nearly flawless game with no penalties, just one turnover, and unrelenting defensive discipline. The game's only score came with just 12 seconds left in the first half, after two costly back-to-back personal foul penalties on Refugio moved the ball deep into their red zone. Hurt connected with Lee on a 17-yard touchdown pass in the back of the end zone, giving Ganado a 6-0 lead. The extra point attempt failed, but it didn't matter - Ganado's "bend-but-don't-break" defense held strong through the second half. Standouts Fabian Benavides, Chad Green, and Anthony Galindo anchored the defensive line, shutting down the interior running game and neutralizing Refugio's bootleg plays. This victory was widely regarded as one of the biggest upsets in Texas high school football that year. Ganado, a team that few had even predicted to make the playoffs, had just eliminated a perennial state power with far more tradition and playoff experience. It was a testament to the Indians' grit, preparation, and resilience, shaped by a challenging schedule and hardened by previous battles. With a 14-0 record, the Indians had now punched their ticket to the state semifinals - the final four - and were just one win away from reaching the state championship game. Against all odds, Ganado was rewriting school history, and the dream was still alive.

In the Class 2A state semifinals, the Indians faced off against the storied Groveton Indians at the Houston Astrodome, marking the most significant game in Ganado football history up to that point. Groveton was a powerhouse program, having won state championships in 1984, 1989, and 1990, with NFL player Rodney Thomas a key figure on their last two title teams. For Ganado, playing in the iconic Astrodome felt surreal - but it was very real, and the town embraced every moment of it. Leading up to the game, excitement swept through Ganado. The team practiced at the Astrodome midweek and borrowed turf shoes from El Campo ISD to adjust to the stadium's artificial surface. A massive community pep rally was held Thursday night at the stadium, and fans traveled to the game on chartered buses. In a show of sportsmanship, East Bernard ISD even sent a congratulatory letter to Ganado for their success and for representing the district, highlighting the unity among the schools. As game time arrived, the Ganado team entered the field with energy and smoke, fired up and ready to fight for a berth in the state championship. Early in the game, Ganado had a golden opportunity to strike first after recovering a Groveton fumble, but Hurt's pass was intercepted in the end zone after a slip by his intended receiver. Offensively, Ganado struggled all night, as Groveton's defense was exceptionally fast and disruptive at the line of scrimmage. Hurt passed for only 9 yards and threw two interceptions, while the running game was held to 125 total yards, with Holt accounting for 68 of them. Groveton took the lead midway through the second quarter following a turnover, capitalizing with a 2-yard touchdown run by Chris Spivey. Ganado entered halftime down 7-0, having managed just 46 yards of offense. The second half began with a devastating blow for Ganado, as star player Greg Lee injured his ankle on the kickoff return and was unable to return - a massive loss for the team both offensively and defensively. Groveton extended their lead on their first possession of the second half, marching 64 yards in 11 plays, with Jim Bird finishing the drive from one yard out to make it 14-0. With time slipping away, Ganado refused to quit. Holt recovered a Groveton fumble late in the fourth quarter, and Barry Dunlap set up the Indians with a 12-yard reverse. Watson capped the drive with a 4-yard touchdown run to cut the deficit to 14-6, though the two-point conversion attempt failed. The Indians had another shot when Heath Bures ripped the ball from Spivey's hands at the Ganado 45-yard line, giving them possession with just over three minutes left. They converted a key first down on another reverse by Dunlap, but their comeback effort ultimately fell short. On fourth-and-two from the Groveton 36-yard line with just 1:19 left, Holt was tackled a yard short of the marker, and Groveton ran out the clock. Ganado's remarkable season came to an end with a hard-fought 14-6 loss. Though the dream of a state championship fell just short, the Indians finished the year with a historic 14-1 record, having defied expectations and captured the hearts of their community and beyond. The 1996 team became a symbol of perseverance, unity, and belief - leaving a lasting legacy in Ganado football history.

The Ganado Indians concluded their historic 1996 football season with a hard-fought 14-6 loss to Groveton in the state semifinals, but their performance left a lasting impact on the program and the community. Despite being outgained 259-134 in total yards, the Indians held a high-powered Groveton offense - which had scored 69 points the week before against Arp - to just 14 points, a major defensive achievement. Groveton would go on to lose in the state championship to Iraan, 14-7, and their quarterback/linebacker Jim Bird was named the 1996 Class 2A Defensive MVP. The semifinal game was shaped by a key injury to Ganado's standout player Greg Lee, whose absence in the second half limited the team's offensive and defensive capabilities. Some later speculated that had the game been played on a natural grass field instead of turf, the outcome might have been different - but that remains an unanswerable "what if." Regardless, the season was nothing short of extraordinary. The team united the school and town in a way that had not been seen in years, and the Indians earned widespread respect throughout the state for their performance, resilience, and determination. The 1996 season firmly placed Ganado on the Texas high school football map, establishing a standard of excellence and igniting a hunger to go even further in the years ahead. It marked the beginning of a new era, as the Indians would go on to make the playoffs in eight consecutive seasons, transforming the program into a perennial powerhouse. The legacy of the 1996 team lives on - not just in the wins, but in the pride, unity, and tradition it inspired for years to come.

1997

Following a highly successful 1996 season, the Ganado Indians used the revenue from playoff ticket sales to fund the construction of a new weight room, located next to the field house at The Hill, which would be operational by the start of the 1997–1998 school year. The athletic program as a whole continued to thrive, with the boys' basketball team - composed largely of football players - reaching the regional finals for the second consecutive year. The girls' basketball team also made notable progress, advancing to the playoffs for the first time since 1987, and the spring saw the introduction of a girls' softball program.

As the 1997 football season approached, expectations were high. Many predicted the Indians would contend for the district title, challenge for a regional championship, or even win a state title. However, the path to the playoffs would not be easy, as Ganado remained in what was considered the most competitive 2A district in the state. East Bernard, ranked #7 in the state by *Dave Campbell's Texas Football*, was the district favorite, with strong teams like Industrial and Tidehaven also in the mix. A major focus for the Indians was maintaining the same level of discipline and determination as the previous season, avoiding complacency after prior success. Although the team lost key offensive players - receiver Greg Lee, 1,000-yard rusher Doug Holt, and quarterback Bryan Hurt to graduation - they returned seven starters on offense. Junior Sterling Watson, who had rushed for over 1,000 yards the previous season with an average of 8.4 yards per carry, returned at tailback. Junior Heath Bures, whose brother Jamie had previously played quarterback for the Indians, stepped in to replace Hurt, and junior B.J. Hicks took over at fullback. Senior receivers Chris Hajovsky and Barry Dunlap provided experience in the passing game. The offensive line was strong despite the loss of tackle Brock Larson, anchored by seniors Chad Green (6-3, 307 lbs.), along with guards Caleb McCain and Adam Galindo, tight end Jarrett Lambert, center Philip Ledwig, and juniors Brandon Bures and Seth Brezina. On defense, returning starters included Lambert and Anthony "Bully" Galindo on the line, with Green, McCain, and Brandon Bures also contributing at defensive tackle. Trey Lechuga took the other defensive end spot. The linebacker corps was largely new, except for Michael Tristan, who transitioned from cornerback, with Adam Galindo and Jon Pruitt expected to step in. In the secondary, all-state safety Heath Bures returned, with Hicks, Sam Chanek, Dunlap, Hajovsky, and Watson rotating at cornerback and halfback positions. Overall, the Indians returned a solid core of experienced players from a successful program, positioning them well for another competitive season.

The Indians began their 1997 football season with a dominant 34-13 road victory over Yorktown. Sterling Watson led the offense with 151 rushing yards and two touchdowns, while B.J. Hicks added 56 rushing yards and a score. Quarterback Heath Bures contributed 107 passing yards, including a touchdown to Chris Hajovsky. The Indians completely controlled the game, outgaining Yorktown 432-189 in total offense and building a commanding 34-0 lead by the end of the third quarter before allowing two late touchdowns in the fourth. In their home opener, the Indians continued their strong performance by overwhelming Shiner 48-8. Bures again played a key role, rushing for 83 yards and two touchdowns, and passing for another score to Barry Dunlap. The final non-district game was Ganado's homecoming against a very young Flatonia team with only one senior. The Indians delivered a lopsided 69-0 victory, gaining all 348 of their total yards on the ground without attempting a single pass. Special teams and defense contributed significantly, with Sam Chanek returning a fumble for a touchdown on the opening kickoff, Trey Lechuga recovering a fumble in the end zone for a score, Watson and Hicks each scoring on punt returns, and Bures returning an interception for a touchdown. The team also scored five offensive touchdowns in the rout, pushing their record to 3-0 heading into district play.

As District 28-2A competition began, the Indians faced Boling on the road. Ganado jumped out to a quick 14-0 lead in the first quarter and maintained control for a 27-6 victory. Hicks scored two rushing touchdowns, Watson added another, and Bures connected with Dunlap for a passing touchdown. Back at home, Ganado dominated Van Vleck, building a staggering 53-0 halftime lead and eventually winning 56-6. The Indians racked up 397 total yards compared to Van Vleck's 136. Hicks rushed for 160 yards and three touchdowns, while Watson contributed 116 rushing yards and four touchdowns. Jarrett Lambert added a 22-yard field goal to cap off the scoring. The Indians continued their dominant run by improving to 5-0, extending their district win streak to 14 games over two seasons.

Despite their success, the team had yet to be seriously challenged. Ranked #4 in the state, Ganado was set to face their toughest test yet in a pivotal matchup against #9 East Bernard, a team coming off a surprising 13-7 loss to Industrial that had dropped them from #2 in the rankings. East Bernard still had the trio of terror in the offensive backfield with quarterback Marlon Blunson and running backs Lee Davis and Lenter Thomas. In a game played in persistent rain and before a packed, standing-room-only crowd at East Bernard, the contest lived up to its high expectations. The Indians struck first with a 50-yard touchdown pass from Heath Bures to Kevin Garcia late in the first quarter. East Bernard responded with a methodical 14-play, 67-yard drive capped by a 5-yard touchdown run from Blunston, tying the game 7-7 midway through the second quarter. Both teams missed scoring opportunities - East Bernard on a missed 29-yard field goal and Ganado after a fumble at the East Bernard 31 - but the Indians seized momentum at the end of the half. With time expiring, Hicks intercepted a pass and returned it 81 yards for a touchdown, giving Ganado a 14-7 halftime lead. The third quarter was scoreless, setting up a wild fourth quarter. East Bernard tied the game early in the fourth with a 21-yard touchdown run by Thomas. Ganado answered with a time-consuming 14-play, 73-yard drive that included a critical 33-yard pass from Bures to Watson on second-and-26. Bures finished the drive with a one-yard touchdown run, putting Ganado back on top 21-14 with just over four minutes remaining. East Bernard struck back quickly, as Blunston connected with Rolind Brown for a 54-yard touchdown pass to tie the game at 21-21. With just over three minutes left, Ganado began their final drive at the East Bernard 35. Watson converted a crucial fourth-and-three, then broke free for 20 yards down to the two-yard line. After two unsuccessful plays, Ganado called a timeout with eight seconds remaining. On the next play, Hicks powered into the end zone for the game-winning score. Jarrett Lambert added his fourth extra point of the night, and Ganado sealed a dramatic 28-21 victory. Hicks, who had battled an upper respiratory infection all week, delivered a heroic performance with 106 rushing yards, the game-winning touchdown, and a pick-six. It was a true team win, as Ganado became the first team all season to score more than 21 points on East Bernard. The victory improved Ganado's record to 6-0 overall and 3-0 in district, while East Bernard fell to 4-2 and 1-2, seriously jeopardizing their playoff hopes. Coach Althaus praised his team for stepping up when it mattered, despite concerns about their conditioning due to a lack of prior challenges.

Riding high from the East Bernard win, Ganado handled Brazos with ease in a 44-7 home victory. Watson rushed for 95 yards and three touchdowns and opened the second half with a 95-yard kickoff return for a score. The following week, despite a slow start against Danbury that saw them leading just 24-0 at halftime, the Indians erupted for 27 points in the third quarter on their way to a 57-0 shutout. Watson rushed for 114 yards and two touchdowns. Hicks had another standout game, scoring three touchdowns - one rushing, one on a punt return, and one on an interception return. Lambert added a defensive touchdown by stripping the ball and returning it 27 yards, Chad Green blocked a punt for a safety, and lineman Anthony Galindo scored on a rare rushing touchdown. With an 8-0 record and full momentum, the stage was now set for the highly anticipated Jackson County showdown against Industrial on Halloween night.

After breaking an 11-game losing streak to Industrial the previous season, the Indians were eager to make it two straight wins in one of the most highly anticipated games of the season. Industrial had been waiting nearly a full year to avenge their 14-7 loss to Ganado on November 1 of the previous year, and the buildup to this Halloween night showdown reached a fever pitch. The excitement around the matchup was so intense that the town of Ganado moved all Halloween festivities to the night before for safety reasons - a decision that made national headlines and was even mentioned on *The David Letterman Show*. Both Ganado and Industrial entered the game undefeated at 8-0 and ranked in the top ten statewide, with Ganado at #4 and Industrial at #9. It was not just a battle of records, but also a clash of styles, with Ganado's potent offense set to face Industrial's elite defense. Adding even more weight to the contest was the likelihood that it would be the final meeting between the two schools, as Industrial was expected to move up to Class 3A in the upcoming UIL realignment. Indian Stadium was packed with a standing-room-only crowd of nearly 5,000 fans. The game was a physical and defensive battle from the outset. Ganado's opening drive reached the Industrial 13-yard line but stalled when Heath Bures was stopped just short on a fourth-and-four fake field goal attempt. Industrial responded with a 90-yard, 14-play drive - all on the ground - capped by a 19-yard touchdown run from James Vaughn with 8:58 left in the second quarter, giving them a 6-0 lead after a missed extra point. In the second half, Industrial continued their ball-control strategy, reaching the Ganado 6-yard line on their opening possession, only to be stopped on fourth down. But they came right back on their next drive and extended the lead to 9-0 on a 20-yard field goal by quarterback Brandon Karl with 9:09 remaining. On their following possession, Industrial sealed the game with a six-play, 38-yard drive that ended with Karl scoring on a one-yard plunge and adding the extra point to make it 16-0 with 4:55 to play. Ganado finally mounted a response late in the game, driving 80 yards behind the arm of Bures and the legs of Watson, who rushed for 80 yards. Watson scored on a 2-yard run with 1:37 left to avoid the shutout, but the Indians failed on the two-point conversion. An unsuccessful onside kick allowed Industrial to run out the clock and claim a 16-6 victory. Industrial's game plan of suffocating defense and a clock-controlling ground game proved decisive, as they held the ball for 32:03 and ran 61 offensive plays (56 of them rushing), compared to Ganado's 43. The loss snapped Ganado's 22-game regular season winning streak and their 16-game district winning streak. With their record now 8-1 overall and 5-1 in district, the Indians faced a must-win situation in their final regular season game against Tidehaven to secure a playoff spot. Ganado rose to the challenge in El Maton, relying on a dominant rushing attack and strong defensive effort. Watson led the way with 192 yards and a touchdown, while Hicks contributed 95 rushing yards. Bures added a touchdown pass to Barry Dunlap and scored on a run himself. The Indians took a 20-0 lead into the fourth quarter before Tidehaven answered with a 66-yard touchdown by Peter Quinn. Still, the Indians maintained control and finished with a 27-13 win, clinching the district runner-up spot and a second consecutive trip to the playoffs. Ganado closed the regular season at 9-1, resilient after their only setback, and ready for postseason play.

In the bi-district round of the playoffs, the Indians faced a formidable opponent in the Schulenburg Shorthorns at Yoakum. Schulenburg entered the game with a 6-4 record, having struggled early in the season but gaining momentum as district champions. A powerhouse in Class 2A throughout the 1990s, Schulenburg had captured nine consecutive district titles from 1990 to 1998, won back-to-back state championships in 1991 and 1992, and finished as state runner-up in 1994. Ganado knew it would take a strong performance to advance. However, the Indians came out flat, and Schulenburg took immediate control. On their opening possession, Schulenburg marched 74 yards in four plays, scoring on a 49-yard touchdown pass from Joel Blansitt to Clarence Irving. After a Ganado punt, Schulenburg capitalized on a 41-yard punt return and extended their lead to 14-0 with another Blansitt touchdown pass, this time to Victor James. The Shorthorns continued their dominance in the second quarter when Thomas Runnells broke free for a 66-yard touchdown run, pushing the lead to 21-0 with under nine minutes left in the first half. Ganado's defense finally made a stop just before halftime, blocking a 26-yard field goal attempt with 19 seconds left. The Indians quickly moved the ball into Schulenburg territory on three straight passes from Heath Bures, but time expired before they could score. Still, the late drive provided a spark and shifted the momentum slightly in Ganado's favor heading into the locker room. The Indians began the second half with renewed energy and a sense of urgency. They put together a 71-yard scoring drive, kept alive by a gutsy 8-yard run by Watson on a fake punt on fourth-and-six. Shortly after, Bures connected with Barry Dunlap for a 40-yard touchdown pass, putting Ganado on the board at 21-7 with 9:34 remaining in the third quarter. After a defensive stop and another punt exchange, Ganado struck again. Watson took a pitch from Bures, broke four tackles, and raced 75 yards down the sideline for a touchdown. Though the extra point was blocked, the Indians had cut the deficit to 21-13 with just over a minute left in the third. With their defense continuing to hold strong, the Indians got the ball back and quickly mounted another drive. Bures found tight end Lambert for a critical 21-yard gain, followed by a clutch 36-yard reception on third-and-19. Bures then hit Dunlap for a 29-yard touchdown, and Watson powered in the two-point conversion to tie the game at 21-21 with 5:34 left. The Ganado sideline erupted with belief and energy, and the defense came up with another stop, forcing a three-and-out. The Indians offense seized the opportunity, driving 54 yards in seven plays. Watson capped the drive with a 6-yard touchdown run, and Lambert's extra point gave Ganado its first lead of the game, 28-21, with just 1:15 remaining. Schulenburg wasn't finished yet. They managed to convert a desperate fourth-and-15 to keep their final drive alive. But the comeback was sealed when Sam Chanek intercepted a Blansitt pass with 31 seconds left, allowing the Indians to complete a remarkable comeback victory. Coach Althaus praised his team's character, stating how fortunate they were to come back against such a high-caliber opponent. After the final whistle, one player passionately shouted, "We Believe!" - a fitting summary of Ganado's resilient performance. Statistically, Bures had an outstanding game, completing 10 of 17 passes for 226 yards and two touchdowns. Lambert came up big in the receiving game with four catches for 95 yards, while Watson led the ground attack with 172 rushing yards and two touchdowns. The thrilling 28-21 win advanced Ganado to the next round of the playoffs and stood as a testament to their determination and heart.

In the Area round of the playoffs, the Indians faced the undefeated Crawford Pirates (11-0) in Brenham - the same venue where the Indians had defeated Rogers a year earlier. Crawford, a perennial playoff contender, was known for its balanced offense and tough defense. Ganado entered the matchup knowing they would need a complete performance to advance. The Indians came out strong. On their opening drive, they marched 59 yards in five plays, with Watson scoring from three yards out just 1:32 into the game. After an offsides penalty on Crawford during the extra point attempt, Ganado opted for a two-point conversion, and Watson successfully ran it in to give the Indians an 8-0 lead. Crawford responded immediately, driving 68 yards in 14 plays, capped by a one-yard touchdown run by Shawn Massirer. A successful two-point conversion tied the game at 8-8 with 4:35 left in the first quarter. On the ensuing kickoff, Ganado nearly faced disaster when Hicks muffed the ball and Crawford recovered at the Indians' 31-yard line. However, the Ganado defense came through, forcing a fourth down where Chad Rhea threw his first interception of the season, picked off by Chris Hajovsky. Ganado took over and moved the ball efficiently but ended the drive with an interception thrown by Bures at the 10-yard line as the first quarter ended. The Indians' defense held Crawford to their first punt of the game, and Ganado quickly capitalized. Watson, who would score all of Ganado's touchdowns, found the end zone again on a 15-yard run. With Lambert's extra point, Ganado regained the lead, 15-8. But Crawford again had an answer. A 30-yard kickoff return set them up for another drive, which ended with Massirer scoring his second one-yard touchdown of the game. The extra point tied it 15-15 with 4:35 left in the half. Ganado drove into Crawford territory but fumbled at the 30-yard line. Crawford couldn't capitalize and punted, and Ganado managed to reach midfield before time expired, sending the teams into halftime deadlocked at 15. Crawford opened the second half with a punt, but soon intercepted Bures for the second time, setting up a potential go-ahead drive. They reached the Ganado 13-yard line, but a delay of game penalty pushed their 30-yard field goal attempt back five yards. Daniel Dysinger's 35-yard attempt came up just short, and Ganado took over. The Indians seized the moment with an 80-yard drive, capped once again by Watson, this time on a 10-yard touchdown run. Lambert's extra point gave Ganado a 22-15 lead with 1:09 left in the third quarter. Crawford, aided by a 39-yard kickoff return, reached the Ganado 22 but turned the ball over on downs. Ganado couldn't extend the lead and eventually punted, giving Crawford possession at their own 23. Crawford then executed an eight-play, 77-yard drive, with Rhea connecting with Brady Walker on a 20-yard touchdown pass. Dysinger's extra point tied the game again, 22-22, with 4:34 left. The Indians' offense sputtered on the next series, and they were forced to punt after losing yardage. Fortunately, the defense held Crawford to just two yards and got the ball back with two minutes to play. Michael Tristan recovered a Crawford fumble to give Ganado a final opportunity in regulation, but the offense couldn't capitalize, and the game headed to overtime. Ganado took the first possession in overtime and needed just two running plays for Watson to score his fourth touchdown of the night from nine yards out. However, Lambert's extra point attempt missed wide right, leaving the score 28-22. Crawford then took over and, on their fourth play, ran a flea-flicker that left Paul Szhnalrieda wide open in the end zone for a 15-yard touchdown. Dysinger nailed the extra point, giving Crawford a 29-28 overtime victory and abruptly ending Ganado's playoff run and season.

The heartbreaking loss was especially tough for Ganado's seniors. Although they never trailed during regulation, the Indians were eliminated in the second round, which felt disappointing given the team's high expectations after a semifinal run the year before. Nonetheless, the season was far from a failure. Ganado finished 10-2, competed in one of the toughest 2A districts in the state, and showed resilience and leadership throughout the year. In a twist of fate, district champion Industrial also lost in overtime that same night to Rogers, 34-33. Crawford would go on to lose to Refugio 17-10 in the next round, while Rogers advanced to the state final before falling to Stanton 33-7. Despite the earlier-than-expected exit, this Ganado team was special. It upheld the program's tradition and left a legacy of hard work and leadership. Standout seniors Jarrett Lambert, Caleb McCain, and Chad Green would go on to play at Angelo State, continuing their football journeys beyond a memorable 1997 season.

1998

At the biannual UIL realignment on February 2, Industrial High School was moved up to the 3A classification, prompting a shift in District 27-2A. Brookshire Royal replaced Industrial, which had dropped down from 3A, while the rest of the district - East Bernard, Tidehaven,

Boling, Van Vleck, Brazos, and Danbury - remained unchanged for the next two football seasons. A significant change introduced by the UIL was that each 2A and 3A district would now send three teams to the playoffs. The school with the highest enrollment among the playoff qualifiers would compete in the Division I bracket, while the other two, with smaller enrollments, would enter the Division II bracket. For Ganado, which had the smallest enrollment in the district, this meant any playoff berth would result in placement in Division II.

Expectations were high once again for Ganado, with the primary goal being to secure one of the three playoff spots. The team returned two key offensive weapons from the previous season: quarterback Heath Bures, who passed for 1,007 yards and earned District 28-2A Offensive MVP and second-team all-state honors, and tailback Sterling Watson, who rushed for 1,304 yards and 19 touchdowns, averaging 10 yards per carry. Fullback B.J. Hicks also returned, having rushed for over 800 yards. However, the biggest challenge lay in replacing a standout offensive line, which lost Chad Green, Caleb McCain, and Jarrett Lambert to Angelo State. The new starting offensive line featured senior Rex Reid at center, brothers Travis and Joe Neumann at guard, and seniors Seth Brezina and Brandon Bures at tackle. Michael Tristan took over at tight end. Freshman Matthew Bures, Heath's younger brother, was expected to contribute significantly in the backfield, particularly when Watson lined up at receiver. Defensively, Ganado aimed to improve after struggles in last year's playoffs. Returning players included Hicks at cornerback, Tristan and Jon Pruitt at linebacker, Heath Bures at safety, and Brandon Bures on the defensive line. New starters included juniors Robert Beard and Wesley Lambert at defensive end, junior Joey Neumann and sophomore Will McCain at cornerback, and Watson and junior Greg Hajovsky at halfback. Ganado faced a tough non-district schedule with games against Class 3A schools Yoakum and Hallettsville and top-10 ranked Lexington in Class 2A. Coach Althaus believed that if the team could physically and mentally withstand those early challenges, they would be well-prepared and competitive heading into district play. The strong non-district slate was intended to make the team battle-tested and ready to contend with playoff contenders Royal, East Bernard, and Tidehaven.

The Indians opened their football season at home against Class 3A Yoakum in a tough and physical contest. The defense led the way, with

Heath Bures returning an interception for a touchdown and later setting up one of B.J. Hicks' two touchdowns with another interception. Hicks finished the night with 75 rushing yards and two scores, helping Ganado to a 13-0 halftime lead. Yoakum responded with a one-yard touchdown run by Nathan Bucek in the second half, cutting the lead to 13-6. However, Travis Neumann forced a fumble that Heath Bures recovered and returned for another touchdown, sealing a 20-6 victory. Sterling Watson contributed 79 rushing yards in the win. The following week, the Indians were scheduled to host the #9-ranked Lexington team, but Tropical Storm Frances made landfall near Matagorda Bay, bringing heavy rains that flooded the area and forced school closure on game day. Due to poor field conditions, the game was relocated to Lexington, with an agreement that Lexington would travel to Ganado in 1999. Despite the disruption, the Indians traveled well and delivered a dominant performance, rushing for 283 total yards. Watson led the way with 144 yards and two touchdowns, while freshman Matthew Bures scored his first varsity touchdown on a one-yard run in the third quarter, giving Ganado a 22-0 lead. Lexington scored once in the fourth quarter, but Ganado's defense forced four turnovers, and the Indians secured a 22-6 win. For their final non-district game, the Indians traveled to Hallettsville to face another Class 3A opponent. The field conditions were poor due to continued rainfall from Tropical Storm Frances and a week of steady rain, turning the field into a "pig sty." Trailing 10-7 late in the second quarter, Watson scored just before halftime to give Ganado a 14-10 lead. He finished with 68 rushing yards. In the fourth quarter, Matthew Bures added a one-yard touchdown run to seal a 21-10 victory. With a perfect 3-0 record in non-district play against strong competition, including two 3A schools and a top-10 ranked 2A team, the Indians proved themselves physically and mentally prepared for the challenges of district play. Their successful start established them as a serious contender, battle-tested and ready to compete for a playoff spot.

The Indians began district play on the road against Tidehaven as 18-point favorites, having won three consecutive meetings against them during Coach Althaus' tenure and entering the game with a strong 3-0 record against quality non-district opponents. However, the expected victory did not materialize, as Tidehaven was well-prepared and executed a bruising, ball-control offensive strategy led by quarterback Neil Clements, along with a suffocating defensive effort. Tidehaven dominated time of possession in the second half, holding the ball for 19 minutes and 12 seconds compared to Ganado's 4 minutes and 48 seconds, and ran 70 plays to Ganado's 34. Ganado had an early opportunity to score after driving from their own 45-yard line to the Tidehaven 4, but missed a 21-yard field goal. That would be their only scoring opportunity, as they managed just three more first downs and never advanced past their own 46-yard line for the remainder of the game. Watson was held to just 45 rushing yards, 17 of which came on his first carry. Tidehaven finally broke the scoreless tie late in the third quarter with a 20-yard field goal by Tim Johnson, and sealed the game with an 81-yard, 11-play drive capped by a one-yard touchdown run from Clements. The Indians fell 9-0, starting district play with a disappointing 0-1 record. Coach Althaus acknowledged that Tidehaven simply outplayed them and emphasized the importance of regrouping, as six district games remained. Ganado bounced back in a big way the following week during their homecoming game against Brazos. The Bures brothers led the charge - quarterback Heath Bures threw two touchdown passes to Michael Tristan and Watson, while Watson and freshman Matthew Bures each added rushing touchdowns. All 33 points were scored in the first half, and the Indians shut out Brazos 33-0. The momentum continued on the road against Danbury, where the Indians delivered one of their most dominant performances in school history with a 76-6 victory - their second-highest point total ever at the time. Watson and Hicks both rushed for 152 yards and scored three touchdowns apiece. With two commanding wins under their belt, Ganado had worked its way back into the district race, but tougher opponents were still ahead.

The Indians entered a pivotal point in their district schedule when they hosted district favorite Brookshire Royal, a team fresh off a win against East Bernard and known for its explosive offense and incredible team speed. Royal's standout running back, Thomas Tarver, would eventually rush for over 3,000 yards that season and help lead Royal to the 2A Division I state championship game, where they narrowly lost to Omaha Paul Pewitt, 28-26. The Indians faced significant adversity ahead of the game, as three starting defenders were suspended for disciplinary reasons stemming from a weekend party involving alcohol. Despite the setbacks, Ganado showed resilience. Hicks ignited the crowd with a 75-yard touchdown run in the first quarter, giving the Indians a 7-0 lead. Royal responded with three consecutive scores to take a 19-7 lead, but Hicks struck again with a one-yard touchdown run just before halftime, cutting the deficit to 19-14. In the second half, the Indians regained the lead after Watson scored on a six-yard run, followed by a two-point conversion pass from Heath Bures to Greg Hajovsky, making it 22-19. However, Tarver proved unstoppable, finishing the night with 233 rushing yards and four touchdowns, including a back-breaking 41-yard score on fourth down to seal Royal's 33-22 win. With the loss, Ganado dropped to 2-2 in district and entered must-win territory for the remainder of the season. To qualify for the playoffs for a third consecutive year, the Indians needed to win their final three games - and beat East Bernard by at least 11 points due to tiebreaker rules following the 11-point loss to Royal.

That week, South Texas was hit by the devastating Flood of 1998, with Gonzales, Cuero, and Victoria severely affected by the overflowing Guadalupe River. Despite the challenging weather conditions, Ganado remained focused and practiced well. On the road at East Bernard, the Indians fell behind early when Marlon Blunston scored on a 7-yard run, but the defense tightened and shut down the Brahmas the rest of the night, limiting them to just 170 total yards and seven first downs. The Indians responded with an 11-yard touchdown run by Watson, and, needing every point, converted a two-point play to take an 8-7 lead. In the second quarter, Bures threw touchdown passes to Watson (23 yards) and Michael Tristan (21 yards), with another two-point conversion by Watson sandwiched in between. Ganado led 22-7 at halftime and shut out East Bernard in the second half, using clock management and a ground-heavy attack led by freshman Matthew Bures, who rushed for 142 yards. The 22-7 win met the required margin and revived Ganado's playoff hopes. With momentum back on their side, Ganado traveled to Van Vleck and erupted early, building a 34-6 lead in the first quarter en route to a 47-18 victory. The Indians dominated on the ground, rushing for 348 yards. Watson led the way with 123 yards and three touchdowns, while Hicks added 102 yards and a score. The defense gave up 266 passing yards - including 228 receiving yards to Sherman Abbott - but the offensive explosion proved more than enough. Needing one final win to secure their playoff spot, the Indians hosted Boling in the regular season finale and delivered with a 33-14 win. Hicks starred again, rushing for 118 yards and three touchdowns, as Ganado secured a playoff berth for the third consecutive season. The Indians finished the regular season with an 8-2 overall record and 5-2 in district. Overcoming adversity - including key player suspensions, a flood-affected week of preparation, and a must-win stretch to close the season - the Indians showed resilience, focus, and heart. Now back in the playoffs, the team wasn't satisfied with just making it. They were determined to keep winning and embark on what would become a memorable playoff run.

The Indians entered the playoffs as the top seed in the Division II bracket, with Tidehaven securing the second seed after their loss to East Bernard in the season finale. Royal, having won the district championship and boasting the largest enrollment, advanced to the Division I bracket. Ganado began their bi-district playoffs against Yorktown at Victoria Memorial Stadium. The Indians had easily defeated Yorktown in the past two seasons, winning 55-0 and 34-13. However, Yorktown, with a 5-5 record, was improved this year, notably with a strong running back, Dennis Warwas. Despite rain soaking the area before and during the day of the game, the weather cleared up by game time. In the first half, both teams played physically, with Matthew Bures scoring two touchdowns to put Ganado up 14-0. Yorktown's Warwas answered with a touchdown, cutting the lead to 14-7 by halftime. In the second half, Ganado took control, with Watson scoring three touchdowns and rushing for 197 yards, leading to a 38-13 victory. After the game, the rain returned. Next, the Indians faced Winters, the 11-0, #3 ranked team, in the Area playoffs in Kerrville, marking their longest playoff trip at the time at 240 miles. Winters had a talented quarterback, Kenny Whittenburg, who had thrown for over 1,400 yards and was a contender for the 2A Player of the Year award. Their offensive line averaged 240 pounds per player, making for a challenging matchup. Despite Winters' strength, the Indians' defense dominated. In the first quarter, Tristan and Hicks forced a fumble, which Heath Bures returned 17 yards for a touchdown. Matthew Bures, who rushed for 134 yards, scored three touchdowns. Ganado led 18-0 by the third quarter, but Winters scored once before the Indians sealed the win with a series of turnovers. Watson intercepted two passes, including one that led to Bures' third touchdown. Watson then returned another interception 40 yards for a touchdown to finish the game, leading to a dominant 31-6 victory. The defense was key, intercepting Whittenburg four times and holding him under 100 yards passing, while the offense capitalized on the turnovers. The Indians advanced to play over Thanksgiving weekend for only the second time in school history. In the regional round, Ganado faced Poth, who had just upset Refugio in overtime. Poth, a senior-heavy team with 29 seniors, was big and physical. The game, played in Gonzales, was a hard-hitting, smash-mouth affair. Poth scored first with a three-yard touchdown run by Adam Montez. Ganado responded with a 33-yard touchdown pass from Heath Bures to Tristan, but missed the extra point, leaving them trailing 7-6 at halftime. In the second half, the Indians' offense came alive, particularly with Matthew Bures' powerful running. He converted a fourth-and-two, and a key 14-yard pass from Heath Bures to Dwayne Hinojosa set up a 1-yard touchdown by Bures and a subsequent two-point conversion to give Ganado a 14-7 lead. Ganado's defense dominated in the second half, holding Poth to only three first downs and 37 total yards. A crucial goal-line stand, stopping Poth on first-and-goal at the 5-yard line, kept the lead intact. The game was sealed when Greg Hajovsky recovered a fumble on a punt with 2:44 remaining, securing a 14-7 victory and sending Ganado to the next round of the playoffs.

The Indians were on their way to the quarterfinals, aiming for the Region 4 championship for the second consecutive year. Awaiting them was Goldthwaite, who had recently defeated district rival Tidehaven 33-21 in the area round. Goldthwaite had a strong tradition, having appeared in three straight 2A state championship games from 1992 to 1994, winning back-to-back titles in 1993 and 1994, as well as a 1A title in 1985. Known for their explosive offense, solid defense, and effective running game, Goldthwaite was a formidable opponent. The game was held at Hays Consolidated Rebel Field in Buda, and Goldthwaite controlled most of the game. They dominated for three quarters, building a 16-0 lead, as Ganado struggled to get much possession, with Goldthwaite running 65 plays. The Indians managed to score late in the third quarter, when Heath Bures connected with Watson on a 79-yard touchdown pass to make the score 16-6. Goldthwaite added another touchdown in the fourth quarter to increase their lead to 22-6, but the Indians started to rally. A muffed kick provided Ganado with good field position, and Matthew Bures took advantage, catching a short screen pass from his brother Heath for a 41-yard gain, setting up a touchdown run from Watson from the five-yard line. After a missed two-point conversion, the score stood at 22-12. The Indians' defense then forced Goldthwaite to punt, and Travis Neumann blocked the punt, returning it to the one-yard line.

Watson quickly scored again, and with a successful extra point, Ganado was now within three points, trailing 22-19. With just over a minute to play and the ball at their own two-yard line, it seemed like a miracle comeback was within reach. However, on the first snap, Heath Bures lost the ball, and despite recovering it, the ball bounced away, allowing Goldthwaite to recover it at the 14-yard line. Three plays later, the game was over. The Indians' valiant effort fell short in heartbreaking fashion.

Despite the tough loss, Coach Althaus remained proud of his team. The Indians finished the season with an 11-3 record, and the senior class stood out for their leadership and heart. While the team may not have been the biggest or fastest, their heart and dedication were unmatched. After starting the season with a 2-2 district record and a mid-October loss to Royal, they fought hard and stayed on a mission, making the season memorable. One of the senior leaders, B.J. Hicks would continue his football career at Texas Lutheran in Seguin.

1999

Entering the 1999 season, expectations were once again high for the Ganado football team, with a clear goal of not only making the playoffs but also performing well once there. A record number of 68 players came out for football during the start of two-a-days in August - still the largest turnout in Ganado history. The roster included 37 junior varsity players, allowing for two JV teams, and 31 varsity players. Despite a solid senior class, the varsity team was relatively young and in a rebuilding phase. However, the experience gained from the previous season's playoff run provided valuable preparation for the younger players, many of whom were promoted from JV and considered strong contributors.

Only three offensive starters returned: sophomore running back Matthew Bures and the Neumann brothers - senior Travis and sophomore Joe - at the guard positions. Senior tight ends Robert Beard and Wesley Lambert also returned with experience and started again at defensive end. Senior Jonathan Tristan started at center, with junior Will McCain joining the Neumann brothers at guard. The offensive tackle positions were filled by senior Russ Hunt and juniors Kurt Janica and Tyson Skalicky. Senior Greg Hajovsky led the offense as the starting quarterback, with junior Randy Rakowitz as backup. The backfield featured junior Edward Perez alongside Matthew Bures, with seniors Joey Neumann and Billy Cortez contributing, while the receiving corps included seniors Wesley Miller and Ryan Pape, along with juniors Eric Aguilar, Josh Chambless, Jacob Bures, and Dustin Hicks. On defense, Travis Neumann returned at linebacker, while McCain and Joey Neumann held down the cornerback positions. The defensive line was anchored by junior Bryan Cervenka, Joe Neumann, and returning ends Beard and Lambert. Junior Joey Almarez took over the other linebacker spot, and Matthew Bures filled the safety role vacated by his brother Heath. Hajovsky, the only returning player with experience in the defensive secondary, was joined by Chambless. Although the team experienced some early growing pains, their ability to come together, work hard, and play cohesively ultimately paid off. By the end of the season, their efforts resulted in a successful campaign.

The Indians opened the 1999 football season on the road against 3A Yoakum, a team that returned most of its roster from the previous year and was in better physical condition at the time. Ganado struggled significantly on both sides of the ball and was thoroughly dominated in a 48-0 shutout loss. The Indians were limited to just three first downs and 77 total yards of offense, while Yoakum amassed 350 total yards. This game marked Coach Althaus' first non-district loss since taking over the Ganado program in 1995. In response, the team turned to film study and preparation to regroup. Ganado's home opener came against Lexington, the first of three consecutive home games. The Indians showed improvement and played a competitive first half, entering halftime tied 6-6. However, Lexington took control in the second half, scoring 21 unanswered points to secure a 27-6 victory. Ganado's lone score came from a 9-yard touchdown pass from quarterback Greg Hajovsky to Edward Perez, while Matthew Bures rushed for 80 yards. Lexington's speed and talent proved too much in the end. In their final non-district game, the Indians hosted Hallettsville for Homecoming. Ganado fought hard and showed continued progress, taking their first lead of the season on a 1-yard touchdown run by Hajovsky late in the second quarter. They led 7-0 until the final play of the half, when Hallettsville quarterback Jordan Mullins connected with Kenneth Harper on a 27-yard touchdown pass. The extra point was blocked, and Ganado held a narrow 7-6 lead at halftime. In the second half,

Hallettsville pulled ahead with a third-quarter on another Mullins touchdown pass to Chad Shimek, ultimately winning 14-7. Though the Indians started the season 0-3, they were visibly improving each week despite facing three strong opponents. Offensively, the team had only scored 13 points through the first three games, leading many outsiders to doubt Ganado's playoff potential. However, such skepticism was nothing new for the program, which has a history of facing and overcoming doubt. The early adversity only served to motivate the team further, reinforcing the pride and resilience of the Indians.

Ganado opened district play as significant underdogs against undefeated 3-0 Tidehaven. Adding to the challenge was the emotional weight of the matchup, as most of the senior class had never defeated Tidehaven in their football careers dating back to seventh grade. In contrast, the previous year had seen Ganado enter as heavy favorites, only to suffer a disappointing 9-0 loss. However, with non-district records wiped clean and a fresh start in district play, the Indians were focused and ready. The game turned out to be a tense, defensive battle. While Tidehaven brought a strong defense, it was Ganado's defensive unit that ultimately won the game. A crucial goal-line stand in the second quarter kept Tidehaven out of the end zone, and later in the game, Joey Almarez forced a fumble on a punt return that Ganado recovered to help seal the victory. The Indians' only score came late in the first quarter when Hajovsky connected with Wesley Lambert on a 24-yard touchdown pass. Jose Pena's extra point made it 7-0. Tidehaven responded in the third quarter with a 44-yard touchdown pass from Patrick Hosey to Rocky Galvan, but the extra point attempt failed, preserving a 7-6 Ganado lead that would hold as the final score. The victory was especially meaningful for the senior class, marking their first-ever win over Tidehaven and giving the Indians a 1-0 start in district play. The win also reignited Ganado's season and silenced early-season doubters.

Building on that momentum, Ganado's defense continued to shine in the following two games, posting back-to-back shutouts. The Indians traveled to Brazos and dominated, holding an explosive offense to just 86 total yards in a 21-0 win. On offense, Ganado also began to find its rhythm, rushing for 291 yards. Edward Perez led the way with 124 yards, and Matthew Bures added 95 yards and a touchdown. Bures also showcased his versatility by throwing a 21-yard touchdown pass on a halfback pass to Lambert. The next week, at home against Danbury,

Ganado's defense delivered another dominant performance, limiting Danbury to only 63 total yards - all on the ground - and just two first downs. The Indians even added a safety when a Danbury punt rolled into their own end zone. On offense, Ganado rushed for 315 yards, with Perez gaining 158 yards and a touchdown, and Bures contributing 82 yards and two scores. By this point, the Indians had improved their overall record to 3-3, but more importantly, stood undefeated at 3-0 in district play. The team was playing their best football at the perfect time, setting the stage for a pivotal matchup against #8-ranked Brookshire Royal, the defending 2A Division I state finalist. The game was expected to have major implications for the district championship.

The Indians' defense faced a tough challenge as Royal struck first with a 5-yard touchdown pass from Sean Eason to Andy Leahey in the first quarter. Ganado responded early in the second quarter with a 1-yard touchdown run by Matthew Bures to tie the game at 7-7. Royal regained the lead with a 9-yard rushing touchdown by Patrick Shalow, but the Indians answered right back with a 44-yard touchdown run by Perez. A missed extra point left Ganado trailing 14-13. Just before halftime, Shalow scored again from 11 yards out, giving Royal a 20-13 lead at the break. The second half shifted into a defensive battle, and Ganado appeared poised for an upset late in the game. With 3:23 remaining, Bures - who finished with 91 rushing yards - scored on a 4-yard run. On the ensuing extra point attempt, the Indians executed a fake as holder Hajovsky threw a successful two-point conversion pass to Robert Beard, giving Ganado a 21-20 lead. However, Royal drove down the field in the final moments, and with just three seconds left, Willie Sierra kicked a 30-yard field goal to give Royal a heartbreaking 23-21 win. The narrow loss was tough to accept, as many players were visibly emotional after coming so close to a major upset. The defeat gave Royal sole possession of the district lead, but Ganado remained firmly in the playoff hunt.

Rather than being deflated by the loss, the Indians used it as fuel. The following week at home, Ganado played its most complete game of the season in a dominant 34-13 victory over East Bernard, a playoff-bound team. For the first time all season, both Matthew Bures and Perez rushed for over 100 yards - Bures with 151 yards and two touchdowns, and Perez with 130 yards and three scores. The Indians built a 27-0 lead by the third quarter and never looked back, reestablishing themselves as serious contenders. In their home finale against Van

Vleck, the Indians were tested by an athletic opponent. Ganado took a 12-0 lead in the second quarter, but Van Vleck's quarterback Rowdy Patterson heated up, throwing touchdown passes to Sherman Abbott and Vonchess Griggs, cutting the lead to 19-15 by the end of the third quarter. Ganado responded in the fourth with clutch touchdowns from Joey Neumann and Bures, who rushed for 179 yards on the night, to secure a 32-15 win. Defensively, the Indians were strong against the run, holding Van Vleck to just 56 rushing yards and limiting standout back Griggs to only 32 yards. More importantly, the win clinched a playoff berth for Ganado, marking their fourth consecutive postseason appearance. On that same night, Tidehaven shocked Royal with a 24-7 upset, creating a three-way tie atop the district standings between Ganado, Royal, and Tidehaven. Ganado then closed out the regular season with a dominant 41-6 win at Boling. Hajovsky had a perfect passing night, completing all four of his attempts for 192 yards, including two long touchdown passes to Perez for 72 and 68 yards in the second quarter. Perez added two more touchdowns on the ground in the third quarter, finishing the night with four total scores. Boling's lone touchdown came with just eight seconds left, preventing a shutout. This win was particularly significant as it marked Coach Les Althaus' 50th career victory at Ganado. The Indians finished the regular season with a 6-4 overall record and a 6-1 district mark, sharing the district title with Royal. However, East Bernard's upset win over Tidehaven that same night knocked Tidehaven out of the playoffs despite their 8-2 record. With East Bernard earning the final playoff spot, Ganado was awarded the top seed in the Division II bracket. This favorable outcome meant the Indians avoided facing undefeated district champion Shiner in the bi-district round - an opponent they likely would have drawn had the district ended in a three-way tie.

The Indians opened the bi-district round of the playoffs with a matchup against Weimar in Wharton. The game began poorly for Ganado, as the Indians fumbled on their first offensive play, and Weimar quickly capitalized when quarterback David Fuchs connected with Donald Levinski for a 36-yard touchdown, giving Weimar a 7-0 lead. Ganado struggled to find rhythm early on offense, but their defense provided the spark when Travis Neumann blocked a punt and returned it 27 yards for a touchdown to tie the game 7-7 late in the first quarter. In the second quarter, Ganado's offense came to life. Matthew Bures, who rushed for a game-high 239 yards, scored three touchdowns, propelling the Indians ahead. Although Fuchs added a rushing touchdown for Weimar before halftime, Ganado took control with a 28-14 lead at the break. The second half was all Ganado, as Perez, who finished with 122 rushing yards, scored two third-quarter touchdowns. Gerald Lee, a player recently promoted from the JV squad, capped off the scoring with a 22-yard touchdown run in the fourth quarter. Ganado dominated the game after the early fumble, piling up 494 rushing yards and attempting only one pass, which was completed for six yards. The Indians cruised to a commanding 49-14 win. In the Area round, Ganado faced Little River Academy at Giddings. Academy had pulled off an upset over Goldthwaite the week before, and the Indians knew they were facing a tough opponent. The game was a defensive battle from the outset, with no touchdowns scored through the first three quarters. Ganado took a 3-0 lead in the first quarter on a 34-yard field goal by Pena. Academy responded in the second quarter with a 27-yard field goal by Luke Bargainer, tying the game 3-3. Bargainer would later join the Ganado coaching staff from 2019 to 2021, while his father, Grady Bargainer, had been Academy's head coach from 1994 to 1998. The first touchdown of the game came in the fourth quarter when Academy's Aaron Pressley connected with Bargainer on a 15-yard pass, giving Academy a 10-3 lead with 8:33 remaining. As they had all season, the Indians responded under pressure. Matthew Bures broke loose for a 34-yard touchdown run to bring the score to 10-9, but the two-point conversion failed. With just under seven minutes left, Ganado's defense held firm and gave the offense one final opportunity. The Indians then orchestrated a 12-play, 64-yard drive that consumed nearly five minutes. Bures finished the drive with a one-yard touchdown plunge with just 53 seconds remaining to give Ganado a 15-10 lead. Another two-point attempt failed, but the game was sealed when Josh Chambless intercepted a pass with 18 seconds left, securing the win. The 15-10 comeback victory sent Ganado to the regional round for the third time in four years. It was a testament to the team's grit, resilience, and toughness, especially as several players had battled illness during the week and still managed to play through adversity to earn the win.

The Indians found themselves playing football over Thanksgiving for the second consecutive year and the third time in four seasons - a clear indication of the program's growing success. As expected in the later rounds of the playoffs, the level of competition intensified, and

Ganado's next opponent, Refugio, was a formidable powerhouse. Refugio came into the matchup with a dominant defense that had recorded seven shutouts, including not allowing a single point in district play. Offensively, they were explosive, with quarterback Zach Edwards and running back Alex Boyd leading a fast and powerful attack, supported by a massive offensive line. Defensively, they were anchored by junior linebacker Matt McKinney, a relentless force all over the field. Coach Althaus understood the challenge and implemented a game plan centered around sustaining drives and controlling the clock to limit Refugio's offensive possessions. Adding to the intensity was Refugio's desire for revenge after a painful 6-0 playoff loss to Ganado in 1996. The game was played on a Saturday night at Victoria's Memorial Stadium. Refugio opened the scoring with a field goal, but Ganado answered immediately as Matthew Bures returned the ensuing kickoff 80 yards for a touchdown, giving the Indians a 7-3 lead - unfortunately, their only score and lead of the night. Refugio responded with 17 more unanswered points in the first half to take a 20-7 lead into halftime. In the second half, especially in the fourth quarter, things unraveled for Ganado. Refugio completely took control, dominating the rest of the game and rolling to a 54-7 victory. Refugio racked up 348 total yards, all on the ground, led by Edwards, who rushed for 167 yards and three touchdowns. Their defense forced four turnovers - two fumbles and two interceptions - including a fumble recovery in the end zone for a score. Ganado was held to just 101 total yards and six first downs. Refugio would go on to defeat Mason 42-6 in the regional finals before falling 14-13 to Elysian Fields in the state semifinals.

Despite the lopsided loss, Ganado had much to be proud of. The Indians opened and closed the season with blowout defeats, but what happened in between truly mattered. After starting the season 0-3, many doubted the team's potential. However, Ganado, with a young and relatively inexperienced roster, matured quickly and never stopped believing. The team rallied behind a strong senior class that embraced their leadership roles, guiding the Indians to an 8-5 overall record, a share of the district championship, and a deep playoff run that took them to the third round. This season was a testament to the values of hard work, resilience, and perseverance. The 1999 Ganado Indians showed what could be achieved when a team refuses to give up, proving that belief, effort, and unity can lead to something special -

even in the face of early setbacks and tough odds. Wesley Lambert, would go on to play at Angelo State, following in his brother's footsteps.

2000

The biannual UIL realignment that took place on February 1, Ganado was placed into a six-team district for the first time since 1995. This structure meant the Indians would play five district games and five non-district games, the latter serving as preparation for their tough district competition. Historically, Ganado's district had been among the most competitive in the state in Class 2A throughout the 1990s. The newly formed District 28-2A included familiar rivals Tidehaven and Van Vleck, who were anticipated to be the most formidable opponents, along with Boling, Danbury, and Louise, which had moved up from Class 1A. Meanwhile, East Bernard, Royal, and Brazos exited the district and were set to be potential bi-district playoff opponents. Ganado prepared for the rigorous district schedule with a challenging non-district lineup, facing three Class 3A teams - Yoakum, George West, and Palacios - as well as former rival East Bernard and state-ranked Refugio, the team that eliminated them from the playoffs the previous year. As scheduling luck would have it, both Ganado and Refugio were available in the final week of non-district play and agreed to face off, making for a potential playoff preview. Ganado's goal was to emerge from this tough early schedule healthy, competitive, and confident heading into district play.

The team entered the 2000 season in much better shape than the year before, bolstered by a large and experienced group of returning players, including 18 seniors. In the backfield, junior Matthew Bures and senior Edward Perez both returned after 1,000-yard rushing seasons. They were supported by sophomore running backs Tim Neumann and Gerald Lee, as well as senior Joey Almarez. The receiving corps was deep with seniors Eric Aguilar, Josh Chambless, Jacob Bures, Scott Lee, and Dustin Hicks. Ganado's offensive line was also senior-laden, with tackles Kurt Janica and Tyson Skalicky, guard Will McCain, and center Manuel Gonzales. Junior Kirk Fowler played the other guard spot, while junior Joe Neumann moved from guard to tight end. Additional line depth came from seniors Brett Peters, Chris Peters, and Mark Waits. The starting quarterback role was awarded to senior Randy Rakowitz after a preseason competition with junior Clayton Hayden.

Defensively, the Indians were strong and experienced. Matthew Bures returned at safety, Almarez at linebacker, McCain and Jacob Bures at cornerback, and Chambless and Scott Lee at halfback. On the defensive line, Bryan Cervenka was the only returning starter at tackle, joined by junior Arthur Rodriguez. Defensive ends Joe Neumann and junior Colin Pittman, with support from Chris Peters, rounded out the line. Fowler played linebacker alongside Almarez, while Tim Neumann served as backup safety. On special teams, senior Jose Pena resumed his role as kicker. Overall, Ganado entered the season with a well-rounded, experienced roster and a difficult schedule designed to sharpen the team for a competitive district run.

The Indians opened the 2000 football season at home against Class 3A Yoakum under extreme heat conditions, with practice during the week limited due to heat indexes exceeding 110 degrees. Coach Althaus implemented cooling strategies, including ice towels for players during frequent breaks in practice. Despite the harsh weather earlier in the week, game night brought cooler but very humid conditions. Unlike the previous season's 48-0 loss to Yoakum, Ganado entered the matchup better prepared. Edward Perez gave the Indians an early 7-0 lead with a 20-yard touchdown run, though two scoring opportunities were missed on dropped halfback passes from Matthew Bures. Yoakum took control in the second half, tying the game 7-7 on a 69-yard drive capped by a Lester Lewis touchdown. Lewis finished with 127 rushing yards. However, Ganado responded with an 11-play, 69-yard drive ending in a 3-yard touchdown run by Gerald Lee. Jose Pena's extra point put Ganado ahead 14-7 with just over ten minutes remaining. A critical turning point came when Yoakum, threatening to score again, fumbled inside Ganado's 5-yard line. Despite this miscue, Yoakum scored with 40 seconds left on a short pass, but the extra point attempt missed wide left. Ganado recovered the onside kick and held on for a 14-13 victory. Coach Althaus acknowledged the team's effort and fortune, praising their resilience. Bures led Ganado with 111 rushing yards, followed by Lee with 63 and Perez with 52. The win proved significant as Yoakum went on to win their district and their only other loss was in the regional playoffs to eventual state champion La Grange. The next week, Ganado traveled to face perennial 3A playoff contender George West. The teams were evenly matched statistically, but Ganado was plagued by 12 penalties for 100 yards, which repeatedly stalled their momentum. Despite this, the Indians led late in the game after a

15-yard touchdown run by Bures, who rushed for 84 yards. However, George West responded with a 75-yard drive, scoring with 38 seconds left to win 16-13. The close loss dropped Ganado to 1-1 and was seen as a missed opportunity, but one that offered valuable lessons. Ganado returned home the following week to face another 3A team, Palacios, for their homecoming game. Palacios entered the matchup undefeated at 2-0 and boasted one of the most experienced rosters in 3A, with wins over Ganado district opponents Tidehaven and Van Vleck. However, the Indians' defense stepped up, forcing three interceptions on quarterback Ryan Kubecka, and keeping Palacios out of the end zone. Ganado took the lead just before halftime on a 35-yard touchdown pass from Clayton Hayden to Eric Aguilar. Bures added a 7-yard touchdown run in the third quarter, finishing the game with 137 rushing yards. Ganado won 13-0, earning their first shutout of the season and improving to 2-1.

After a successful 2-1 record against three tough 3A schools, the Indians felt confident heading into the final stretch of their non-district schedule. However, they knew the next two opponents - familiar 2A rivals - would be a real challenge. The first of these opponents was East Bernard, a former district rival, who brought a strong, speedy offense to town. With quarterback Brandon Black and running back Jonus Blunston leading the charge, along with a powerful offensive line, East Bernard struck first. After receiving the opening kickoff, East Bernard quickly moved the ball down the field, with Black, capping the drive with a 3-yard touchdown run to take a 7-0 lead. Black would rush for 118 yards. Ganado's offense struggled on their first possession, going three-and-out and giving the ball back to East Bernard. The Indians were flat to start, but in the second quarter, they began to find their rhythm. Matthew Bures finally sparked the offense with a 15-yard touchdown run, and Pena's extra point tied the game at 7-7. The Ganado defense stepped up next, stopping East Bernard deep in their territory, and the Indians took over at their own 10-yard line. On just the second play of the drive, Bures broke free for an electrifying 90-yard touchdown run, putting Ganado ahead 13-7. Bures went on to have a career game, rushing for 227 yards, adding another score in the third quarter, and even intercepting a pass. The Ganado offensive line performed their best blocking of the year, giving the offense much-needed support. While East Bernard still managed to gain yards, the Indians' defense made key stops when necessary. Ganado held on to win 19-7, improving their record to 3-1 as they prepared for their final non-district game against Refugio. Refugio, ranked #3 in the state at the time, presented an even tougher challenge. With explosive quarterback Alex Boyd, a state track medalist, and a big and powerful line on both sides of the ball, Refugio was a formidable opponent. The field conditions also posed difficulties, as 2.5 inches of rain had fallen before the game, leaving it soggy. Unfortunately for Ganado, the game started disastrously. On their first four offensive plays, Ganado lost two fumbles, both of which led to Refugio touchdowns, and the Indians quickly found themselves down 14-0. Refugio's defense and offensive power continued to dominate, and by the second quarter, Ganado trailed 21-0 after another fumble led to a score. Boyd, who would finish the game as the leading rusher with 150 yards, scored on two touchdown runs and a punt return, and Refugio went on to win 41-7. Ganado's only bright moment came in the third quarter when Gerald Lee broke free for a 50-yard run, setting up a Perez touchdown to put the Indians on the board. However, the turnovers and the superior play of Refugio proved to be too much for Ganado, resulting in a lopsided defeat. Despite the tough loss, Ganado's performance in non-district play, finishing with a 3-2 record, was respectable given the challenging schedule. With their non-district slate behind them, the Indians were now ready to face the challenges of district play.

After nearly a decade of competing in one of the toughest 2A districts in the state, the Indians found themselves in a much weaker district in 2000. They dominated their district opponents, shutting them out in every game with a combined score of 213-0, setting a school record for shutouts with six during the regular season. The Indians' impressive streak began with a 32-0 victory over Tidehaven, a team that had fallen to a 2-8 record after a strong decade in the 90s. In the game, Ganado raced to a 25-0 halftime lead, with Perez rushing for 112 yards and two touchdowns and Matthew Bures rushing for 120 yards and two touchdowns. The offense amassed 304 rushing yards, and the defense held Tidehaven to just 82 total yards while intercepting three passes. The following week, on game day, the team faced tragedy when they learned that Coach Althaus' mother had passed away in a house fire in Fredericksburg. After the news was shared by offensive coordinator Andy Bridges and principal Steven Saldivar, who coached under Althaus, Coach Bridges took over as the interim head coach, while assistant coach David Grewe called the defense. Despite the emotional loss, Ganado came out strong, dominating Van Vleck with a 31-0 lead at halftime. The final score remained 31-0, with Bures leading the way, rushing for 167 yards and three touchdowns. The Indians' powerful ground game totaled 357 yards, and Pena kicked four extra points and a 19-yard field goal. With a 2-0 record against the two teams that were expected to be their biggest challenges, Ganado showed resilience and strength. The following Monday, most of the team traveled to Fredericksburg for Coach Althaus' mother's funeral, showing support for their coach. Despite the loss, the team returned home in time for evening practice, and Coach Althaus was back at school by Tuesday, as they began preparing for their next opponent, the 6-1 Danbury Panthers.

Danbury had shown significant improvement in the 2000 season after a decade of struggles, where they had failed to win a district game throughout the 1990s. They broke their losing streak with a 28-12 win over Boling in their district opener but came off a narrow 25-21 loss to Louise. While Danbury had not faced strong competition in their non-district schedule, they were about to face the formidable Indians, who traveled on a long bus ride to Danbury. In what was likely their best performance of the season, Ganado dominated in all three phases of the game, winning 50-0. They led 35-0 by halftime, and their defense completely stifled Danbury, allowing only 63 total yards and forcing them to cross midfield only once late in the game. The Ganado offense was also in full swing, with Matthew Bures rushing for 104 yards, Perez and Gerald Lee combining for 143 yards, and all three scoring touchdowns. Additionally, Perez caught a 70-yard touchdown pass from Hayden. Next up for Ganado was the "Battle of Mustang Creek," their rivalry with the Louise Hornets. The two teams had not met in five years, and Louise, which had moved up in classification, had a competitive team with lots of speed and the district's leading rusher in Keith Edwards. Despite the hype from Louise's principal and local radio predictions from Clinto Robinson on *KULP'S Crystal Ball*, about the game being close, Ganado made it clear from the start that it would not be a contest. The Indians won 51-0, with three backs rushing for over 100 yards in a total of 409 team rushing yards. Gerald Lee led the way with 137 yards and two touchdowns, while Perez rushed for 101 yards and Bures added 100 yards and three scores. Ganado's defense held Edwards to just 37 yards and limited Louise to only 85 total yards and 4 first downs. With the win, Ganado improved to 4-0 in district play and clinched a share of the district title. Ganado finished the regular season with a 49-0 shutout of Boling, securing their fifth consecutive shutout. Despite Boling's winless record, they had shown potential in close games. However, Ganado's focus remained sharp after a slow start, and they dominated in the second quarter by scoring 28 points. A major setback occurred when Matthew Bures suffered a high ankle sprain during the game, limiting his contributions for the remainder of the season going into the playoffs. He would undergo surgery in the offseason to fix the injury. Tim Neumann stepped in to replace Bures at running back and safety for the upcoming playoffs. With the district title secured, Ganado entered the playoffs as the top seed in the Division II bracket, while Louise advanced as the runner-up. Van Vleck, another district competitor, entered the Division I bracket. This marked Ganado's first outright district title since 1996 and their fourth district championship since 1995.

The Indians faced East Bernard for the second time in one season during the bi-district playoffs. Having defeated East Bernard 19-7 earlier in the regular season, the Indians knew it would be tough to beat them again. Both teams were missing key players, with Ganado's Matthew Bures limited by injury and East Bernard without their starting quarterback, Brandon Black. The game was played at Ricebird Stadium in El Campo under cold, wet, and rainy conditions, which made the field slippery. Despite some early miscues and East Bernard having good field position, neither team could score in the first half, as East Bernard fumbled twice and missed a field goal. The score was 0-0 at halftime. In the second half, Ganado's only successful drive came right after the break, as they marched 75 yards down the field and capped it off with a 15-yard touchdown run by Tim Neumann. This would be the only score of the game. Ganado's defense held strong the rest of the way, shutting out East Bernard for a 7-0 victory. The Indians' defense was outstanding, limiting East Bernard to just 94 total yards and recovering two fumbles. This marked Ganado's sixth consecutive shutout, and they were set to face #9 Rogers in the Area round at Moorehead Stadium in Conroe. Rogers, with a 10-1 record, came into the game balanced offensively, led by quarterback Bart Harris and a solid defense. They had just defeated #8 Comfort the previous week in the bi-district round, and they quickly set the tone in the game. Rogers recovered a Ganado fumble early and returned it 41 yards for a touchdown, then extended their lead to 14-0 with another touchdown run by J.D. Young. This was the first time since the Refugio game that Ganado had allowed any points. In the second quarter, Hayden injured his hand, and senior Randy Rakowitz stepped in to finish the game. Rakowitz threw a 15-yard touchdown pass to Aguilar in the third quarter, marking Ganado's only touchdown of the game. Rogers would add one more touchdown in the fourth quarter, securing a 20-6 win over Ganado.

The loss ended Ganado's season with a 9-3 record. Despite the defeat, the team set two school records: 7 shutouts and 18 interceptions. For the senior class, this season was particularly special, as they had been part of Ganado's football program since seventh grade, playing all their years under Coach Althaus. This class had faced challenges, including a difficult junior high experience where they didn't win many games, but through hard work and improvement, they earned two district championships in their junior and senior years. Their commitment to hard work, discipline, and doing the little things right contributed to the team's success in winning five straight playoff berths and establishing a strong football tradition at Ganado.

2001

In the spring of 2001, a significant change occurred in the Ganado football program when coach Althaus resigned in March to become the athletic director and head football coach at 3A Columbus. Althaus left behind a remarkable legacy, compiling a 61-15 record and becoming the winningest coach in Ganado's history. On April 17, Keith Wright was announced as the new athletic director and head football coach at Ganado. Wright had previously served in the same roles at Kerens High School for six years, where he achieved a 48-19 record. A former Memphis college football player and brief NFL player for the Cleveland Browns - where he led the AFC in kickoff returns in 1978 - Wright expressed his respect for Ganado's established success and emphasized that he intended to build on it, not dismantle it.

Wright implemented a smashmouth, tailback-oriented offense using the I-formation and brought in Mark Byrd as defensive coordinator to maintain the aggressive, attacking style established under Althaus. Wayne Rushing also joined the coaching staff as an assistant. Wright inherited a relatively young team following the graduation of 18 seniors, including key members of the offensive line and defensive secondary. Returning senior Matthew Bures resumed his role as tailback, though concerns remained about his recovery from offseason surgery due to a high ankle sprain. Senior Clayton Hayden returned at quarterback, supported by Kirk Fowler at offensive guard and Joe Neumann at tight end. Junior Tim Neumann stepped in at fullback. The offensive line featured junior Brandon Morales at center, though sophomore Blake Schlueter eventually claimed the starting spot and also contributed at defensive end. Seniors Colin Pittman and Matthew Rosalez started at tackle, while sophomores Noe Guerrero and Kevin Poulton played at guard. Junior Coby Brown backed up Hayden at quarterback and also played at receiver alongside senior Chris Lee, junior Jacob Chambless, and sophomore J.C. Fowler. In the backfield, junior Augie Tristan and sophomore Robert Zajicek provided depth. Defensively, the team was anchored by returning starters Bures at safety, Fowler at outside linebacker, Tim Neumann at inside linebacker, and linemen Arthur Rodriguez, Froylan Enriquez, Joe Neumann, and Pittman. However, injuries sidelined Rodriguez and Enriquez during the season, prompting Neumann to shift to tackle and giving opportunities to Schlueter, Guerrero, and Chambless at defensive end. Rosalez played at tackle, while Zajicek filled in at inside linebacker. The secondary included senior Tim Mamerow, junior Chad Guidry, Lee, Brown, and J.C. Fowler. Sophomore Juan Enriquez handled the kicking responsibilities on special teams.

Coach Wright's tenure at Ganado began with a challenging start, as the Indians opened the 2001 season with a 21-0 loss on the road against Yoakum. The offense struggled significantly, managing only 114 total yards and five first downs, while the defense allowed several big plays - something Coach Althaus had always emphasized preventing. Yoakum's speedy running back, Anthony Harrison, was the standout, rushing for 196 yards and scoring all three touchdowns, including long runs of 69 and 50 yards. The loss marked the Indians' first game under Wright and dropped them to 0-1. Shortly after, the nation was shaken by the tragic events of September 11. On that Tuesday morning, normal routines came to a halt as the World Trade Center attacks unfolded on live television. The country entered a period of mourning, with flights grounded and most major sports events - including college and professional football - canceled for the weekend. However, high school football continued, and Ganado hosted its home opener and homecoming game against George West that week. In a display of both school spirit and national unity, the Indians delivered a resounding 33-6 win. Matthew Bures put to rest any doubts about his health by rushing for 237 yards and scoring four touchdowns. Ganado carried that momentum into the following week, defeating Palacios 25-7 and improving their record to 2-1. The next challenge was a road trip to East Bernard, a team Ganado had beaten seven consecutive times under Coach Althaus, including twice the previous season. However, East Bernard finally broke the streak, handing Ganado a 14-0 loss. Despite a strong effort by the defense, offensive struggles and key mistakes - including a safety and a turnover that led to East Bernard's points - proved costly. Bures rushed for 115 yards, including a 55-yard run in the fourth quarter, but the drive ended with a fumble, the Indians' third of the game, which sealed the defeat. The shutout marked Ganado's second of the season, a rarity not seen since 1993, and raised concerns about the offense's consistency. These offensive issues were largely attributed to the team adjusting to a new system and unfamiliar blocking schemes. Still, the Indians remained hopeful, knowing the pieces for a complete team were in place. Next on the schedule was a highly anticipated non-district game against the Refugio Bobcats in Ganado. However, severe weather and lightning forced the cancellation of the game just before kickoff. With both teams set to begin district play the following week, they chose not to reschedule. Many speculated that this might have worked in Ganado's favor, given their recent offensive struggles, while others believed a playoff rematch between the two teams was possible later in the season. Ganado entered district play with a 2-2 record and lingering questions, particularly on offense. However, confidence remained high, and those doubts were soon to be answered.

The Indians entered district play in 2001 facing a much-improved slate of opponents compared to the previous season, when they had gone undefeated and unscored upon. In their district opener, however, the Indians showed no signs of struggle, cruising to a dominant 56-8 victory over Tidehaven. The offense, which had been inconsistent in non-district play, found its rhythm, led by Bures, who scored five touchdowns - including one on a kickoff return - and rushed for 179 yards. Quarterback Clayton Hayden contributed by throwing touchdown passes to both Tim and Joe Neumann. The defense was equally impressive, holding Tidehaven to just five first downs and showcasing the complete team Ganado was becoming. The next week brought a highly anticipated district showdown against the undefeated 6-0 Van Vleck Leopards, a game with major implications for the district championship. Van Vleck entered with a talented roster, including quarterback Daniel Kubecka and a massive offensive line averaging over 250 pounds per player. After a scoreless first quarter, Ganado built a 10-0 lead in the second quarter. However, on the final play of the half, Kubecka connected on a 47-yard touchdown pass, trimming the Indians' lead to 10-7 at halftime. In the second half, Van Vleck struck quickly, scoring 10 points in the third quarter to take a 17-10 lead. Ganado responded late in the fourth quarter, when Bures punched in a one-yard touchdown with 3:41 remaining. Juan Enriquez's extra point tied the game at 17-17, sending it to overtime - reminiscent of Ganado's 1996 overtime game against East Bernard for the district title. Van Vleck had the first possession in overtime and managed to score on a broken play when Kubecka fumbled in the end zone and a teammate recovered the ball for a touchdown. However, Kubecka, who had earlier kicked a 21-yard field goal, sprained his ankle during overtime, and his extra point attempt missed wide, giving Ganado a window of opportunity. On Ganado's first play in overtime, Bures broke free on a 25-yard dive play for a touchdown to tie the game. Enriquez then calmly kicked the game-winning extra point, giving the Indians a thrilling 24-23 overtime victory. The win proved pivotal, ultimately deciding the district championship and handing Van Vleck their first and only regular-season loss. After the defeat, Van Vleck improved dramatically and remained unbeaten until falling to Refugio in the regional playoffs. Bures had another standout performance, rushing for 179 yards and three touchdowns on 38 carries. Hayden also had a solid game, spreading the ball to five different receivers for 98 passing yards, reflecting the team's growing offensive balance. Despite the high of the Van Vleck win, Ganado suffered a setback with season-ending knee injuries to two senior defensive linemen, Arthur Rodriguez and Froylan Enriquez. However, the team's depth showed as other players stepped up to fill the void. Most importantly, the Indians stood at 2-0 in district play and firmly on track in their quest for the district title.

Returning home for their next district matchup, the Ganado Indians faced an improved and determined Danbury team. Danbury employed a deceptive power running offense similar to the slot-T formation, featuring linemen aligned foot-to-foot and backs positioned close to the line of scrimmage. This made it difficult for the defense to identify the ball carrier, requiring aggressive line play to control the line of scrimmage. Danbury made an early statement, scoring on their first play with a 65-yard sweep, and would go on to rush for 247 total yards. However, Ganado responded immediately as Bures broke free for a 65-yard touchdown run on the Indians' first offensive snap, tying the game. Ganado then surged to a 28-7 lead in the second quarter and maintained control throughout the rest of the game, trading scores with Danbury but never losing the upper hand. The offense, which had struggled in non-district play, was now performing at a high level. Bures had another explosive performance, rushing for 255 yards and four touchdowns. Hayden had his best game passing for the season, completing 12 of 18 passes for 175 yards and a touchdown without throwing an interception. In total, the Indians racked up 498 yards of offense. Their offensive approach had clearly evolved into a physical, aggressive philosophy of running straight at opponents, daring them to try and stop it. On defense, the unit - nicknamed "The Rock" by Sheila Brown, a football mom and local sports writer for the *Jackson County Herald Tribune* - began tightening up, delivering two consecutive shutouts in their final regular season games. Against Louise, Ganado clinched at least a share of the district title with a commanding 42-0 victory. The highlight of that game was a 103-yard punt return touchdown by Bures, who also rushed for 195 yards and two additional scores. The regular season finale on senior night against Boling started close, with Ganado holding just a 7-0 lead at halftime. However, the Indians pulled away in the second half, scoring 21 unanswered points to seal a 28-0 win and officially claim the district championship. Bures once again led the way with 221 rushing yards and three touchdowns. By the end of the regular season, Ganado was playing the dominant, balanced football that Coach Wright had envisioned, and they headed into the playoffs for the sixth consecutive year. The Indians secured the top seed in the Division II playoff bracket, while Van Vleck took the runner-up spot. Boling, a winless team the previous season, entered the Division I playoffs with a 3-7 record. According to the *Victoria Advocate*, Matthew Bures finished the regular season as the area's leading rusher with 1,657 yards and 23 touchdowns. With momentum on their side, Ganado was primed for an exciting playoff run.

In the bi-district round of the 2001 playoffs, the Indians faced Brazos at Ricebird Stadium in El Campo - the same location where they had played East Bernard in the same round the previous year. The game was held on a Saturday evening due to Brazos' volleyball team competing in the state tournament on Friday. Despite losing their standout running back David Randle to a season-ending knee injury during a preseason scrimmage, Brazos remained a dangerous and athletic team, entering the playoffs as the runner-up behind district champion East Bernard. Notably, Brazos fielded one of the largest offensive lines Ganado had ever encountered, with linemen averaging between 280 and 300 pounds per man. Ganado came out strong, taking a 21-7 lead at halftime behind two rushing touchdowns from Bures and a trick play touchdown pass from Bures to Coby Brown. The Indians nearly extended their lead with two additional scoring opportunities before halftime, but they were unable to capitalize. In the second half, Brazos took advantage of two Ganado fumbles and tied the game at 21-21. With just over a minute left, Hayden connected with tight end Joe Neumann for a crucial touchdown at the goal line with 42 seconds remaining, giving Ganado a 28-21 lead. On Brazos' next play from scrimmage, Brown intercepted quarterback Patrick Oliver and returned it for a touchdown with 20 seconds left, making it 35-21. Though Oliver responded with a 44-yard touchdown pass on the final play of the game, Ganado held on for a thrilling 35-28 victory in what was a highly physical and hard-fought contest. The win was significant, as the Indians were clearly overmatched in size and speed but still managed to prevail. In the Area round, Ganado faced Comfort the day after Thanksgiving in Columbus, continuing what had become a postseason tradition for the team - playing football during the holiday weekend for the fourth straight year. Comfort was a young but talented team with many sophomores and few upperclassmen. They struck first, but Ganado quickly took control. Comfort ran a similar offensive scheme to Danbury's, which had previously given Ganado some trouble, but like that game, they couldn't contain the Indians' offense. Bures responded with a touchdown to spark a run that saw Ganado lead 28-7 at halftime. The Indians poured it on in the second half, highlighted by a 97-yard touchdown run from Bures, who finished with 211 rushing yards and four touchdowns. Ganado dominated with 411 yards of offense, including 364 rushing yards, en route to a 49-17 win. The regional round brought Ganado back to Columbus to face Stockdale, this time as the visiting team. What followed was one of the most remarkable individual performances in school history. Ganado won 48-6 despite only running 21 offensive plays. Matthew Bures touched the ball just 13 times but scored seven touchdowns - five rushing, one on a punt return, and another on a kickoff return. He finished with 222 rushing yards and surpassed the 2,000-yard mark for the season. After the game, Coach Wright praised Bures' performance as one of the most memorable he had ever witnessed, emphasizing that it was only possible through a complete team effort, particularly the blocking and tackling from the rest of the squad. With their record now at 10-2, the Indians advanced to the regional quarterfinals for a much-anticipated showdown against the powerhouse Refugio Bobcats for the Region IV championship.

Ganado and Refugio were originally scheduled to meet in their final non-district game on October 5, but the game was canceled due to lightning. Many had speculated that these two teams would face off again in the playoffs, and that prediction came true. Refugio, under new head coach Rick Keese (who replaced George Harris), was coming off two consecutive semifinals appearances and had dominated Ganado in previous playoff meetings, including a 54-7 victory in the 1999 regional playoffs and a 41-7 win in a non-district game the year before. Although Refugio had graduated a large senior class, they remained a powerful team with a rich tradition, defeating Van Vleck 29-14 the week prior - Van Vleck being the team Ganado had beaten in overtime to win the district title. This was the third playoff meeting between Ganado and Refugio, and the game was held at Victoria's Memorial Stadium, with Ganado being the "home team." The stadium was packed with nearly 9,000 fans from both sides. The Indians came out strong in the opening drive, with Tim Neumann gaining 28 yards on just two carries, but he was injured and would not return. Ganado stalled at the Refugio 19-yard line, and Enriquez missed a 43-yard field goal attempt. Despite two failed 4th-and-1 attempts on the Refugio 15 and 22-yard lines, Ganado finally found the end zone in the fourth quarter on another 4th-and-1 attempt at the 12-yard line, with Bures rushing for 125 yards and the lone score of the game. With Neumann injured, Bures had to switch between the fullback and tailback positions. The Indians outgained Refugio in total yards, 152 to 118, all of which were on the ground. Ganado's defense, known as "The Rock," dominated the Bobcats, recording three interceptions. Both teams had nine first downs, but Ganado emerged as Region 4 champions, advancing to the semifinals for only the second time in school history. While the victory was sweet, the work was far from over. In the semifinals, Ganado faced Garrison at Bryan Viking Stadium. Garrison was a strong team with a huge line that averaged nearly 250 pounds per man. The game began poorly for Ganado, as Garrison returned the opening kickoff for an 83-yard touchdown. Ganado responded with a 32-yard field goal by Enriquez, but trailed 7-3 after the first quarter. Garrison then scored on a 55-yard pass to take a 14-3 lead at halftime. Despite being down, Ganado's defense played well, holding Garrison's rushing attack to just 64 yards. In the fourth quarter, Ganado had a chance to gain momentum when Joe Neumann blocked a Garrison punt at the 30-yard line, with the ball rolling dead at the 12-yard line. The Indians capitalized, with Gerald Lee scoring on a one-yard run, though the two-point conversion failed, leaving the score 14-9. Ganado's defense continued to shine, stopping Garrison on their next possession and forcing a turnover on a fake punt, giving the Indians the ball at the 16-yard line with six minutes left. Bures, who had rushed for 90 yards in the game, ran for an 11-yard gain, but the Indians faced a critical fourth-and-goal from the 3-yard line. Bures was stopped just shy of the end zone, and Garrison took over possession. Garrison put the game away with a 99-yard touchdown pass, the second of the game over 50 yards, a distance they had not reached all season. The big plays were the backbreakers for Ganado, as Garrison won the game 21-9. Despite the loss, Ganado had fought hard and left everything on the field. Garrison advanced to the state championship game, where they gave Celina a tough challenge, but Celina ultimately won 41-35, securing their fourth straight Class 2A state title from 1998 to 2001.

Ganado finished the season with an impressive 11-3 record, a remarkable achievement for the team. After the semifinal loss, Coach Wright addressed the players, telling them that they were "pound-for-pound the best football team to ever come through Ganado." Despite falling short, Wright expressed his immense pride in what the team had accomplished, emphasizing that the season, especially in his first year as head coach, was incredibly special. From early-season struggles to winning the district championship and reaching the semifinals, the team's success was a testament to their hard work and dedication. Matthew Bures had an exceptional senior year, setting school records by rushing for 2,395 yards and scoring 37 touchdowns, both of which remain unbroken to this day. His recovery from offseason surgery was nothing short of remarkable, and he proved himself to be one of the best athletes in Ganado's history. Bures' achievements earned him the Victoria Advocate's Offensive Player of the Year honor. He would go on to play at Texas A&M, continuing his football career at the collegiate level. Joe Neumann, another key player, would go on to play at Blinn College before transferring to Syracuse, where he completed his collegiate career. While the season was filled with triumphs, it was also marked by tragedy. On the way to the semifinal game, the Carroll family was involved in an accident. Their six-year-old son, Blaine, a first grader at Ganado Elementary, was critically injured in the crash and tragically passed away the following morning. His loss was deeply felt by the community, and he is remembered fondly by many. Despite the heartbreak, Blaine's spirit continued to be a source of inspiration, symbolizing another angel watching over the team as they continued their pursuit of a state championship in the years to come.

2002

In February, the district underwent changes due to the biannual realignment. Boling and Danbury were no longer part of the district, and Louise dropped down to Class 1A. Ganado retained its rivals Tidehaven and Van Vleck, but also reintroduced the rivalry with Industrial, which had spent the last four years in Class 3A before dropping back down to Class 2A. Newcomers to the district included Schulenburg and Weimar, teams that had never been in Ganado's football district before. Additionally, this marked the first season in which Ganado did not play East Bernard in the regular season, ending a streak of matchups that had been ongoing since 1981.

The 2002 Ganado football team featured a mix of new faces and familiar ones, with high expectations following their successful semifinal appearance the previous year. The team was small in terms of senior leadership, with only six seniors: Coby Brown, Tim Neumann, Chad Guidry, Jacob Chambless, Augustine Tristan, and Brian DeSpain. DeSpain, a transfer from Falls City, was an all-district performer, and his father, Ray DeSpain, had recently become the new high school principal. Alongside the seniors were 14 juniors and several impactful sophomores, who were expected to contribute significantly. Replacing

15 lettermen and five graduated all-district performers, including district MVP Matthew Bures, was a major challenge. However, the experience gained by the underclassmen from their five-game playoff run the previous season was crucial. Additionally, the team boasted a strong group of players from the previous year's undefeated JV squad, which recorded seven shutouts. Defensively, the strength of the team was in the inside linebacker positions, where Neumann, the district defensive MVP, and junior Robert Zajicek, an all-district selection, anchored the defense. DeSpain filled in at outside linebacker, with support from Guidry, juniors Juan Enriquez and Kevin Poulton, and sophomores Johny Lesak and Andrew Callis. Junior Blake Schlueter, the district defensive newcomer of the year, returned as a defensive end, with Chambless starting at the other end position and sophomore Bradley Salas as his backup. The defensive tackle positions were manned by juniors Noe Guerrero and Jacob Tristan, while the secondary was comprised of Brown, juniors J.C. Fowler, Ross Chumchal, and Derek Grudzieski, and sophomore Jacob Alvarez. Offensively, Brown, an all-district wide receiver the previous season, stepped into the starting quarterback role. Neumann moved from fullback to tailback, with Callis and Zajicek also contributing at fullback, and Tristan and Alvarez providing depth as backups. The offensive line returned significant bulk with Schlueter at center, Poulton and DeSpain at guards, and Guerrero, sophomore Derek Dunbar, and Darren Ellison playing tackle. Chambless started at tight end, with Guidry and junior Ryan Bailey at wide receiver. Special teams were bolstered by the presence of two all-district kickers, Enriquez and DeSpain, and Brown returning as the punter. This team, filled with a blend of seasoned players and promising underclassmen, was poised to make another strong run, building on the success of the previous year.

Ganado opened the 2002 football season with a strong 35-7 victory on the road against Bloomington. Tim Neumann had an impressive debut, rushing for 130 yards and two touchdowns, while Coby Brown sparked the defense with an interception return for a touchdown. The Indians then faced a challenging home opener against 3A Hallettsville, known for their strong running game. Although Ganado struggled against Hallettsville's rushing attack, yielding 228 yards on the ground, the defense rose to the occasion when it mattered most. Blake Schlueter made a significant impact, returning a fumble 28 yards for a touchdown in the second quarter. Neumann continued to shine, rushing for 303 yards and three touchdowns, leading the Indians to a 2-0 record. Next, Ganado faced a crucial early-season test against Refugio, a team they had eliminated in the playoffs the previous year. The Indians controlled most of the game, leading 9-0 for the first 44 minutes. However, Ganado was without starting quarterback Brown, who was sidelined due to injury, and Chad Guidry stepped in at the position. Neumann put together a stellar performance, rushing for 205 yards on 35 carries. However, a critical fumble in the fourth quarter, while Ganado was driving to put the game away at the Refugio 17-yard line, turned the momentum. Refugio capitalized on the turnover, with Ray John Silvas scoring on a 77-yard run, narrowing the lead to 9-6. Refugio then recovered an onside kick and marched down the field for a winning drive. The Bobcats converted two fourth-down attempts, the last of which came on a fourth-and-five at the Ganado 18. Refugio quarterback Jarvis Edwards, under pressure, threw a desperate pass that was caught by tight end Andrew Brown in the end zone for the game-winning touchdown. Refugio came from behind to win 13-9, a devastating loss for Ganado. The defeat hit hard, with some players visibly upset, but the season was far from over. Despite the loss, Ganado remained resilient and focused on the rest of the season. The Indians quickly bounced back in their homecoming game against Palacios, where Neumann was unstoppable, rushing for 278 yards and three touchdowns in a 28-14 win. In their final non-district game at 3A Ingleside, Ganado dominated once again, winning 41-7, with Neumann rushing for 187 yards and four touchdowns. By the end of non-district play, the Indians had a solid 4-1 record and were ready to challenge for the district championship and a spot in the playoffs.

Up next proved to be an incredibly challenging time for the Ganado football team, testing their strength and character both on and off the field. On Monday, October 7, Robert Zajicek, a junior on the team, tragically lost his stepmother, Vanessa Zajicek, to a sudden illness at the age of 33. Just days later, on Wednesday, October 9, during the Jackson County Fair when the students were out of school, Rachel Wright, the 17-year-old daughter of Coach Wright and school counselor Jane, was critically injured in a car accident in Victoria. Rachel passed away from her injuries the following morning. This was the third consecutive year the team and community had faced a tragedy, and the weight of the losses was felt deeply. Despite the emotional hardship,

Ganado remained resilient and came together in their grief. Coach Wright, understandably, went to be with his family, and the assistant coaches stepped in to fill his spot. On Friday, October 11, the football team attended Vanessa Zajicek's funeral before playing their district opener against Weimar that evening. The game was incredibly emotional, but Ganado played with heart, winning 24-7. Neumann, Brown, and Andrew Callis each scored a touchdown, while Juan Enriquez added a 30-yard field goal. The defense put together a strong performance, yielding only 89 yards and seven first downs. The next day, two charter buses were arranged to take members of the team and community to Rachel Wright's funeral in Kerens, a five-and-a-half-hour drive away. It was an incredibly tough week, and no one should have to endure such hardship. The community, however, found strength and comfort in knowing that two angels, Rachel and Vanessa, were watching over them.

Despite the emotional toll, the team managed to pull together and play through the pain. Coach Wright returned to the team the following week as the Indians prepared for their district showdown against Industrial, marking their first meeting since the infamous Halloween game in 1997. Ganado took control early, leading 21-13 at halftime thanks to two touchdown runs from Neumann, who rushed for 115 yards, and a key interception return for a touchdown by defensive lineman Jacob Tristan. However, Industrial fought back, with Klint Evans, who rushed for 124 yards on the night, scored on a 51-yard touchdown, and quarterback Patrick Mercer connecting with Shane Stuart for a 47-yard touchdown just before the half. In the third quarter, Ganado went up 27-13 with a 5-yard quarterback keeper from Brown. Industrial responded with a passing attack, as Mercer threw for 150 yards and two touchdowns. Industrial scored 14 points in the fourth quarter, with Evans' second touchdown run and Mercer's second touchdown pass to Stuart, tying the game at 27-27 and sending it into overtime. Industrial received the first possession in overtime but was unable to convert after an illegal procedure penalty moved them back to the five-yard line, followed by an incomplete pass and a missed 20-yard field goal. Ganado then had their chance, and on the third play of their overtime possession, Brown threw a 21-yard touchdown pass to tight end Jacob Chambless, clinching the 33-27 victory. Chambless earned the nickname "Cobra killer" for his game-winning play. After the game, Coach Wright reflected on the significance of the victory, saying, "This does not take away the pain, but being around his kids and playing like they did makes it seem like two different worlds. The unreal world happened to us last week, and this week is the real world." The team had managed to persevere through one of the most difficult weeks in their lives and emerged victorious, proving their resilience and strength.

At 2-0, the Indians were preparing for a crucial district showdown against Van Vleck, which, like the previous season, appeared to be a battle for the district title. The weather during the week had been rainy, leaving the field in wet conditions. Ganado initially took control of the game, leading 15-0, including a spectacular 93-yard touchdown run by Neumann, who finished the night with 203 rushing yards on 34 carries. However, Van Vleck responded late in the second quarter when quarterback Daniel Kubecka, who passed for 149 yards, connected with Buck Austin, who had 110 yards on six receptions, narrowing the lead to 15-8 at halftime. During the break, due to the wet conditions, Ganado had to change from maroon to white pants, which disrupted their ability to rest, adjust, and prepare for the second half. Van Vleck came out strong after halftime, with Kubecka picking apart the Ganado secondary and finding Austin for two more touchdowns. Van Vleck scored 20 unanswered points in the second half, securing a 28-15 victory. This loss marked Ganado's first district defeat since October 1999, and it was the first time Van Vleck had beaten Ganado since 1993. While some wondered if this signified a shift in the district's power, it was clear that Van Vleck had a talented team, having advanced to the regional semifinals the previous season and eventually making it to the quarterfinals that year. The district had often been decided by the winner of the Ganado-Van Vleck matchup, with Ganado winning the previous two seasons, but this time it was Van Vleck's turn.

After the loss, Ganado returned home for their final home game against Schulenburg and secured a dominant 45-12 victory, which also clinched their seventh consecutive playoff berth. In this game, seniors Neumann and Brown shined. Neumann rushed for 115 yards and three touchdowns, while Brown had a standout performance, returning an interception for a touchdown and passing for 78 yards and another touchdown. With the win, Ganado was back on track. In the season finale, Ganado narrowly defeated a 3-7 Tidehaven team 7-0 in a tough matchup in El Maton. Despite dominating the game statistically with

313 rushing yards, Ganado lost three fumbles. The defense, however, was outstanding, holding Tidehaven to just 72 total yards and four first downs, earning their first shutout of the season. With an 8-2 record, Ganado finished as the runner-up in the Division II bracket, while Van Vleck took the district championship. Industrial finished in third place and earned the Division I playoff spot. Ganado's solid season continued as they advanced to the playoffs.

Ganado returned to Ricebird Stadium in El Campo for the third consecutive year to compete in the bi-district playoffs, a venue where they had previously enjoyed success with a 2-0 record. Once again, they faced the East Bernard Brahmas, whom they had defeated 7-0 in the 2000 bi-district playoffs. East Bernard boasted a strong defense led by Darrell Gander, and both teams struggled offensively in the first half. The first half saw five punts and two turnovers for Ganado. One of those turnovers was particularly costly when Brown connected with J.C. Fowler on a pass, but an East Bernard defender popped the ball loose, and Gander scooped it up, returning it 67 yards for a touchdown, giving East Bernard a 7-0 lead. Gander, the Brahmas' best player, was also their leading rusher, accumulating 86 yards in the game. However, Ganado responded before halftime. Tim Neumann found Fowler for a 27-yard halfback pass, tying the game 7-7 at the break. The second half was dominated by Ganado. Neumann rushed for 141 yards on 30 carries and scored a touchdown, while Enriquez connected on two field goals, one from 32 yards and another from 31 yards. With a strong second half performance, Ganado won the game 20-7, advancing to the next round. Later, it was revealed that East Bernard's head coach, Rick Bivins, was so surprised by the loss that he came to Ganado the following week to watch one of their workouts. In the Area round, Ganado faced a tough Rogers team at New Braunfels Canyon Stadium. The game started off with Ganado leading 5-0, thanks to a safety by Zajieck and a 28-yard field goal by Enriquez in the first quarter. Rogers took a 6-5 lead in the second quarter and increased their advantage to 9-5 with a field goal in the third quarter. In the fourth quarter, Neumann regained the lead for Ganado with a touchdown, making it 12-9. Neumann finished the game with 140 yards on 43 carries, and Ganado rushed the ball 64 times for a total of 234 yards.

However, Rogers responded with a 50-yard touchdown run by Josh Smith to take a 16-12 lead, which proved to be the final score. Despite having more first downs (17-9) and more total yards (281-212), Ganado's five turnovers - three interceptions and two lost fumbles - were the deciding factor. Rogers had no turnovers, and that difference ultimately led to Ganado's loss. Despite their hard-fought effort, the Indians came up short in a close game.

Coach Wright reflected on the season with immense pride, acknowledging the team's resilience in the face of adversity. He highlighted that the challenges they encountered throughout the year were far tougher than anyone could have anticipated, yet the determination and heart of the young coaches and players never faltered. Despite these difficulties, they remained committed to the pursuit of winning a state championship. Coach Wright referred to the football program as a "circle," emphasizing that this bond would only grow stronger as the Indians aimed for the 2A State Championship in 2003. He praised both the coaching staff and players for their dedication, effort, and never-give-up attitude. The season taught valuable life lessons and values, and the character of the team was repeatedly tested. However, each member of the team responded like champions, demonstrating resilience and perseverance throughout the season.

2003

In the spring of 2003, Coach Wright met with his upcoming high school football team and presented them with an ambitious yet achievable goal: if they worked hard, they could potentially go undefeated with a 16-0 record and win the state championship. This dream had been in the making for years, as evidenced by a moment from my junior year in geometry class, where a player from the team had written "2003 State Champions" on the blackboard - demonstrating the long-standing aspirations of the team, which had been envisioned since their 8th grade year. By August, the Indians fielded one of their most experienced teams in recent memory, consisting of 15 seniors and 16 juniors, which led to high expectations for the season. One question going into the season was who would play quarterback? The position went to Robert Zajicek, a senior transitioning from fullback but who had previous quarterback experience in junior high. At tailback, the team considered senior J.C. Fowler and junior Jacob Alvarez - both quick and elusive runners, though not as physically dominant as past players like Matthew Bures or Tim Neumann. The offensive line featured experienced seniors such as Blake Schlueter at center, along with Kevin Poulton and Noe Guerrero at guard, while juniors Darren Ellison and Derek Dunbar held down the tackle positions. Schlueter, also the team's deep snapper on punts, was drawing attention from college scouts due to his impressive size (6'4", 240 pounds) and speed (4.8-second 40-yard dash). The receiving corps was made up of seniors Ryan Bailey, Derek Grudzieski, and Fowler, with junior Bradley Salas playing tight end. In the kicking game, senior Juan Enriquez stood out as one of the best kickers in school history, particularly notable at the 2A level, with consistent field goals from distances of up to 47 yards. On defense, the Indians featured a strong line with senior tackles Jacob Tristan and Eric Salazar, joined by Schlueter and Guerrero at the end positions. Zajicek anchored the defense at inside linebacker, while Alvarez and Fowler played cornerback. With a combination of seasoned players, skill, and determination, if all the elements aligned, this team had a real chance at achieving their goal of winning the state championship.

The 2003 football season began with a dominant 46-0 home victory over Bloomington, where the Indians excelled in all aspects of the game. They amassed 482 yards of total offense while limiting Bloomington to just five first downs and 102 total yards. Confidence was high heading into their next game, a road matchup against Class 3A Hallettsville. Ganado started strong, taking a 10-0 lead with a Robert Zajicek touchdown and a 28-yard field goal by Juan Enriquez. However, the momentum shifted when Hallettsville executed a successful fake punt for a touchdown, sparking a run of 34 unanswered points that resulted in a 34-10 defeat for Ganado. The Indians struggled on defense, allowing big plays including two long touchdown passes and a 76-yard touchdown run. To make matters worse, starting tailback Jacob Alvarez suffered a season-ending knee injury. Now 1-1, Ganado returned home for a critical homecoming game against Refugio. In response to the previous loss and Alvarez's injury, the coaching staff made significant changes: Zajicek moved from quarterback to tailback, sophomore Sam Samudio was promoted from JV to start at quarterback, and J.C. Fowler continued to rotate in at tailback. Zajicek performed well, rushing for 125 yards and two touchdowns, giving Ganado a 14-6 halftime lead. But in the second half, the team faltered, allowing 19 unanswered points as Refugio took a 25-14 lead with under five minutes remaining. The situation looked bleak, and questions arose about whether this highly touted team was underperforming. Then came one of the season's most dramatic moments. Samudio connected with Bradley Salas for a 51-yard touchdown, narrowing the gap to 25-20. After forcing a stop and capitalizing on a short punt, Ganado drove again, with Andrew Callis scoring on an 11-yard run to give the Indians a 26-25 lead. On Refugio's next possession, Rusty Rushing intercepted a pass and returned it 16 yards for a touchdown, and Enriquez added the extra point for a 33-25 lead. Refugio's final drive ended with another interception, this time by Fowler, sealing an improbable comeback victory. The Indians improved to 2-1, and this win marked a pivotal turning point in the season, revitalizing team confidence. Ganado built on that momentum, winning their next two non-district games convincingly. On the road against Palacios, Zajicek rushed for 170 yards and three touchdowns, and Enriquez added a 47-yard field goal in a 32-14 victory. They then closed non-district play with a commanding 48-6 home win over Class 3A Ingleside, where Zajicek continued his strong performance, rushing for 131 yards and four touchdowns. With a 4-1 record heading into district play, the Indians were focused and determined to reclaim the district title that had slipped to Van Vleck the previous year.

The Indians opened district play in dominant fashion with a 49-0 shutout win at Weimar. Despite a modest 14-0 lead at halftime - and a brief power outage during the marching band's halftime performance - the Indians exploded in the second half. Zajicek rushed for 167 yards and three touchdowns, while quarterback Sam Samudio threw for 102 yards and connected with Ryan Bailey for a touchdown. The defense was equally impressive, holding Weimar to just three first downs. The following week brought one of the season's most memorable games against their Jackson County rival, the undefeated Industrial Cobras. Facing a 6-0 team on the road in Vanderbilt on October 17, the Indians rose to the occasion. As noted by the *Victoria Advocate*, "Industrial had Hummers in the parking lot, but Ganado had one on the field" - referring to Zajicek, who bulldozed his way to 155 yards on 28 carries and scored four touchdowns. The offensive line, described as a fleet of Humvees, paved the way for a total of 359 yards of offense in a 50-6 rout. The defense allowed only 106 total yards and six first downs, prompting Coach Wright to compare this team's dominance to the 2001 squad that reached the state semifinals. The game ended with a rallying cry: "Who's House? OUR House!" - a phrase that would echo through the rest of the season. With a 2-0 district record, the Indians prepared to face Van Vleck - a team that had beaten them the year before for the district title and had handed them their only loss in 8th grade. This time, the game was in Ganado, and the seniors declared, "OUR time in OUR house!" The Indians backed it up by building a 21-0 halftime lead and extending it to 28-0 before Van Vleck scored two late touchdowns in the fourth quarter, long after the outcome had been decided. Ganado won 28-14, moving to 3-0 in district. Samudio threw two touchdown passes, while Fowler scored three different ways: receiving, rushing, and on a punt return - an all-around team effort. The Indians clinched a playoff spot the following week with a 35-7 victory at Schulenburg on Halloween night. After falling behind 7-0, Ganado responded with 35 unanswered points, racking up 411 rushing yards, including 157 from Zajicek, who scored twice. The team was playing with undeniable momentum and intensity, and nothing appeared to be standing in their way. In the regular-season finale and final home game against Tidehaven, Ganado capped off their district run with a commanding 44-7 victory to claim the district championship. Zajicek rushed for 132 yards and three touchdowns, while Enriquez added field goals from 36, 25, and 39 yards. The win solidified a perfect 5-0 district record and a 9-1 overall mark. Remarkably, this group of seniors had never lost a home game in their high school careers - a testament to their consistency, grit, and leadership. Throughout district play, no opponent came within 14 points of the Indians, underscoring their dominance. Now, with district conquered, the team was fully prepared to begin their long-anticipated playoff run in pursuit of a state championship.

Ganado opened the 2A Division II playoffs with a thrilling bi-district matchup against Hitchcock in Angleton. Hitchcock was one of the most athletic and physically gifted teams the Indians had ever faced, featuring impressive speed and size across the board. Their backfield was anchored by the dynamic Lowe brothers, Marqus and Marquis, and nearly all of their skill players ran 40-yard dashes in the 4.5-second range. As the teams warmed up, Hitchcock players high-stepped onto the field, pointing their fingers while taunting the Indians with confidence, signaling they believed they had the game won before it even began. However, Ganado wasn't intimidated. The Indians struck first in the second quarter on a touchdown run by Zajicek. Hitchcock answered quickly with a 62-yard explosive touchdown run by Marquis

Lowe, showcasing their speed. Ganado regained the lead on a clutch 47-yard field goal by Enriquez, making it 10-7. Just before halftime, Hitchcock scored again with only three seconds left, taking a 14-10 lead into the break. The second half was a tightly contested battle. Late in the fourth quarter, Zajicek scored his second touchdown of the night to give Ganado a 17-14 lead. But with just over four minutes remaining, Hitchcock completed a short touchdown pass to retake the lead, 20-17, and their band began playing the song "Na Na Hey Hey Goodbye," assuming the game was in hand. Yet, Ganado wasn't finished. With time running out, Samudio launched a deep 65-yard pass to Derek Grudzieski, moving the Indians into scoring position in dramatic fashion. With just one second left on the clock, Enriquez delivered again, this time with a 32-yard field goal to tie the game 20-20 and force overtime. In overtime, Hitchcock had the ball first but was stopped by Ganado's defense, and then missed a field goal attempt. The Indians' offensive possession in overtime didn't advance far, but they still had their secret weapon - Enriquez. He was called on once more and calmly drilled a 41-yard field goal, which likely would've been good from 60 yards, giving Ganado an incredible 23-20 overtime victory. Though Hitchcock was clearly the more athletic team, Ganado proved to be the more disciplined and resilient group, playing with heart and determination. This victory marked Ganado's eighth consecutive appearance in the playoffs and their eighth straight first-round win - an enormous accomplishment and a defining moment of the season.

In the Area round of the playoffs, the Indians faced undefeated 11-0 Junction in Seguin. Led by Zajicek, who rushed for 216 yards on 30 carries, Ganado broke open a tight 6-3 halftime lead when Zajicek scored the game's only touchdown in the third quarter. Enriquez added three field goals from 39, 27, and 23 yards to help secure a 16-3 victory. While the score appeared close, the game was largely dominated by Ganado. The Indians' defense held Junction to just 148 total yards and six first downs, intercepting three passes. However, turnovers - including two fumbles and a missed field goal before halftime - kept the score from being more lopsided. The next challenge came in the regional round against Poth on Thanksgiving weekend. A large and supportive crowd gathered at Victoria's Memorial Stadium the day after Thanksgiving to cheer on the Indians. Ganado took immediate control of the game, as Zajicek returned the opening kickoff

92 yards for a touchdown. He would go on to rush for 185 yards and two more scores. Samudio passed for 127 yards and added a rushing touchdown, while Enriquez hit two more field goals from 38 and 40 yards. Despite allowing 324 passing yards - including 256 yards on six catches to tight end Shaun Ramirez - the Indians cruised to a 48-6 win, thanks to two interceptions and overall dominance on offense and special teams. With the win, Ganado advanced to the state quarterfinals for the first time since 1998 and only the third time in school history. Their opponent was a familiar playoff rival: the Rogers Eagles, who had eliminated Ganado two out of the last three seasons. The stakes were high, as the winner would claim the Region 4 championship and move on to the state semifinals, possibly for a rematch with Garrison. The game took place at Seguin's Matador Stadium - the same location where Ganado had defeated Junction two weeks earlier - and the Indians appeared confident and ready. On a cold night, Ganado jumped out to a 10-0 lead with a 40-yard field goal from Enriquez and a touchdown pass from Zajicek to Ryan Bailey. However, momentum shifted when Zajicek suffered a concussion and was ruled out by halftime. Rogers quickly capitalized, blocking a Bailey punt and returning it for a touchdown. Two plays later, Ganado fumbled deep in their own territory, and Rogers scored again to take a 14-10 lead. A field goal just before halftime extended Rogers' advantage to 17-10. In the second half, Ganado mounted a promising drive that stalled at the one-yard line after a costly fumble. Rogers responded with a long drive of their own, scoring to make it 23-10. Despite the setbacks, Ganado continued to fight. Samudio led a 74-yard scoring drive that ended with a touchdown pass to Bailey, and Enriquez's extra point brought the score to 23-17 with 9:28 remaining. However, that would be as close as the Indians would get. Rogers sealed the game with a short touchdown run by Jacob Bane with just over two minutes left, securing a 29-17 victory and ending Ganado's remarkable playoff run. Though the season ended in heartbreak, the 2003 Ganado Indians left a lasting legacy. They finished as district champions, reached the quarterfinals, and played with grit, heart, and unity - just as Coach Wright had envisioned at the start of the season.

After the game, Coach Wright expressed no disappointment, hugging each of his players and thanking them for their hard work. He told them he wouldn't trade this group of kids for all the state championships in the world. He acknowledged that they had given everything they had, and though they came up short, he was proud of their effort. The Indians finished the season with a 12-2 record, marking the second most total wins in school history at the time. This team was special, a testament to hard work, dedication, and perseverance. Blake Schlueter, one of the standout players, would go on to play at TCU before being drafted by the Denver Broncos in the 7th round of the 2009 NFL Draft. He signed with Denver but was waived before the start of the season. Schlueter then briefly joined the Seattle Seahawks for eight days before being signed to the Atlanta Falcons' practice squad toward the end of the 2009 season. However, he was released prior to the start of the 2010 NFL season. This period in Ganado football marked a golden era for the program. The team enjoyed nine consecutive winning seasons, made the playoffs for eight consecutive years, won multiple playoff games, and reached the semifinals twice. Prior to 1995, the program had little success, but this era represented a major turning point. As the community reflected on the glory years, the big question remained: would this winning tradition and playoff success continue in the years to come?

Chapter 5

Protecting the Tradition

2004

In the spring of 2004, several significant changes took place at Ganado ISD. Coach Wright resigned to take the position of athletic director at Farmersville after compiling an impressive 32-8 record over his three years as the head coach at Ganado. On May 3, the Ganado school board appointed Mark Byrd as the new athletic director and head football coach. Byrd, who had been the Indians' defensive coordinator for the past three years, had worked with Wright since 1999 and was also his defensive coordinator at Kerens before they both moved to Ganado. Byrd had a background as an assistant coach at Winnsboro, Pearsall, and Newton, and interestingly, Wright's father had given Byrd's father his first coaching job in 1968 at Gilmer. With the coaching change, came more adjustments, particularly on the offensive side of the ball. Byrd transitioned the team from the power-run I-formation offense used under Wright to a more diverse offensive system that incorporated motion and passing. This shift was made to better suit the team's personnel, as they no longer had the large back capable of powering through defenses. Byrd also promoted Wayne Rushing, who had been an assistant coach for the past three years, to the role of defensive coordinator. Additionally, long-time assistant coach Andy Bridges decided to step away from coaching to become the assistant high school principal, leaving a vacancy in the staff. Ganado ISD also experienced changes at the administrative level. Superintendent Donald Egg resigned by the end of the school year, and after a brief search, a new superintendent was hired in early May. However, the new hire left shortly thereafter for a position at Cuero. Finally, in July, Jeff Black from Tom Bean was appointed as the new superintendent at Ganado ISD. Despite the changes, everything seemed to be in place, and when two-a-day practices began in early August, the program was ready to continue its tradition of excellence.

In 2004, Coach Mark Byrd inherited a team with a strong foundation, built on the experience and winning tradition established by former coaches Keith Wright and Monte Althaus. The senior class had an impressive track record, going undefeated on the JV team as freshmen with a 9-0-1 record, which meant they were already well-versed in winning. Byrd's decision to change the offensive system quickly became a topic of discussion in the community, as fans watched the new style unfold during practices. Some of the key returnees that Byrd inherited was the return of junior quarterback Sam Samudio. Senior Andrew Callis was also returning as the fullback in the backfield, along with Jacob Alvarez, who had been sidelined the previous season due to a torn ACL. Junior Devon Morales was expected to step in at tailback. The team's receiving corps featured senior tight ends Bradley Salas and Rusty Rushing, along with senior Robert Lauer and junior Drew Bridges. On the offensive line, the team had experienced players, although the line had lost some size compared to previous years. Seniors Johny Lesak and David Lee Bures returned as guards, with Derek Dunbar back at tackle. Senior Cody Englemohr was moved from tight end to replace the graduated all-state Blake Schlueter at center. On the defensive side of the ball, Salas and Englemohr returned as ends, while Bures and junior Michael Lara played at tackle. Callis, Rushing, and Lauer were expected to play linebacker, and Samudio, along with senior B.J. Novak, was set to start in the secondary. A significant challenge for the team was replacing Juan Enriquez, the clutch kicker from the previous year's playoff run. Ruben Pena and Mauricio Ramos were the leading candidates for the kicking position going into the season. There was little doubt that the team had the talent to continue the tradition of success. With a talented roster in place, the 2004 season was poised to be another strong campaign for the Indians.

Ganado began the 2004 season with a dominant 48-0 victory over Bloomington. The team showcased their traditional strength in the running game, racking up 341 rushing yards and scoring six touchdowns on the ground. Defensively, they were just as impressive, limiting Bloomington to only 108 total yards and four first downs. With a 1-0 record, the team faced a tough test the following week against Hallettsville at home. Despite solid defensive play, the offense struggled to find any rhythm. Hallettsville capitalized on big plays, including a punt return for a touchdown in the second quarter and an 88-yard touchdown run from Parris Brown late in the fourth quarter after Ganado turned the ball over on downs. The 14-0 loss marked the first shutout for Ganado since 2001 and their first home loss since

1999, snapping a 29-game home winning streak. With the record now at 1-1, the Indians traveled to Refugio for their next game, but things did not improve. They trailed 20-6 at halftime, turning the ball over four times, and struggled defensively, giving up 325 rushing yards. The game ended in a 27-6 defeat, leaving Ganado with a 1-2 record. However, the team wasn't ready to give up. They bounced back the following week at home for homecoming against Boling, where they played perhaps their best game of the season. Quarterback Sam Samudio ran for two touchdowns, rushed for 82 yards, and passed for 117 yards. Running back Andrew Callis added 97 rushing yards, and the defense intercepted Boling's passes three times. Despite the victory, the team suffered a significant loss with Drew Bridges breaking his ankle, ending his season. At 2-2, Ganado traveled to East Bernard for their final non-district game. East Bernard, winless at 0-4, proved to be a tougher opponent than anticipated. Ganado struggled in the first half, trailing 7-6 after giving up a 65-yard touchdown run on the first play from scrimmage. However, the Indians improved in the second half, with Samudio throwing two touchdown passes to Devon Morales and Cody Parker. Ganado managed to secure a 25-13 win, entering a bye week with a 3-2 record. This set the stage for their district opener at home against Schulenburg.

Ganado entered their district opener against Schulenburg with high expectations, especially after Schulenburg had been struggling, allowing 36 points per game and suffering a heavy loss to Hallettsville the week before by a score of 52-6. The previous two seasons had seen easy victories over Schulenburg, so the team anticipated a straightforward win. However, things didn't go as planned. Despite the extra week off due to their bye, Ganado came out flat and struggled throughout the game. Offensively, they were dominated by Schulenburg's defense, managing only five first downs and punting seven times. A defensive nose tackle for Schulenburg was consistently in the backfield, causing havoc for Ganado's offensive line. Coach Byrd attempted a unique move early on by putting their largest offensive lineman, Michael Lara, in the backfield on the first play, but it resulted in a loss of yards, setting the tone for a frustrating offensive performance. The Indians rushed for just 30 yards on 29 carries, with some of those being negative yardage. Defensively, Ganado performed well, creating five turnovers, but the offense was unable to capitalize on those opportunities. The game ended in a 7-7 tie, forcing overtime. In a controversial decision, Coach Byrd chose to have Cody Englemohr, who had not been the regular kicker and had limited experience with field goals, attempt a game-winning field goal. The attempt was unsuccessful, and in the second overtime, Schulenburg's kicker, Carlos Lara, who was considered one of the best in the district, made a 37-yard field goal to win the game 10-7. The loss left many fans dissatisfied, as it was clear that this Ganado team was not performing at the level they were used to. The inconsistency and struggles on offense marked a significant departure from the dominant teams of previous years. The loss to Schulenburg was a tough setback for the Indians, who now faced serious questions about their ability to turn their season around.

The following week, Ganado traveled to Cobra Field in Vanderbilt, the site of their dominant 50-6 victory over rival Industrial the previous year. Determined not to be stopped again, the Indians came out strong and took control of the game, leading 21-7 at halftime. Defensively, they were solid, allowing only five first downs and forcing five turnovers. Industrial managed to stay in the game, scoring twice in the fourth quarter - once on a fumble recovery in the end zone and again on a kickoff return. However, Samudio sealed the victory with an interception return for a touchdown, leading Ganado to a 35-20 win and improving their district record to 1-1. The Indians followed up with a 27-12 home victory over Tidehaven, improving to 2-1 in district play. In the win, two players rushed for over 100 yards: Morales, who gained 152 yards, and Callis, who rushed for 103 yards and scored a touchdown. Although Tidehaven initially took the lead with an 80-yard touchdown after blocking a field goal attempt, Ganado controlled the rest of the game. Next, the Indians faced Van Vleck in their final home game of the season, a crucial district matchup. In the past four years, the district championship had often been decided by the winner of the Ganado-Van Vleck game, and Ganado had won three out of the last four meetings. A victory here, combined with other favorable results in the district, would secure Ganado a playoff berth. However, Van Vleck's quarterback Derek Lewis tore apart Ganado's secondary in the first half, passing for 326 yards and five touchdowns on only 10 completions for the night. The Indians trailed 20-7 at halftime. Coach Rushing ripped the defensive secondary at halftime, which motivated the entire team. The Indians came out in the second half as a new team. They fought back to tie the game at 27-27, with two touchdowns from Samudio and one from Morales, who rushed for a game-high 138 yards. Ganado played a clean game with no turnovers, while Van Vleck turned the ball over four times, including a crucial interception from defensive tackle Zeke Kuehn in the fourth quarter. With time winding down, it seemed like the game would go into overtime, as Van Vleck had the ball at their own 20-yard line. However, instead of taking a knee, Lewis launched a long pass down the left sideline. The ball was caught by William Thompson for an 82-yard touchdown as time expired, giving Van Vleck a dramatic 33-27 victory. This crushing loss left Ganado heartbroken, with players and coaches collapsing on the field in disbelief. The defeat set up a winner-take-all scenario in the season finale against Weimar, where the third and final playoff spot in the district would be on the line.

The loss to Van Vleck seemed to take a toll on the Ganado football team, as they struggled to get anything going offensively in their final regular-season game against Weimar. The game turned into a defensive battle, with neither team able to generate much offense. Ganado's defense held strong for most of the game, keeping them in it, but the team trailed 7-0 at halftime. In the early part of the fourth quarter, Weimar had a chance to extend their lead, but B.J. Novak intercepted a pass to stop the threat. Ganado managed to mount a successful drive, going 80 yards, with Morales scoring a 15-yard touchdown to tie the game at 7-7, thanks to an extra point from Mauricio Ramos. The game seemed to be on the verge of a dramatic finish, but with just 1:39 left, Weimar's Brandon Burley broke free for a 79-yard touchdown run, putting Weimar up 14-7. The Indians had one final opportunity to respond, but their last-ditch effort was thwarted with an interception. The 14-7 loss ended Ganado's season and eliminated them from playoff contention. With a final record of 5-5, the team missed the playoffs for the first time since 1995, snapping an eight-year playoff streak. Coach Byrd expressed his disappointment, acknowledging that while the team had the talent to continue their playoff tradition, they had some lapses at key moments that prevented them from achieving that goal. The three district games that Ganado lost were all close and could have gone either way. Despite the disappointment, Byrd continued to emphasize the team's hard work and determination. Though some fans expressed frustration and criticized the coach, Byrd remained committed to doing the best he could with the players at his disposal. The season came to an end, and the team faced a long offseason ahead, with hopes of returning to the playoffs in 2005.

2005

As Coach Byrd entered his second season as the head coach of Ganado, his primary goal was to lead the team back to the playoffs and continue the winning tradition that had been established a decade earlier. The team saw the return of several key players, including offensive tackle Michael Lara, running back Devon Morales, receivers Drew Bridges and Cody Parker, as well as defensive tackles Zeke Kuehn and Ben Castillo, linebackers Joseph Perez and Max Herrera, and defensive back Sam Samudio. Coach Byrd decided to keep the offense simple after a season of growing pains, aiming to focus on utilizing the team's two key weapons: running back Morales and quarterback Samudio. One significant change was that Samudio switched positions to play both receiver and running back, a move that proved to be effective. The team faced the challenge of determining who would play quarterback, and during two-a-days, the competition came down to junior Preston Morales and sophomore Ike Kuehn. Ultimately, Kuehn was named the starting quarterback heading into the season.

The Indians kicked off the 2005 season with an impressive 54-0 victory over Bloomington, showcasing a dominant performance on both offense and defense. The offense was firing on all cylinders, amassing 445 total yards, with Devon Morales rushing for 169 yards and six touchdowns, while quarterback Ike Kuehn passed for 186 yards and two touchdowns. Defensively, the Indians allowed only eight first downs and 160 total yards, while also forcing three turnovers. However, the following week in Hallettsville, the team faced a stark contrast in a 20-0 loss. The high-powered offense that had excelled the week before was shut down, managing only 96 total yards and five first downs. The team also struggled with penalties, committing eight for 60 yards, while Hallettsville's Parris Brown rushed for 180 yards and two touchdowns. Ganado returned home to face Refugio, but the game was marked by adversity. With two starters, Sam Samudio and Zeke Kuehn, out, Refugio took control early, leading 36-0 at halftime. Despite this, the Indians showed resilience, not allowing any points in the second half and scoring two touchdowns to make the final score 36-14. With a 1-2 record, Ganado had two weeks to regroup before the start of district play. The team found their rhythm the next week in Boling, where their offense came alive. Kuehn had his best passing game of the season, throwing for 252 yards and three touchdowns. Samudio was a key contributor, receiving for 168 yards on eight receptions, including three touchdowns, and also running for another score in a 28-14 win. This victory brought the Indians to 2-2. As the team prepared for their final non-district game against East Bernard, Hurricane Rita became a major concern. The storm, a Category 4 hurricane, was expected to make landfall near Matagorda Bay on Friday night. With the game canceled due to the storm, Jackson County was placed under an evacuation order. The storm ultimately made landfall between Texas and Louisiana as a Category 3 storm, sparing Ganado. The game against East Bernard was never rescheduled, and Ganado had a bye week to rest and recover. While the break was beneficial for the team's health, there was concern that it might throw them off rhythm heading into their district opener against undefeated Schulenburg.

Schulenburg entered the game as an explosive offensive team, averaging 40.6 points per game, led by the dual threat of quarterback Jared Trojacek, who was effective both running and passing, and talented receivers like Colby Wilson and all-state tight end Casey Moore. Despite being vulnerable on defense, Schulenburg's offense had enough firepower to outscore nearly anyone. The Indians came out strong, taking the lead in the first quarter with a Morales touchdown run, followed by a two-point conversion from Kuehn to Samudio, giving them an 8-0 lead. The defense also made plays, with Drew Bridges batting down a pass intended for Moore, showing they were ready for the challenge. Schulenburg responded with two touchdowns, taking a 14-8 lead, but Samudio answered back with a spectacular 90-yard kickoff return for a touchdown to tie the game at 14-14. Schulenburg regained the lead with another Trojacek touchdown, and Ganado was able to keep it close, as Mauricio Ramos kicked a 37-yard field goal just before halftime, making the score 22-17. Despite their strong efforts, Schulenburg took control in the second half, scoring 16 unanswered points, and Ganado fell 38-23. Morales rushed for 176 yards and two touchdowns, while Kuehn passed for 102 yards, but the Indians came up short against the high-powered Schulenburg team. The following week, Ganado faced their rivals, Industrial, in a crucial district game. Industrial's staff included former Ganado head coach Monte Althaus as the defensive coordinator, and this added extra significance to the matchup. The game was a defensive battle, with Ganado managing 327 rushing yards but only scoring one touchdown. Morales rushed for over 300 yards, and Kuehn threw an 11-yard touchdown pass to Samudio late in the first quarter. Industrial tied the game at 7-7 with a touchdown just before halftime. The game came down to a dramatic finish, with Ramos kicking a 25-yard field goal with 1:26 left in the game to give Ganado a hard-fought 10-7 victory, evening their district record at 1-1. The Indians followed up with a dominant 50-14 win over Tidehaven, racking up 510 yards on the ground. Kuehn, Samudio, and Morales each rushed for over 100 yards, and Ganado improved to 2-1 in district. The next three weeks would be crucial, as they set the stage for the defining moments of their season.

Ganado traveled to Van Vleck needing a win to stay in playoff contention. Van Vleck, struggling with a 2-5 record, seemed vulnerable, making this game a crucial opportunity for the Indians. However, Van Vleck played one of their best games of the season, and despite Ganado's strong efforts, they had trouble stopping the powerful running of Eddie Quiroga, who rushed for 225 yards. With 1:43 left in the game, Van Vleck extended their lead to 33-20 after a Quiroga touchdown. Things looked bleak for Ganado when Kuehn threw an interception on the following possession, and the stands began to empty. But then the comeback began. On the very next play for Van Vleck, Joseph Perez blitzed and knocked the ball loose from Quiroga, and Brandon Mercer scooped it up and ran 49 yards for a touchdown. The score was now 33-26, and hope was revived. On Van Vleck's next play, Justin Peters stripped Quiroga of the ball again, and Ganado recovered the fumble. Kuehn then threw a 27-yard touchdown pass to Samudio with 28 seconds left, tying the game at 33-33. Mauricio Ramos successfully kicked the extra point, sending the crowd into a frenzy. On the ensuing kickoff, Ramos kicked deep, and Van Vleck fumbled once again, with Ganado recovering near the goal line. Kuehn completed a pass to Samudio, but he was pushed out of bounds just short of the end zone. The Indians planned to spike the ball to set up Ramos for a potential game-winning field goal with only 7 seconds left, but in a controversial moment, the officials did not stop the clock and ruled that Kuehn's spike was a fumbled snap, causing time to expire and sending the game into overtime. Ganado received the ball first in overtime, and Morales scored on a 17-yard run, with Ramos' extra point giving the Indians their first lead of the game, 40-33. Now it was up to the defense. Van Vleck attempted a pass in their overtime possession, but Seth Labay intercepted the ball in the end zone, sealing the victory for Ganado with a dramatic 40-33 comeback win. The win was especially sweet, with a sign in the field house reading, "48 minutes to play, a lifetime to remember (every second counts)," a reminder of the heartbreaking loss to Van Vleck the previous year when the game had ended in the final two seconds. The Indians displayed incredible character, never giving up and fighting until the very end. With this victory, Ganado was now in position for a playoff berth, setting up a crucial final game against Weimar at home.

The season finale between Ganado and Weimar was a dramatic and strange game, as it had serious playoff implications for both teams. The previous year, Ganado had lost to Weimar in a winner-take-all game for the third and final playoff spot. This time, the scenario was reversed, as Weimar still had a chance to make the playoffs, but only if they won by at least 9 points. If they won by a smaller margin, Ganado would take the playoff spot. Ganado controlled their own destiny, needing a win to secure a spot in the playoffs. Weimar started strong with their talented quarterback Drew Quinney, who threw two touchdown passes to Hank Janecka in the first half, giving Weimar a 12-0 lead. Things looked bleak for Ganado, but turnovers became the story of the game. Ganado's defense intercepted Weimar five times, with Bridges snagging three and Labay taking two. Bridges not only excelled on defense but also contributed offensively, with 71 yards receiving on five catches. Morales had a stellar performance, rushing for 168 yards on 32 carries, but Ganado could only manage one touchdown. Kuehn connected with Labay for an 11-yard touchdown pass in the fourth quarter to cut Weimar's lead to 12-6. With the game now within reach, Ganado had control of their playoff fate. Weimar's leading rusher, Brandon Burley, was contained by the Ganado defense, though he still rushed for 103 yards before re-aggravating an ankle injury that forced him out of the game. After Ganado's touchdown, they managed to control the clock for 4:22, getting three first downs and leaving Weimar with just 1:30 to respond. In the final moments, it was Bridges who sealed the game for Ganado, intercepting Quinney for the third time with 50 seconds left. Though Weimar won the game 12-6, they failed to win by the required margin, and Ganado clinched the playoff spot due to the tiebreaker rules. The game was controversial in the final moments, with some Ganado fans booing, possibly not understanding the scenario, when the team didn't down the ball to kill the clock, despite being down by six points with less than a minute left. Despite the confusion, the end result was a victory for the Ganado players, who had battled through adversity and got their shot at the playoffs once again, a sweet redemption after the loss to Weimar the previous year.

The 2005 bi-district playoff game between Ganado and Refugio was a highly anticipated rematch that took place at Sandcrab Stadium in Port Lavaca on November 11, Veterans Day. The first meeting between these two teams in September had been a dominant win for Refugio, with Ganado missing two key starters. However, this time Ganado was at full strength and had a solid game plan in place. This playoff appearance marked Ganado's ninth in the past ten seasons, and they had never lost a bi-district playoff game during that stretch. The team was determined for revenge, especially after Refugio had come into Ganado earlier in the season and disrespectfully staked their flag at midfield before the game. In addition to the motivation on the field, the week leading up to the game had a personal significance for me. While I was deer hunting that week, I had shot two bobcats (Refugio's mascot) and took this as a good omen for the game. Interestingly, I also participated in a local football pick contest for the first time and won first place, picking a score close to what the final outcome would be. The game itself was a defensive battle, with Refugio initially taking the lead in the first quarter on a 27-yard touchdown pass from quarterback Collin Avery to Carl Swain. However, a penalty on the extra point attempt pushed Refugio back and caused the kick to be missed, leaving them with a 6-0 lead. The defenses then took over, with both teams playing tough, and neither offense able to find much rhythm. With just 23 seconds left in the first half, Ganado struck back when Kuehn connected with Devon Morales on a 37-yard touchdown pass. Ramos successfully kicked the extra point, giving Ganado a 7-6 lead at halftime. In the second half, Ganado controlled possession for much of the third quarter but was unable to score again. However, the defense continued to shine, with Mercer intercepting a pass and Bridges recovering a fumble. Refugio had one last opportunity in the fourth quarter, advancing to the Ganado 30-yard line with their passing game, but the drive ended when Zeke Kuehn recovered a fumble to secure the win for Ganado. The Indians ran down the clock from the 40-yard line, and the final score was 7-6 in favor of Ganado. This win was especially sweet for Ganado, as no one had expected them to come out on top, particularly after the heavy loss to Refugio earlier in the season. The victory was a moment of redemption and set the stage for a deep playoff run. This game would go down as one of the most memorable in the season, alongside the dramatic comeback against Van Vleck. It also marked the last time Ganado would defeat Refugio until 2023, when they once again knocked them out of the playoffs in a quarterfinal match.

With the win, Ganado moved on to the area round, where they would face Skidmore-Tynan at Victoria Memorial Stadium. Skidmore-Tynan, though not typically a football powerhouse, had a strong team in 2005, led by head coach Adam Arroyo, a former player on Cuero's 1987 Class 3A state championship team and a former Baylor player. His experience in winning was evident, and his team posed a significant challenge for Ganado in the area round of the playoffs. This game was played on a Saturday night, which gave the Indians that Friday night off, and while they had reason to feel confident after their big win over Refugio, were they too confident? The game began on a high note for Ganado as they quickly took a 7-0 lead with a touchdown run from Morales on their first possession. After a Skidmore-Tynan punt, Ganado seemed poised to extend the lead, but an interception stopped the drive. Skidmore-Tynan responded with a touchdown and a successful two-point conversion to take an 8-7 lead. Ganado answered back with an 11-yard touchdown pass from Kuehn to Bridges, but the two-point conversion failed, and Ganado led 13-8 with 4:55 left in the first half. However, Skidmore-Tynan capitalized on a Ganado fumble and scored before halftime, regaining the lead at 14-13. With all the momentum on their side, Skidmore-Tynan came out strong in the second half, extending their lead to 21-13. Ganado struggled to find their rhythm, and Skidmore-Tynan continued to build their lead, eventually going up 28-13 in the fourth quarter. The game ended with a third interception off of Kuehn, sealing a 28-13 win for Skidmore-Tynan and ending Ganado's season. Despite Kuehn passing for 110 yards, the three interceptions proved to be costly for Ganado. Morales rushed for 93 yards in his final game as a senior. After the game, Coach Byrd reflected on the season, stating, "We were happy to be here, we took a group of young men who had a chance and made them better." This team had been doubted throughout the season, but they successfully brought Ganado back to the playoffs after a year's absence, continuing the tradition of postseason success. They may have fallen short in the area round, but Coach Byrd and his staff had done an excellent job developing the team, particularly the young players.

Though they didn't know it at the time, significant changes were on the horizon for the program in the near future.

On Friday, December 16, as school was letting out for the Christmas holidays, a shocking and unexpected event unfolded at Ganado ISD. Mark Byrd, the athletic director and head football coach, was reassigned to an assistant coaching position, a decision that stunned many. This news came as a surprise to both students and staff, as Byrd had only been in the position for two seasons, compiling an 11-10 record. Superintendent Jeff Black was questioned about the decision but offered little explanation, later stating that a change in leadership was needed in the athletic department. This change sparked a significant uproar at the school, with protests taking place both on campus and around town in the days that followed. Byrd was well-liked by many, though some fans had expressed dissatisfaction with his coaching style. Despite the controversy, Byrd had made notable contributions, including taking the girls' powerlifting team to state in 2005 and being part of the team that won a state championship in 2006, alongside coach Sherri Hicks. Tragically, the unsettling news didn't end there. On Christmas Day, the community was hit with the devastating loss of Coach Mike Flynn, who passed away from drowning while fishing in the Lavaca River. Flynn, who had been the boys' basketball coach for the past seven years and an assistant coach for the football team, was beloved by many. His passing left the school in mourning. The remainder of the basketball season was dedicated to his memory, and every team Ganado played against showed respect with a moment of silence before each game. Assistant coach Joey Rosalez stepped in as interim head coach for the boys' basketball team for the rest of the season. Coach Flynn had joined Ganado ISD in 1996 and was deeply respected by students and colleagues alike. He had been an influential figure in the school community, coaching many students, and taught Biology in high school. Known for his laid-back nature, Flynn was also disciplined and had a strong desire to win. He was a mentor who helped shape the character of every player he coached, making them better people both on and off the field. Outside of his coaching duties, Flynn had a passion for playing the guitar and was a big fan of Jimmy Buffett. He was always there when needed, offering friendship and support to anyone who crossed his path. His untimely passing left a hole in the community, and his memory lived on through the impact he had on everyone around him. In the face of these challenges, the Ganado community remained resilient, staying strong and united through difficult times. The unexpected changes and tragedies that occurred in such a short period left many questioning the events, but as always, the people of Ganado pulled together and supported each other.

Chapter 6

Rebuilding

2006

On January 26, Mike Rabe was officially hired as the new athletic director and head football coach at Ganado ISD. Although this was Rabe's first role as an athletic director, his background in successful football programs made him a strong and promising choice for the position. Rabe had played under the legendary coach Mickey Finley at Cuero High School, where he was an all-state offensive lineman on a team that reached the state finals in 1993. He went on to play one season of college football at Tarleton State before graduating from Sam Houston State University. Rabe began his coaching career with a one-year stint as an assistant at Huntsville High School. He then joined Finley's staff at Arlington High School for two seasons and followed him to Cleburne, where he coached for the next three years. Rabe planned to bring Clint Finley, Mickey Finley's son, to Ganado as his defensive coordinator. Clint brought an impressive resume of his own, having played quarterback and defensive back at Cuero, continuing his career at the University of Nebraska, and later with the Kansas City Chiefs in the NFL. One of Rabe's first priorities at Ganado was to get to know the student-athletes and begin implementing his vision for the football program, which centered on an option-based offensive system. At the same time, he had to closely monitor the upcoming UIL biannual realignment, scheduled for the following week. Ganado was on the cusp of potentially dropping from Class 2A to Class 1A, which added another layer of complexity and importance to Rabe's early decisions as he began his tenure with the program.

On February 2, the outcome of the biannual UIL realignment came down to just five students, as Ganado's reported enrollment of 200 narrowly exceeded the Class 1A cutoff of 194, keeping the school in Class 2A. This slim margin had major implications for the football program and overall athletic competition. To further complicate matters, schools such as Edna, Hallettsville, and Rice Consolidated dropped from Class 3A to 2A, joining Ganado in what quickly became a highly competitive district alongside Schulenburg, Weimar, Industrial, and Tidehaven. As one of the smallest schools in the district for the next two years, Ganado faced an uphill battle, particularly as student enrollment continued to decline and the program was already thin in both talent and depth. Coach Rabe acknowledged the difficulty of the situation, stating, "we will take what we get," while noting that Ganado had traditionally held its own at the 2A level. However, he also recognized that this season would present a serious challenge. Adding another twist to the evolving district landscape, Rabe's former mentor Mickey Finley accepted the athletic director and head football coach position at Schulenburg, a new district rival, and was joined by his son Clint, who had initially planned to coach at Ganado, as Schulenburg's defensive coordinator. In response, Coach Rabe hired Bobby Schuman to serve as Ganado's new defensive coordinator. Schuman's wife, Rachel, joined Rabe's wife, Teri, on the girls' coaching staff, helping to round out the athletic department and bring stability amid the shifting dynamics of a challenging new district.

Despite low numbers and a highly competitive district, Ganado approached the 2006 football season with its trademark toughness and resilience, ready to face any opponent on the schedule. Coach Rabe inherited a very young team, with only seven seniors on a 25-player varsity roster. Junior quarterback Ike Kuehn returned to lead the offense, having guided the Indians to a playoff appearance and victory the previous season. However, the team lacked experience at running back, with the position to be filled by junior Derek Hicks and sophomores John Meyer and Joe Salinas. Kuehn possessed a strong arm, and if the Indians needed to rely on the passing game, they had capable targets in junior receivers Seth Labay and Joseph Janecek, along with senior tight end Justin Peters. Peters, one of the few large players on the roster, also served as a vital blocker on the offensive line, working alongside senior Dillon Lesak and junior Ryan Taylor. Defensively, Labay contributed in the secondary, Peters moved from the line to play middle linebacker, and Lesak and Taylor anchored the defensive front. The remaining positions were filled by other members of the young roster, who stepped up as needed. Although faced with challenges, the team embraced the season with determination and a fighting spirit.

Ganado opened its 2006 football season at Patti Welder Stadium in Victoria with a 21-0 loss to St. Joseph. The young team faced early growing pains, which would be a recurring theme throughout the season as players continued to develop and learn. While the Indians showed moments of promise, inconsistency ultimately led to their defeat, despite a competitive overall effort. In the home opener the following week - also homecoming, Ganado's offense showed signs of life, scoring three touchdowns in a 34-19 loss to Boling. Derek Hicks, Ike Kuehn, and Kevin Smith each found the end zone, but Boling's standout player, Wayland Griggs, ran for 140 yards and four touchdowns, which proved too much to overcome. Heading into their final non-district matchup, a rivalry game against Louise, the Indians were determined to earn their first win. Louise entered the game undefeated at 2-0, and both teams struggled offensively in the early going. The game became a defensive battle, with the turning point coming in the second quarter when the Louise punter dropped the snap and was tackled in the end zone for a safety, giving Ganado a 2-0 lead. In the third quarter, the Indians extended their lead with a short touchdown run by Oscar Cantu, although the two-point conversion attempt failed, leaving the score at 8-0. Louise responded late with a touchdown of their own, but the Indians' defense held firm, stopping the two-point attempt thanks to a crucial tackle by Dillon Lesak. Ganado secured a narrow 8-6 win - its first of the season - in a game that was nearly even in total yardage, with Ganado edging Louise 163 to 154. The victory improved the Indians' record to 1-2 and provided a boost of momentum heading into their bye week before entering the tough district portion of their schedule.

During the bye week, Ganado made key position changes to strengthen the team. Derek Hicks moved from running back to quarterback, while Ike Kuehn shifted from quarterback to tight end. The Indians opened district play with a strong showing against Hallettsville. Hicks led an impressive opening drive that ended in a touchdown, followed by a two-point conversion from Joe Salinas to Carlos Arriaga, giving Ganado an early 8-0 lead. Hallettsville responded with a touchdown but failed on their two-point attempt, allowing Ganado to hold an 8-6 advantage. Midway through the second quarter, Kevin Smith scored another touchdown, and Julio Ramos added the extra point, pushing the lead to 15-6. However, a costly penalty on the Ganado defense late in the first half allowed Hallettsville to score again, tightening the game to a 15-13 halftime lead for the Indians. In the second half, Ganado's offense stalled, and Hallettsville scored the only touchdown to secure a narrow 19-15 win. The following two games were tough back-to-back blowout home losses - 47-7 to Tidehaven and 40-0 to Industrial - dropping Ganado to 0-3 in district play. Despite the losses, the team continued to fight. Ganado traveled to Weimar for another hard-fought battle. The Indians took a 6-3 halftime lead after Derek Hicks, before being injured, connected with Kuehn on a 36-yard pass that set up the team's only touchdown, which Kuehn then ran in after taking over as quarterback. In the second half, Weimar took the lead with a touchdown in the fourth quarter to make it 10-6. Ganado had one final chance to score, but a late interception ended the drive. With one second left and the game already decided, Weimar's coaches controversially called a timeout and threw a final touchdown pass to win 16-6. This decision angered many Ganado fans, and tensions rose postgame as words were exchanged between a Ganado fan and a Weimar coach. Ganado fell to 1-6 overall and 0-4 in district, and the tough stretch continued through the final three games of the season. The Indians lost to Edna (40-6), Rice Consolidated (45-20), and district champion Schulenburg (36-7), finishing the 2006 season with a 1-9 record and winless in district play for the first time since 1989. Despite the record, the young team showed heart and determination throughout the season. Coach Rabe emphasized the importance of facing adversity and learning from it, praising the team for battling every week and never giving up. It was a rebuilding year full of valuable lessons for a group that gained experience and character through perseverance.

2007

Coach Rabe entered his second season as head football coach at Ganado in 2007 with optimism, noting that the team had matured significantly through the challenges and growing pains of the 2006 season. One of the key changes heading into the new year was at the quarterback position. Senior Jared Atzenhoffer, who is the brother-in-law of defensive coordinator Bobby Schuman, earned the starting role under center. Former quarterback Ike Kuehn, who started as a sophomore in 2005 and weighed 170 pounds at the time, had grown to 225 pounds by his senior year and transitioned to playing offensive guard. Kuehn embraced the move without complaint, embodying the selflessness, toughness, and team-first mindset that defined the character of the Indians. While the players could not control their physical size, school enrollment, or the fact that they competed in one of the toughest districts in the region - if not the state - they remained committed to improvement. The team benefited from the experience gained by underclassmen the previous year, as four freshmen and several sophomores had seen playing time in the final game of 2006. This experience proved valuable heading into the new season. Sophomore Kevin Smith returned to the backfield after starting at tailback as a freshman, bringing both speed and experience. He was joined by senior Derek Hicks and sophomore Donovan Foster to round out a solid group of running backs. The receiving corps featured returning senior Seth Labay, and the offensive line was expected to be a strength with experienced seniors including center Hunter Hlavaty, guards Ryan Taylor and Kuehn, and tackle Brady Engelmohr. Defensively, the Indians were determined to improve after surrendering 40 or more points in four district games the previous season. John Meyer returned at defensive tackle, while Engelmohr and Kuehn brought experience to the defensive end positions. In the secondary, Labay and junior Joe Salinas provided leadership and coverage ability. With greater maturity, returning experience, and a strong commitment to growth, the Indians looked to take meaningful steps forward despite the continued challenges of a tough district.

The Indians kicked off their football season at home against St. Joseph. The Indians started strong, taking a 20-8 lead at halftime with touchdowns from Derek Hicks, Donovan Foster, and Joe Salinas. However, St. Joseph came out energized in the second half, with Brett Stafford scoring on a 52-yard run on their first snap, shifting the momentum in their favor. Despite a solid effort from Ganado, St. Joseph outscored them 21-0 in the second half, ultimately winning 29-20. Stafford had an impressive performance for St. Joseph, rushing for 175 yards and two touchdowns. In the next game against Boling, Ganado struggled to hold onto the football, committing four fumbles and an interception that led to points for Boling. B.W. McLeod dominated for Boling, rushing for 191 yards and five touchdowns. Ganado trailed 26-7 at halftime but closed the gap to 26-21 in the third quarter, thanks to touchdown runs from Foster and Smith. However, Boling sealed the victory with a 28-point fourth quarter, winning 54-21.

As a result, Ganado started the season 0-2 for the second year in a row, with a big home game against rival Louise on the horizon. In the final non-district game, Louise, who was 2-0, came to Ganado, and the game lived up to expectations. Louise stunned the home crowd when Antwon Parson returned the opening kickoff for a touchdown, giving them a 7-0 lead. Louise suffered a significant blow when their quarterback Nick Barrera was injured in the first quarter and was unable to return. Despite the injury, Louise extended their lead to 13-0 by halftime. Ganado responded in the second half when Atzenhoffer connected with Hicks for a touchdown, narrowing the gap to 13-6. In the final seconds of the third quarter, Tim Bridges made a spectacular catch on an Atzenhoffer pass, energizing the crowd and shifting momentum in Ganado's favor. The Indians continued their comeback in the fourth quarter with a touchdown from Donovan Foster, and Julio Ramos added the extra point to tie the game at 13-13. The Ganado defense stepped up, preventing Louise from advancing further and giving their offense a chance to score. In the closing minutes, Oscar Cantu made a critical catch on an Atzenhoffer pass, and with the ball at the five-yard line and only 10 seconds left, Atzenhoffer rushed for a touchdown to give Ganado a thrilling 20-13 victory. This comeback win improved their record to 1-2 as they headed into their bye week before preparing for their district opener against Hallettsville. Louise, which had a strong season, went on to reach the playoffs and finished with an 8-4 record after losing to D'Hanis in the Area round.

District play for Ganado began with a home game against a strong Hallettsville team. Hallettsville quickly took control, building a 21-0 lead in the second quarter. Ganado managed to score just before halftime on a Salinas touchdown run, but despite a more competitive second half, they ultimately fell short, losing 27-6. The following week, Ganado traveled to El Maton to face Tidehaven. In a lineup change, sophomore Donovan Foster made his debut at quarterback. Ganado dominated in time of possession and first downs, recording 33 first downs to Tidehaven's 14 and rushing for 374 yards on 59 attempts. However, Tidehaven had a huge offensive night as well, totaling 209 rushing yards and 255 passing yards. Quarterback Jared Ramirez threw four touchdown passes, and JaCorey Fisher rushed for 176 yards and two touchdowns, including a 96-yard score. Tidehaven defeated Ganado 49-20, dropping the Indians to 0-2 in district play. Despite the losses, Ganado remained determined and hungry for a win as they faced county rival Industrial at Cobra Field in Vanderbilt. Industrial had crushed Ganado 40-0 the year before, but this time, the Indians turned the tables. In a tightly contested game, Ganado capitalized on three turnovers and controlled the ground game with 333 rushing yards on 54 attempts. Kevin Smith and Foster scored the game's only points in the second quarter with touchdown runs, leading to a 14-0 Ganado victory. Both players surpassed the 100-yard mark, with Foster rushing for 217 yards on 32 carries and Smith adding 122 yards on 20 carries. Defensively, Ganado delivered their best performance of the season, holding Industrial to just 201 total yards and earning their first district win in two years. With renewed momentum, Ganado returned home to face Weimar, a team that had beaten them three straight years in competitive matchups. Despite Weimar being winless in district play, they had athletic talent, including a 270-pound fullback. Ganado responded with what was arguably their best game of the season, dominating in a 42-12 victory. The Indians rushed for 406 yards, with Smith running for 220 yards and two touchdowns, and Foster adding 106 yards, including a 70-yard touchdown run in the fourth quarter. The defense also continued to impress, holding Weimar to just 150 total yards and showing noticeable improvement. With back-to-back district wins, Ganado was gaining momentum and confidence on both sides of the ball.

By the end of the season, Ganado had established itself as having the top-ranked defense in the district - an impressive accomplishment considering the strength of their competition. With a district record of 2-2, the Indians remained in the playoff race, but the final stretch of the season featured a tough slate of opponents, including Edna and Rice Consolidated, both of whom would finish as co-district champions and advance to the playoffs. Ganado's next game was a short trip west on Highway 59 to face rival Edna in a highly anticipated "Cowboys vs. Indians" matchup. The Indians came out strong, scoring on their opening drive with a Foster touchdown run and a successful extra point by Ramos to take an early 7-0 lead. The defense held Edna to a punt on their first possession, fueling early momentum for Ganado. However, after a Ganado punt, the game turned quickly. Edna's Fletcher Robinson tied the game 7-7, and the Cowboys dominated from that point on, scoring 35 unanswered points, including a 28-point second quarter, to take a 35-7 lead at halftime. The teams traded touchdowns in the second half, but Edna emerged with a 48-20 win, effectively eliminating Ganado from playoff contention. In their final home game of the season, Ganado hosted a talented Rice Consolidated squad, which featured standout athletes like quarterback Taylor Cook, a University of Miami commit, and running back Zacchaeus Foster, who would go on to play at Blinn College. Rice jumped out to a commanding 38-0 lead before Ganado added two second-half touchdowns - one a 67-yard run by Donovan Foster and the other by Smith - to make the final score more respectable. Foster from Rice finished the game with 131 rushing yards and scored the team's first two touchdowns. Ganado concluded the season on the road against Schulenburg. Despite putting up a fight, the Indians fell 49-28, finishing the season with an overall record of 3-7. While the year had its ups and downs, the development of an improved defense and strong individual performances gave the program a solid foundation to build on for the future.

The 2007 Ganado football team showed significant improvement from the previous season, both in performance and overall competitiveness. Although the final record may not fully reflect it, the team won two more games than the year before and consistently played hard against a challenging schedule. The players showed determination and resilience, never giving up regardless of the opponent. Despite missing the playoffs, many believe that this team would have likely qualified had they competed in a different district or especially in Class 1A. Over the past two seasons, Ganado competed in a highly competitive district filled with talented programs, most of which were from larger schools. This made every game a tough battle, yet Ganado continued to hold their own. The 2007 squad was also notably young, with many underclassmen gaining valuable playing experience that would benefit the program moving forward. With the expected drop to Class 1A during February's UIL realignment, there was growing optimism about the team's future potential. One standout, Brady Englemohr, continued his football journey at the collegiate level, going on to play for Mary Hardin-Baylor. Overall, the 2007 season laid the foundation for future success and marked a turning point for a program on the rise.

Chapter 7

Back to the Playoffs: The Second Run

2008

On February 1, a highly anticipated and significant event occurred when Ganado was reclassified, moving from Class 2A down to Class 1A. This change had been eagerly awaited during the previous two alignment periods and was expected to benefit the athletic program by allowing Ganado to compete against schools of a more similar size. Although the reclassification was seen as an advantage, the new district Ganado entered remained highly competitive. It included perennial playoff contenders such as Shiner and Flatonia, as well as a strong Burton team. Additionally, Ganado's local rival, Louise, was placed in the same district, along with Somerville, another school that had also dropped a classification.

Ganado entered the season well-prepared for a strong playoff run, led by an experienced backfield that featured junior quarterback Donovan Foster and running backs junior Kevin Smith and seniors Joey Arriaga and Joe Salinas. Foster and Smith formed a dynamic offensive duo, with Foster rushing for 1,014 yards and Smith adding 1,027 yards in the previous season. The receiving corps also brought experience, with seniors Tim Bridges and Matt Hajovsky, along with junior Ross Rakowitz. However, the offensive line required rebuilding after losing several senior starters from the previous year. Potential replacements included seniors Chance Bothe at center and Fabian Garcia and Jonathan Fowler at the guard positions. On the defensive side, senior linemen John Meyer and Garcia returned at tackle, while the linebacker group was anchored by seniors David Brito, Fowler, Arriaga, and Hajovsky. The secondary featured returning players Bridges, Salinas, Rakowitz, and Foster, all of whom had experience from a defense that ranked first in one of the toughest Class 2A districts the previous year. With this depth and experience, the team was motivated and ready to return to the playoffs, especially now that they would be facing schools of similar size in their new district alignment.

Ganado opened the season with a dominant 44–6 home victory over Bloomington, showcasing a powerful rushing attack and a strong defensive performance. The Indians amassed 523 rushing yards, led by Kevin Smith with 159 yards and a touchdown, Donovan Foster contributed 124 yards and a touchdown, while Roy Sophus added 98 yards and a touchdown. Joey Arriaga scored two touchdowns, and Matthew Hajovsky also added a score. Defensively, Ganado was equally impressive, with John Meyer recording a sack for a safety in the third quarter. The only touchdown allowed came late in the fourth quarter, long after the game was decided. The following week, Ganado improved to 2–0 with a hard-fought 22–14 road win over Nixon-Smiley. In a physical contest, the Indians' defense forced seven turnovers, including five interceptions - three of which were made by Ross Rakowitz. For the second consecutive week, Ganado's defense scored a safety, this time when David Brito tackled Nixon-Smiley quarterback Cody Box in the end zone. The win marked the first time since 2002 that Ganado started a season with two straight victories. However, the momentum was briefly interrupted by the looming threat of Hurricane Ike. On Monday, September 8, attention turned to the storm as it moved from Cuba into the Gulf of Mexico, appearing to head directly toward the central Texas coast. By the following day, preparations and evacuation orders were underway, leading to the cancellation of Ganado's upcoming game against Boling, which was also scheduled to be the homecoming game. Fortunately, by September 11, Hurricane Ike shifted eastward and made landfall near Galveston as a strong Category 2 hurricane on the morning of Saturday, September 13. Ganado was once again spared major impact, just as it had been during Hurricane Rita in September 2005.

After a week off due to the cancellation from the pending hurricane, Ganado resumed play against their Jackson County rival, Industrial, in Vanderbilt. The game quickly spiraled out of control for the Indians, as Industrial capitalized on two blocked punts by Glenn Sparkman to gain favorable field position and jump out to a 13–0 lead. Foster briefly shifted the momentum by racing 87 yards for a touchdown early in the second quarter, cutting the deficit to 13–7. However, Industrial responded with a dominating stretch, scoring 22 unanswered points in a span of seven minutes to take a commanding 35–7 lead at halftime. Industrial's Matt Anderson was the key difference-maker, rushing for 154 yards and three touchdowns, with 140 of those yards coming in the first half. Industrial extended their lead to 42–7 in the third quarter before Smith added a short touchdown run in the fourth, closing the scoring at 42–14. Foster finished with 122 rushing yards, but Ganado suffered their first loss of the season, falling to 2–1. Looking to bounce back, Ganado hosted Danbury in their rescheduled homecoming game. Danbury, who had not played in three weeks due to the impact of Hurricane Ike, came out energized and quickly built a 19–7 lead early in the second quarter. A stunned home crowd watched as Ganado struggled early, but the Indians' defense stiffened, and the offense responded. Smith scored two touchdowns late in the second quarter to give Ganado a narrow 22–21 halftime lead. During the halftime festivities, Megan Diaz was crowned homecoming queen, and the Ganado community came together to donate school supplies to Danbury in support of their recovery efforts. The second half began with a spark as Smith returned the opening kickoff 85 yards for a touchdown, extending Ganado's lead to 28–21. Danbury would later add a safety after tackling Foster in the end zone, cutting the score to 28–23. However, Smith sealed the game with his fourth touchdown of the night, capping off a stellar performance in which he rushed for 157 yards on 19 carries. Ganado rallied from a 12-point second-quarter deficit to secure a 34–23 homecoming win, improving their record to 3–1 heading into a bye week before the start of district play.

Entering district play in a new classification meant new opponents, unfamiliar stadiums, and longer travel distances for Ganado. In their district opener, the Indians made a lengthy trip to Somerville to face a team with a matching 3–1 record. The game was played at Yegua Stadium - also known as "The Rock" - a unique venue bordered by a distinctive stone wall, offering a different atmosphere than what Ganado was used to. The Indians got off to a slow start offensively, struggling to reach the end zone in the early stages of the game, but the defense remained strong throughout the night. Late in the second quarter, Ganado finally broke through with back-to-back touchdowns by Sophus and Smith, giving the Indians a 14–0 halftime lead. Somerville answered quickly to open the second half with a 60-yard scoring drive capped by a touchdown run from quarterback Cody Holliday. However, on the ensuing extra point attempt, Ganado freshman Josh Labay made a momentum-shifting play by blocking the kick and returning it 95 yards for two points, extending the lead to 16–6. From there, the Ganado defense shut down Somerville for the remainder of the game. On offense, Foster connected with Jason Staff for a 30-yard touchdown pass, and Smith added an 18-yard touchdown run to seal the victory. Ganado went on to win 30–6, earning their first district win as a Class 1A program and improving to 4–1 on the season.

Next on the schedule was a highly anticipated district showdown as undefeated 5–0 Shiner traveled to Ganado in what would become one of the district's fiercest rivalries in the years to follow. Though the two teams had scrimmaged annually on Saturday mornings from 2002 to 2007, this marked their first official meeting since a 1997 non-district game, which Ganado had won convincingly, 48–8. With both teams eyeing a possible district title, the stakes were high. Ganado came out energized and dominated the first half, jumping out to a 21–7 lead by halftime. Smith opened the scoring on the Indians' first possession with a 31-yard touchdown run. Later in the first quarter, Foster broke free for an 83-yard touchdown run, shocking Shiner and putting Ganado up 14–0. Shiner responded early in the second quarter with a touchdown from Matthew Hibbs to make it 14–7, but Foster answered quickly with another big play - a 47-yard touchdown run - to restore a two-score lead and give the Indians control heading into the break. However, the second half told a very different story. Shiner came out of the locker room with renewed focus and completely took over the game, scoring 35 unanswered points and finding the end zone on all six of their second-half possessions. Running back Josh Greathouse led the charge with three third-quarter touchdowns on runs of 1, 44, and 35 yards, accounting for 161 of his 223 total rushing yards in that quarter alone. Shiner's Hibbs and Lance Otto each added touchdowns in the fourth quarter, sealing a 42–21 comeback victory. The statistical contrast between the two halves was striking. Ganado had racked up 237 yards in the first half but was held to just 93 yards after halftime. Meanwhile, Shiner gained 243 of their 320 total yards in the second half. Smith finished with 156 rushing yards on 20 carries, and Foster ended the night with 103 yards on 14 carries. Notably, Foster had 141 yards and two touchdowns on five carries in the first half but was tackled for losses on six of his nine second-half attempts. The game was a tale of two halves, and Shiner's halftime adjustments proved decisive. For many Ganado fans, the fourth quarter was tough to watch, as their team, once in control, was overwhelmed on its home field. While the loss was disappointing, Coach Rabe emphasized that the game was a learning experience for a team not accustomed to this level of competition in recent years. He reminded everyone that there was still a lot of football left to play and that the outcome of this one game would not define the season.

With a 1–1 district record and looking to rebound from a tough loss to Shiner, Ganado hit the road once again, this time traveling to face a strong and physically imposing Burton team. Burton was had lots of talent and size, highlighted by lineman Jon Hodde, who stood 6'7" and weighed 285 pounds - a visual contrast captured in a memorable photo featured in the 2009 *Chieftain* yearbook, showing Hodde towering over Ganado's Tim Bridges during the coin toss before the second half. This game was critical for Ganado, not only to stay in the district race but also to regain momentum after the previous week's collapse. From the opening kickoff, it was a hard-fought battle. The first quarter ended scoreless as both defenses held strong. Early in the second quarter, Ganado struck first when Foster scored on a 12-yard run. Julio Ramos, who would later play a key role, added the extra point to give the Indians a 7–0 lead. Burton responded after capitalizing on a Ganado turnover, as Gabriel Patterson scored a touchdown, and the extra point tied the game at 7–7. After a series of defensive stops and quick possessions, Ganado found themselves with the ball and only 51 seconds left in the half. With just one second remaining, Foster launched a pass into the end zone, and despite tight coverage, Jason Staff came down with the ball for a dramatic touchdown. Ramos' extra point gave Ganado a 14–7 halftime lead. The second half mirrored the intensity of the first. After a scoreless third quarter, Burton tied the game when Daniel Patterson scored with just over eight minutes remaining. On the extra point attempt, Ganado blocked the kick, but an offside penalty gave Burton a second chance, which they used to successfully convert a two-point play by quarterback Bobby Mathis, giving Burton a 15–14 lead. Ganado's offense stalled, and they were forced to punt, handing the ball back to Burton. However, a series of costly penalties pushed Burton backward, leading to a critical fourth-down situation at their own 30-yard line. Ganado's defense made a huge stop, giving the offense one last chance. The Indians drove down the field and reached the 5-yard line. With just 15 seconds remaining, Coach Rabe called a timeout to set up a potential game-winning field goal. Ganado ran one more play but failed to score. With one second left, Ramos stepped onto the field and calmly delivered a perfect field goal as time expired, lifting Ganado to a dramatic 17–15 victory. The buzzer sounded, and the crowd erupted in celebration as Ganado improved to 2–1 in district play. Coach Rabe praised the team's resilience, composure, and unity, calling it a huge win and a great example of overcoming adversity through teamwork.

Ganado faced another critical district matchup on Halloween night, hosting long-time Highway 59 rival Louise in the annual "Battle of Mustang Creek." The atmosphere was charged, but whether it was the eerie feel of Halloween or simply Louise's determination, the night belonged to Louise. Although Ganado had edged Louise in close non-district games the two previous seasons, this time things went the other way. Both teams moved the ball in the first half but failed to find the end zone until midway through the second quarter, when Chico Vasquez stunned the Ganado crowd by intercepting a Foster pitch and returning it 84 yards for a touchdown. Louise missed the extra point, giving them a 6–0 lead. Ganado answered with a short touchdown run by Joe Salinas, and Ramos added the extra point to give the Indians a narrow 7–6 halftime lead. The second half turned into a defensive battle, but the momentum shifted decisively in the fourth quarter. Ganado appeared to gain control with a goal-line stand, but a blocked Louise field goal attempt was nullified by a personal foul penalty. Given a second chance, Louise scored on the next play as Kyle Lawson ran it in and added the two-point conversion to put Louise ahead 14–7 with 5:22 left. Ganado unraveled in the final minutes, as Lawson scored two more touchdowns, capitalizing on Indian penalties, poor field position, and turnovers. The 28–7 loss left the home crowd stunned and added another chapter to a season full of highs and lows - one week bringing a big win, the next a tough loss.

Despite the setback, the season came down to a winner-take-all finale against Flatonia for the final playoff spot. It was a situation eerily similar to 2004, when Ganado faced Weimar on the road in a must-win game to advance. Again, Ganado had to travel, and again the stakes were clear: win and move on. Flatonia entered the game with the district's top-ranked offense and leading rusher, Adrian Lighteard, whose status was uncertain after missing the previous game with an injury. Lighteard did play and scored Flatonia's first touchdown, giving them an 8–2 lead after Ganado opened the scoring with a safety. Smith responded with the first of his two touchdowns, part of a 200-yard rushing performance, to give Ganado a 9–8 lead. Flatonia answered before the half and went into the locker room with a 14–9 advantage. Ganado opened the second half with a statement drive, marching 95 yards on 12 plays, capped by Smith's second touchdown of the night. Foster then connected with freshman Case Silliman on a successful two-point conversion, putting Ganado ahead 17–14. Both defenses clamped down from there. Flatonia made a crucial goal-line stand with 6:24 left, stopping Ganado inches from the end zone. On the next Flatonia drive, Rakowitz came up with a key interception. Ganado was later forced to punt, giving Flatonia one last shot with just over a minute remaining. But Arriaga sealed the game with another interception, and Ganado held on for a thrilling 17–14 victory. The win secured Ganado a spot in the playoffs for the first time since 2005, ending a two-year absence. District 27-1A, which included Ganado, Shiner, and Burton as its playoff representatives, received a bye in the bi-district round. This break provided a much-needed opportunity for players to rest and recover, as well as additional time to prepare for their area round opponents. The emotional victory over Flatonia gave the team momentum and new life heading into the postseason.

Ganado entered the playoffs with a 6–3 record and faced 7–4 Chilton in the area round on Saturday, November 22, in Navasota. As has often been the case in past postseasons, the Indians elevated their level of play when it mattered most. Ganado capitalized on three Chilton turnovers and recovered an onside kick, turning those opportunities into a dominant 21–0 halftime lead, with all three touchdowns scored by Smith. Chilton managed to score once on its first drive of the second half, but the Ganado defense shut them down for the remainder of the game. The Indians controlled the tempo, ran out the clock, and secured a 21–6 victory to advance to the regional round. In the next round, Ganado faced Mason on the Friday after Thanksgiving at Bob Shelton Stadium in Buda. It marked the Indians' return to Thanksgiving weekend football for the first time since 2003, rekindling a cherished tradition. A spirited community pep rally at the town square sent the team off with energy and pride. Mason, playing without their star running back Jared Hudson due to a broken arm, struggled against a tenacious Ganado defense. Turnovers once again played a pivotal role, as Mason fumbled deep in Ganado territory three times, threw two interceptions, and mishandled a punt - errors that Ganado took full advantage of. Ganado built a 16–0 lead on touchdowns from Arriaga and Foster, along with a 23-yard field goal by Ramos. Mason found some life in the third quarter, scoring on a 13-yard touchdown pass from quarterback Justin Yonker to receiver Dustin Tatsch, cutting the deficit to 16–8. Tatsch proved to be Mason's most effective weapon, finishing with five receptions for 118 yards. However, the momentum shifted again when Smith, having his best performance of the season, broke loose for a dominant 264-yard rushing effort on 24 carries, including a key touchdown late in the third quarter to extend Ganado's lead to 23–8. Mason added a late score with just 45 seconds left, but it wasn't enough as Ganado held on for a 23–14 victory. The win not only extended the Indians' playoff run but also marked their return to December football for the first time since 2003. Against the odds and proving critics wrong, Ganado demonstrated once again that when the postseason arrives, the Indians are ready to rise to the occasion.

In the regional final and Class 1A Division I state quarterfinals, Ganado faced Falls City at Victoria Memorial Stadium on a cold night with a large, enthusiastic crowd in attendance. The first half was tightly contested and passed quickly - lasting only about an hour - with neither team able to score despite several opportunities. Falls City advanced as far as the Ganado 15- and 23-yard lines but turned the ball over on downs, while Ganado missed a 30-yard field goal attempt, leaving the score tied 0–0 at halftime. Falls City struck first in the second half after forcing a Ganado three-and-out on their opening drive. The Beavers put together a 68-yard, 13-play drive, capped by a fourth-and-goal touchdown from quarterback Will Kirchoff to Luke Mynier, putting Falls City ahead 7–0 with 3:59 left in the third quarter. Ganado responded with a determined 70-yard, 11-play drive. A key fourth-and-2 conversion by Foster at the 10-yard line kept the drive alive, and Foster also connected with Staff on a crucial 38-yard pass. Smith finished it off with a 3-yard touchdown run, and Ramos added the extra point to tie the game 7–7 early in the fourth quarter. Moments later, Foster came up big again on defense, making a leaping interception at the Ganado 35-yard line. The Indians capitalized, needing just six plays to score, with Smith punching it in from seven yards out to give Ganado a 14–7 lead with 7:57 left. Smith had an impactful night, rushing for 114 yards, including a key 43-yard run from Ganado's 4-yard line to help burn the clock. Falls City got the ball back with 1:15 remaining but never advanced past their own 25-yard line. Ganado's defense held firm, and the Indians secured a thrilling 14–7 victory. After the game, senior Joey Arriaga summed it up simply: "TEAMWORK." Coach Rabe had consistently emphasized that teamwork was the foundation of their playoff success, and it was on full display as the Indians won their third straight playoff game. With the win, Ganado advanced to the state semifinals for only the third time in school history - previously falling short in 1996 to Groveton (14–6) and in 2001 to Garrison (21–9). The semifinal matchup was set for Saturday, December 13, exactly 12 years to the date of Ganado's first semifinal appearance.

The Indians would face a talented 12–2 Cayuga team at A&M Consolidated's Tiger Stadium in College Station. Cayuga had just knocked off top-ranked Maud in the quarterfinals and boasted a high-powered offense led by standout running back Traylon Shead, who had rushed for over 3,000 yards and 45 touchdowns, and quarterback Brock January, who had thrown for 1,437 yards and 17 touchdowns. Cayuga had a tremendous amount of speed, scoring ability, and big-play potential. Ganado entered the game riding a wave of momentum with strong playoff performances, especially on defense, and an efficient offense led by Smith, who had rushed for 1,649 yards and 18 touchdowns on the season. However, the team's bus was delayed due to road construction, pushing the start time back nearly 30 minutes - a possible factor in the slow start. Cayuga dominated from the outset, and Shead proved unstoppable, rushing for 250 yards and six touchdowns. Ganado didn't manage a first down until 2:25 remained in the second quarter and trailed 21–0 at halftime, despite reaching the Cayuga 4-yard line and being stopped at the 1-yard line on the final play of the half. Missed scoring opportunities plagued the Indians, including a third-quarter interception at the Cayuga 5-yard line and a fourth-quarter drive that stalled at the 21-yard line. Cayuga took full advantage of Ganado's missed chances, extending the lead to 42–0. Ganado's only score came late in the game when Sophus capped a 45-yard drive with a 4-yard touchdown run, making the final score 42–7.

Although the season ended in disappointment, it marked a remarkable playoff run, a return to the state semifinals, and a year defined by resilience, teamwork, and the rekindling of pride in Ganado football.

Coach Rabe reflected on a season that, at one point, no one expected would lead to success. Despite the doubts, the team came together like a family and fully embraced the lessons they were being taught. Although the season didn't end exactly as the team had hoped, it was still a remarkable journey. The 2008 team was one of the most resilient groups Coach Rabe had ever seen. There were many ups and downs throughout the season, but that's often the nature of both sports and life. The team demonstrated tremendous heart and handled adversity with remarkable poise. Ganado finished the season with a 9-4 record, a significant improvement after back-to-back tough seasons with records of 1-9 and 3-7. This turnaround earned Coach Rabe the Advocate Area's Coach of the Year honors in his third season at Ganado. Additionally, the team featured four freshmen - Josh Labay, Case Silliman, Tyler Gorman, and Trey Thedford - who were part of a talented group with a bright future ahead. These freshmen had already made a name for themselves with undefeated junior high seasons, signaling an exciting outlook for their high school football careers.

Just two months after the football season ended, tragedy struck Ganado ISD once again. On February 18, senior Joey Arriaga was found dead at his home. Joey was not only a star on the football team, but also the class president. He was well-liked by everyone and known for being a genuinely good person. His sudden death was a heartbreaking loss for the school, but the community came together to mourn and support one another. Joey was remembered during graduation ceremonies, which made the loss even more poignant. The 2008-2009 school year was a special one for this senior class, as it marked a significant turning point for them. Despite having faced challenges in previous years, this group of students experienced great success, especially in athletics. The year was a triumph for the entire athletic program, with both the boys' and girls' teams achieving remarkable accomplishments. Joey's legacy was deeply felt, and his memory was honored as part of a year that symbolized resilience and achievement for his class and for Ganado ISD as a whole.

2009

As the 2009 football season began, there was a great deal of anticipation surrounding the Ganado Indians. The team entered the season ranked #7 in the state by *Dave Campbell's Texas Football*

Magazine and was picked to win the district. With a roster filled with experienced players, including several who had been lettermen for two or three years, expectations were high. The goal was clear: to return to the state semifinals and potentially face a rematch with the preseason #1 ranked Cayuga. The team boasted impressive speed, particularly in the backfield, with senior Donovan Foster returning as quarterback for the third year and senior running back Kevin Smith, who had a standout junior season with 1,812 rushing yards and 21 touchdowns. Sophomore Josh Labay was also expected to make a strong impact at running back, having played most of his freshman year on defense. The offensive line included sophomore Tyler Gorman at guard, seniors Tyler Biehle and Rafael Martinez at tackle, and senior Rusty Parker at tackle. On defense, Gorman returned as a tackle, with Silliman and senior Glenn Sparkman at linebacker. The secondary featured Labay, junior Jacob Benavides, Foster, and senior Ross Rakowitz, who had been named first-team all-area defense the previous season and had recorded eight interceptions. Other key players who would contribute throughout the season included sophomores Trey Thedford and Anthony Parks, junior Wesley Demicelli, seniors Glenn Sparkman, Josh Harrison (the son of assistant coach Tim Harrison), Rusty Parker, and Curtis Cox. Additionally, Andy Bridges, the current high school principal, returned to coaching and joined the staff, balancing both his administrative duties and coaching responsibilities. With a solid mix of experienced players and promising new talent, Ganado was poised for a successful season.

Ganado opened the 2009 football season against Bloomington. Originally scheduled to be played at Bloomington, the game was moved to Sandcrab Stadium in Port Lavaca due to structural issues with the light poles at Bloomington's stadium. Despite the change in venue, the Indians dominated the game, securing a 47-0 victory. The team rushed for a total of 439 yards, with Josh Labay leading the charge, rushing for 231 yards and two touchdowns. In their home opener against Nixon-Smiley, Ganado's offense was once again in full gear, delivering a 62-13 blowout to move to 2-0 for the second consecutive year. Labay led the rushing attack with 137 yards, while Kevin Smith rushed for 139 yards and Donovan Foster contributed 103 yards on the ground, also adding 120 passing yards. Ganado then traveled to Boling for their third game, which was marked by off-and-on rain throughout the contest. The game turned into a hard-fought battle, with Ganado leading at halftime. However, the Indians found themselves trailing 27-14 in the fourth quarter. They made a strong rally but ultimately fell short, losing 27-21 for their first defeat of the season. Labay rushed for 107 yards, scoring both a rushing and receiving touchdown. The Indians returned home for their homecoming game against their Jackson County rival, the Industrial Cobras, looking to bounce back from the loss. Despite a packed stadium on both sides, the game was a one-sided affair, with the Cobras rolling to a 37-7 victory. Industrial's quarterback, Austin Smalley, rushed for 164 yards and two touchdowns, while running back Matt Anderson added 69 yards and two touchdowns of his own. The Industrial defense was dominant, limiting Ganado to just 11 first downs and forcing multiple turnovers. The only touchdown for Ganado came late in the game when Smith scored from two yards out, preventing a shutout. Coach Rabe acknowledged that the team struggled with execution on both offense and defense, emphasizing the need for improvements. In their final non-district game, Ganado traveled to Danbury, where they faced the possibility of losing their third straight game. The first half was a disaster, as the Indians trailed 14-0 at halftime. However, the team came out rejuvenated in the second half, scoring 21 unanswered points and shutting out Danbury for the remainder of the game to secure a 21-14 victory. Labay was the star of the game, rushing for 168 yards and scoring two touchdowns. The game was tied at 14-14 with just one-minute remaining when Danbury attempted a fourth-down pass, only for it to be intercepted by Jacob Benavides, who ran it back 54 yards for a touchdown. Brian Bubela added the extra point to seal the victory. This win was a crucial one for the Indians, as it gave them momentum heading into their bye week and preparing for the upcoming district games.

After a week off during their bye, Ganado opened district play against undefeated Somerville, who entered the game with a 4-0 record. Unfortunately for Somerville, they suffered a significant setback on the very first play when their quarterback, Cody Holliday, was injured. Taking advantage of this, Ganado quickly gained control of the game. On the very first play of the Indians' offense, Josh Labay ran for an impressive 77-yard touchdown, setting the tone for the game. Labay finished with 209 rushing yards and two touchdowns, leading Ganado to a dominant 49-14 victory. The Indians amassed 421 rushing yards on the night and began district play with a 1-0 record. Next, Ganado traveled to Shiner for what was expected to be the district championship showdown. The game lived up to the hype, with the score tied 14-14 at halftime. Labay gave Ganado the early lead with a 33-yard touchdown reception from quarterback Foster. Shiner responded with two touchdowns, taking a 14-7 lead, but Labay once again answered with a 57-yard touchdown reception from Foster to tie the game just before halftime. However, the second half was a different story. Shiner came out strong, dominating the second half by outscoring Ganado 30-0. The biggest blow came in the third quarter, where Shiner scored 23 points, largely thanks to the performance of Drew Stafford, who had been battling a 102-degree fever earlier that day. Stafford rushed for 201 yards on the night, with 160 of those yards coming in the second half. Shiner's offensive line and defense were overpowering, rushing for a total of 367 yards and stifling Ganado's offense. The Indians were held to just 9 rushing yards for the game, and Foster was tackled behind the line of scrimmage five times, including a third-quarter safety. In the end, Shiner secured a 44-14 win, continuing their dominance in the second half, much like the previous year's meeting. The game served as a reminder that football is a game of momentum, where teams must play well for all four quarters to succeed.

Ganado learned from their tough loss to Shiner and bounced back the following week with a strong home win over Burton. The Indians raced to a 28-0 halftime lead and held on to win 28-14, improving their district record to 2-1. The next week, they faced their rivals in the "Battle of Mustang Creek" against Louise, where playoff implications were at stake for both teams. It was a hard-fought game, but Louise pulled out a 13-10 victory. Louise's bruising running back, Desmond Pulliam, was the difference maker, scoring both of their touchdowns and rushing for 106 yards. Pulliam opened the scoring with a 35-yard touchdown run on Louise's first possession, giving them a 7-0 lead. Ganado responded with a 32-yard field goal by Bubela in the second quarter, making the score 7-3 at halftime. Pulliam added another touchdown late in the third quarter, and despite a missed extra point, Louise extended their lead to 13-3. The Indians responded with a touchdown run from Smith to close the gap, but it wasn't enough. Smith rushed for 82 yards, and Labay led the team with 96 rushing yards. With a 2-2 district record, Ganado returned home for the season finale and dominated Flatonia 50-7 to secure a playoff spot for the second straight year. The Indians came out strong, scoring 22 points in the first quarter and accumulating 332 rushing yards while holding Flatonia to just 189 total yards. Like the previous season, the district had a bye in the bi-district round, so Ganado's first playoff game was in the Area round against Bartlett.

Ganado finished the regular season with a 6-4 record and faced Bartlett on November 21 at Rutledge Stadium in Converse for the bi-district playoff game. The Indians struck first when Foster ran for a 15-yard touchdown, giving Ganado a 6-0 lead after a missed extra point in the first quarter. Bartlett responded by scoring two touchdowns to take a 12-6 lead by the end of the first quarter, but that would be all the scoring they would do. Ganado then dominated the game with 30 unanswered points, rushing for a total of 480 yards on the night. In the second quarter, Smith ran for a 7-yard touchdown, and Foster added a dazzling 65-yard touchdown run. Foster finished the night with 147 yards. Glenn Sparkman capped off the first half with a 36-yard field goal, and Ganado led 23-12 at halftime. In the second half, Labay scored on a 38-yard run, finishing with 180 yards. Smith added his second touchdown of the night with a 24-yard run in the fourth quarter, and the Indians secured a 36-12 bi-district win. The following week, Ganado returned to Rutledge Stadium in Converse the night after Thanksgiving to face La Pryor in the Regional playoffs. La Pryor led 21-6 in the third quarter, but the Indians staged an incredible comeback. Despite struggling offensively in the first half, Ganado was down 14-0 at halftime. They finally got on the board in the third quarter when Wesley Demicelli scored on a 2-yard run, aided by a 32-yard pass from Foster. La Pryor answered with another touchdown to make it 21-7 with 57 seconds left in the third quarter. In the fourth, Labay scored two touchdowns, and with 5:05 left in the game, the score was tied at 21-21 after a successful two-point conversion play from Labay to Demicelli. The Indians' defense stepped up when needed, and the game went into overtime. La Pryor took the first possession and scored on a 14-yard run, taking a 28-21 lead. Facing a fourth-and-inches from the 5-yard line, Labay ran in for the touchdown to tie the game. Then came the memorable moment of the season - Ganado faked the extra point attempt, and Demicelli threw a pass to Jacob Benavides for the successful two-point conversion, giving Ganado a 29-28 victory. The crowd erupted in celebration, and the "Cardiac Indians" were proving they would win by any means necessary. The team showed incredible heart and character, surviving another week of dramatic playoff football.

Ganado's next challenge came in the quarterfinals, where they faced Falls City, a team they had defeated 14-7 in the same round the previous year to win the region. This year, however, Falls City was an even stronger team, entering the game with a perfect 13-0 record and having shut out six of their opponents. They dominated their district, outscoring opponents 206-0, and boasted a strong defense. On offense, quarterback Will Kirchhoff, son of the coach, led the team with 1,378 rushing yards and 20 touchdowns, along with 1,214 passing yards and 8 touchdowns. The matchup was set at New Braunfels Canyon Stadium on a very cold Saturday evening, with temperatures having dipped significantly, and the weather had even brought snow to Ganado the day before. The Indians struggled in the first half, totaling just 7 net yards and zero first downs by halftime, but they were fortunate to be tied 7-7. The second half remained challenging as Falls City pulled ahead 21-7 with a touchdown by Coli Dziuk, leaving Ganado facing a difficult 8-point deficit with just over 10 minutes left in the game. However, the Indians showed their resilience and "Indian Magic" once again. Foster connected with Cade Cihal on a huge 53-yard pass, setting up a 6-yard touchdown pass from Foster to Trey McDonald. Although the extra point was missed, Ganado closed the gap to 21-13 with 3:46 remaining. The Indians' defense then stepped up, making a crucial stop. On the next drive, Foster connected with Labay on a 20-yard touchdown pass on a fourth-and-12 situation, setting up a pivotal two-point conversion attempt with 1:52 left in the game. Foster found McDonald in the back of the end zone for the conversion, tying the game 21-21. The Ganado defense continued to shine as Tyler Gorman recovered a fumble from Falls City, and Foster found Demicelli to set up a 29-yard field goal attempt by Sparkman. Sparkman, who had missed an earlier extra point, redeemed himself by nailing the field goal with just six seconds left, giving Ganado a 24-21 lead - their first lead of the game. Ganado held onto the lead and won the game, advancing to the semifinals for the second consecutive year. Coach Rabe praised the team for their perseverance, stating that they stayed focused, never lost concentration, and displayed remarkable character. He emphasized that the Indians' belief in themselves was key to their victory. This game, according to the coach, was one of the best he had ever witnessed due to its high stakes and the team's ability to overcome adversity. It was a reminder that, no matter the circumstances, you can never count out the Ganado Indians.

On Saturday, December 12, Ganado faced a rematch with state-ranked #6 Cayuga in the semifinals at Woodforest Bank Stadium in Shenandoah. Cayuga entered the game with a 12-1 record and a roster filled with talent, much like the previous year. The team was led by Traylon Shead, a University of Texas commit, who had accumulated 2,334 rushing yards and 33 touchdowns. Quarterback Maclome Kennedy, committed to Texas A&M, was a dual-threat, passing for 1,422 yards and 19 touchdowns while also rushing for 1,923 yards and 22 touchdowns. For Ganado, Labay, the offensive leader, had rushed for 1,793 yards and 16 touchdowns on the season. The game started with a strong showing from Cayuga, who capitalized on a Ganado turnover in scoring territory. Shead, lining up as a slot receiver, took an end-around and sprinted 57 yards for the first touchdown, giving Cayuga a 20-0 lead in the first quarter. Ganado fought back in the second quarter, with Labay scoring on a 50-yard run, narrowing the deficit to 20-7 at halftime. As the game progressed, Cayuga's Shead responded in the third quarter with a 48-yard touchdown run, putting Cayuga up 28-7. However, Ganado was determined to stay in the game, and Smith rushed for a touchdown to make it 28-13, heading into the final quarter. Smith had a solid performance, rushing for 93 yards, with six of his 14 carries resulting in first downs. Despite Ganado's best efforts, Shead sealed the victory for Cayuga with two additional touchdown runs in the fourth quarter, bringing the score to 41-13. The Indians managed to score one final touchdown when Foster connected with Labay on a 7-yard pass, but the game ended with a 41-19 loss. This marked the second consecutive year Ganado was eliminated by Cayuga in the semifinals.

While the loss was disappointing, history was made during the game. Shead became only the second player in state history to surpass 10,000 career rushing yards, finishing with 226 yards and four touchdowns on the night. He now trailed only Kenneth Hall's all-time record of 11,232 yards. Kennedy also had a strong performance, rushing for 187 yards and contributing to Cayuga's early lead with two big plays - an 88-yard touchdown run and a 42-yard touchdown pass. For Ganado, the season was still a remarkable achievement. This was the team's second consecutive appearance in the semifinals, a first in school history. The 11 seniors, who had experienced a tough 3-7 record as sophomores just two years earlier, had now led their team to two semifinal appearances, cementing their legacy as one of the best senior classes in Ganado football history.

2010

On January 21, Mike Rabe submitted his resignation as athletic director and head football coach at Ganado after accepting the same position at Class 3A Waco Connally. During his four-year tenure at Ganado, Rabe compiled a 22-25 record but was highly regarded for revitalizing the football program, leading them to back-to-back state semifinal appearances, and contributing to the overall success of both the boys' and girls' athletic programs. Just under two weeks later, on February 1, the Ganado school board held a special session and hired Jimmy Thompson as the new athletic director and head football coach. Thompson brought with him 29 years of coaching experience, including 21 years as a head coach, and held an overall record of 156-84-1. His most notable success came during his tenure at Garrison from 1999 to 2004, where he led the team to a state championship in 2003 with a 27-0 win over Bangs. He also coached against Ganado in the 2001 state semifinals, where Garrison defeated them 21-9 before narrowly losing to Celina in the championship. Following his time at Garrison, Thompson coached at Cleveland in 2005 and then at Mount Pleasant from 2006 to 2009, where he led the team to two playoff appearances. Thompson's hiring coincided with the UIL's biannual realignment, which reclassified Class 1A into two divisions based on enrollment. Ganado remained in Class 1A and was placed in District 15-1A Division I, alongside Shiner, Flatonia, Louise, and Yorktown. Burton dropped to Division II, and Somerville was reassigned to another region within Division I.

Ganado entered the 2010 football season with high expectations, ranked #9 in the state by *Dave Campbell's Texas Football Magazine*. Backed by a strong tradition that included consecutive state semifinal appearances and now led by a head coach with two state championship game appearances and one title victory, the team was seen as a legitimate contender if everything came together. Junior Josh Labay was the centerpiece of the team, returning as a running back and defensive back after an outstanding sophomore season in which he rushed for 1,907 yards, scored 17 touchdowns, and recorded 168 tackles. Labay was recognized as one of the top athletes in Class 1A.

Key linemen included juniors Tyler Gorman, who played both offensive and defensive line, and Case Silliman, a tight end and defensive end - both of whom had lettered since their freshman year alongside Labay. Junior Trey Thedford stepped in at quarterback, replacing the graduated Donovan Foster, and also contributed as a linebacker on defense. The roster featured several senior leaders such as running back-linebackers Wesley Demicelli, Roy Sophus, and Brian Gamble; running back-defensive back Jacob Benavides; and receiver-defensive back Trey McDonald. Additional junior contributors included offensive and defensive lineman Anthony Parks, receiver and kicker Brian Bubela, receiver-linebacker Cade Cihal, offensive line-linebacker Anthony Landry, offensive line-defensive end Derrick Hlavaty, and offensive line-defensive lineman Denton Lesak. Sophomore Roman Leal also added depth on both the offensive and defensive lines. With a talented, experienced core and a proven coaching staff, the 2010 Ganado team had the tools to make a deep playoff run.

Ganado began the 2010 football season with a commanding performance defeating Hallettsville 35-2 to open the season 1-0 and make a strong early statement. Josh Labay led the way with 154 rushing yards and three touchdowns, while the defense was dominant, intercepting Hallettsville five times. The only points allowed came from an intentional safety late in the game. The following week, Ganado hosted long-time Jackson County rival Industrial in the home opener. After being dominated by Industrial in the previous two seasons, Ganado was determined to change the narrative. In front of a packed crowd, the game lived up to its billing as a classic rivalry battle. Ganado struck first when Labay broke loose for a 70-yard touchdown run, though the extra point was missed, giving Ganado a 6-0 lead after the first quarter. Industrial responded with a 45-yard touchdown run by quarterback Austin Smalley and took a 7-6 lead into halftime. Ganado came out strong in the second half, marching down the field on the opening drive. Labay capped it off with a 1-yard touchdown run, and Wesley Demicelli added a two-point conversion to give Ganado a 14-7 lead. Industrial answered again with Smalley scoring from the 1-yard line to tie the game 14-14 at the end of the third quarter. The fourth quarter turned into a defensive standoff, sending the game into overtime. In overtime, Ganado scored first as quarterback Trey Thedford ran for 10 yards before Labay punched it in from the 5-yard line. Industrial threatened to respond, but on a crucial pass play, Thedford made the game-saving interception in the end zone to seal a thrilling 20-14 overtime victory. The win not only pushed Ganado to 2-0 but also marked a breakthrough triumph over their rival and served as a major confidence boost early in the season. Notably, both wins came against larger Class 2A Division I opponents, highlighting Ganado's early-season strength despite being a smaller 1A program.

The week following their thrilling overtime win, Ganado faced another tough challenge on homecoming night against the traditionally strong East Bernard team, which also entered the game undefeated at 2-0. Ganado started fast, as Demicelli blocked a punt that set up a 13-yard touchdown run by Josh Labay, giving the Indians an early 7-0 lead. On East Bernard's next possession, Labay intercepted a pass and returned it 76 yards for a touchdown, extending Ganado's lead to 14-0. Although East Bernard responded with a touchdown via their powerful slot-T rushing attack to make it 14-7 early in the second quarter, the Indians continued to dominate defensively. Cade Cihal and Demicelli recovered two East Bernard fumbles, both leading to Ganado scores - a Labay touchdown run on fourth down and a touchdown pass from Thedford to Case Silliman. Ganado entered halftime with a commanding 28-7 lead, although Coach Thompson noted that all the first-half scoring came from short-field opportunities created by turnovers, not sustained offensive drives. In the second half, Ganado answered the challenge with two solid offensive possessions, both ending in touchdowns by Demicelli, as the Indians pulled away for a 41-14 win to improve to 3-0. Next, Ganado traveled to El Maton to face Tidehaven, who had a potent passing attack led by quarterback Sean Dannels and standout receiver Colt Clontz, a 6'7", 220-pound Tulsa commit. The first quarter was evenly matched, with both teams moving the ball but failing to score. Early in the second quarter, Ganado converted a crucial fourth-and-13, leading to a touchdown run by Labay. After a Tidehaven offside penalty on the extra point attempt, Ganado opted to go for two, and Demicelli converted, making it 8-0. Tidehaven quickly answered with a touchdown, but excellent coverage by Thedford on Clontz prevented the two-point conversion, keeping the score at 8-6. A sudden rainstorm then shifted momentum, limiting Tidehaven's aerial attack and playing into Ganado's power-run game. Labay broke free for touchdown runs of 51 and 48 yards, and Brian Bubela added a 22-yard field goal to give Ganado a 24-6 halftime lead. The second half was all

Indians, who forced five turnovers and scored three more touchdowns en route to a dominant 45-6 victory, improving their record to 4-0 and showing signs of being an elite team. Following their impressive start, Ganado entered a bye week before traveling to face Palacios in their final non-district game. The Indians showed no signs of slowing down, piling up 404 total yards - all on the ground. Thedford rushed for 115 yards, including a 45-yard touchdown run, and returned a punt 72 yards for another score. Labay continued his stellar season with 108 rushing yards and two touchdowns. Ganado cruised to a 41-7 win, closing out non-district play with a perfect 5-0 record and heading into district competition with great momentum.

Ganado opened district play at home against a 1-5 Shiner team, a matchup that carried weight despite Shiner's non-winning record. As the defending district champions who had defeated Ganado the previous two seasons, Shiner was not to be taken lightly. The developing rivalry between the two teams set the stage for a hard-fought contest. Shiner struck first, taking a 7-0 lead late in the first quarter, but Ganado quickly responded as Labay broke loose for a 44-yard touchdown run, with Bubela's extra point tying the game at 7-7. Shiner regained the lead before halftime with a passing touchdown from quarterback Joey Game to receiver Blaine Caka, making it 14-7. However, the Indians answered once again in the closing seconds of the half when Thedford connected with Demicelli, who made a tumbling catch in the end zone. Bubela added the extra point to tie the game at 14-14 going into halftime. The second half was just as physical and intense, with both teams battling for control. Ganado's defense stepped up, forcing four Shiner turnovers. Thedford intercepted two passes, and Roy Sophus recovered a key fumble, which set up the go-ahead score. Thedford capped the ensuing drive with a 1-yard touchdown run, giving Ganado its first lead of the game at 21-14 with 7:32 remaining. Later, Brian Gamble recovered another Shiner fumble with 3:32 left, helping to seal the victory. The 21-14 win was a major milestone for Ganado - it marked the team's first win over Shiner since a non-district matchup in 1997. Although Shiner's record suggested a weaker team, they played tough and competitive football throughout. Labay, despite nursing a shoulder sprain suffered the previous week against Palacios, carried the offense with 136 rushing yards on 23 carries and a touchdown. With the win, Ganado remained undefeated at 6-0 and started district play on a strong note.

Ganado continued its impressive season with a pivotal district matchup against Louise in the annual "Battle of the Mustang." The Indians were determined to avenge back-to-back losses from the previous two seasons and move one step closer to a district championship. The first quarter was a defensive battle, with Ganado making several key stops despite spending much of the time on the field. The offense came alive in the second quarter as Thedford threw touchdown passes to Demicelli and Labay, while Labay also added a rushing touchdown. Ganado took a commanding 21-6 lead into halftime and maintained control throughout the second half. Louise's only touchdown came after a Ganado fumble, but the game was never in doubt as the Indians rolled to a 34-12 win, improving to 7-0 and knocking off another opponent who had beaten them the previous two years. Ganado then hosted San Antonio Cornerstone, a TAPPS school, in a non-district game to fill out the schedule. The Indians dominated from the start, scoring easily and pulling the starters after just two possessions. The junior varsity took over and delivered an impressive performance, with Clay Vesely rushing for 139 yards and Billy Jones adding 130 yards on the ground. Ganado cruised to a 42-0 victory, pushing their record to 8-0. Returning home for their final regular-season home game, the Indians faced Yorktown and stayed focused on the task at hand. Ganado delivered a decisive 42-7 win, clinching the district championship for the first time since 2003. Their dominant performance earned them recognition as the *Army Strong Team of the Week* for Class 1A by *Dave Campbell's Texas Football*. With the district title secured, Ganado entered the final regular-season game against 1-8 Flatonia looking to complete an undefeated season. The Indians quickly jumped out to a 14-0 first-quarter lead with two Labay touchdowns. The score held through halftime, and Labay sealed the game in the third quarter with a 52-yard touchdown run, moments after a 39-yard touchdown was called back due to a penalty. Ganado closed out the game and the regular season with a 33-0 shutout victory, finishing 10-0 - their second undefeated regular season in school history and the first since 1996. The flawless run also marked Ganado's first district championship in seven years, and by earning the title, the team received a bye in the bi-district round of the playoffs.

In the Area round of the playoffs, Ganado faced Winters at Marble Falls and showed no signs of rust following their bi-district bye. The Indians dominated from the start, with Labay scoring four first-half touchdowns to propel Ganado to a commanding 35-6 halftime lead. The team maintained control throughout the game, eventually securing a 41-6 victory to remain undefeated and improve to 11-0 on the season. In the regional round, Ganado faced a much tougher challenge in defending state champion Goldthwaite. The matchup carried a sense of déjà vu, mirroring the 1998 playoff path when the Indians also faced Winters and Goldthwaite, including playing at the same site - Bob Shelton Stadium in Buda. In that 1998 game, Ganado narrowly lost after a late comeback attempt, and history would once again bring a dramatic, emotional contest. Goldthwaite threatened early after a Ganado fumble on the opening possession, driving to the 1-yard line. However, the Indians made a massive defensive stand, highlighted by Demicelli's tackle in the backfield on fourth down. Capitalizing on the momentum, Ganado marched down the field and scored on a 1-yard run by Labay, with Bubela adding the extra point to give the Indians a 7-0 lead with 8:58 left in the second quarter. Ganado initially appeared to stop Goldthwaite on their next possession, but was caught off guard when the Eagles executed a successful fake punt for a long touchdown pass to tie the game at 7-7, a score that held through halftime. The second half began with both teams exchanging possessions, but Ganado broke the deadlock with a creative and determined drive. On a crucial fourth-and-ten, Labay pitched the ball to quarterback Thedford, who had reversed roles and caught a 13-yard pass for a first down. Moments later, lineman Tyler Gorman surprised everyone with a 13-yard run, setting up Labay's second touchdown of the night on a 6-yard run. Bubela's kick put Ganado ahead 14-7 with 1:07 remaining in the third quarter. The defense again stepped up as Thedford intercepted a pass to halt Goldthwaite's next drive. However, the momentum shifted dramatically early in the fourth quarter when Thedford's pass was intercepted and returned to Ganado's 9-yard line. Goldthwaite capitalized, scoring on third down to tie the game at 14-14. On the ensuing kickoff, Goldthwaite executed a successful onside kick and recovered the ball at midfield. The momentum swung fully in their favor as they scored again to take their first lead of the night, 21-14, with 5:14 remaining. Ganado put together one final push, but the drive stalled at the Goldthwaite 21-yard line. Goldthwaite then ran out the clock with a couple of first downs, ending Ganado's season in heartbreaking fashion. The Indians had gone toe-to-toe with the defending state champions and were just a few plays away from advancing. Goldthwaite went on to the state final but fell to Mart, 28-7, in the 1A Division I championship game.

Ganado finished the 2010 season with an 11-1 record. Though the playoff run ended sooner than in previous years when the team made back-to-back state semifinal appearances, it was still a season filled with accomplishments. The Indians captured their first district title since 2003, completed an undefeated regular season for only the second time in school history, and played with heart and resilience throughout the year. With only seven seniors - Trey McDonald, Wesley Demicelli, Jacob Benavides, Roy Sophus, Collin Hans, Brian Gamble, and Jonatan Aguilar - graduating, a large and talented junior class was set to return in 2011 with high expectations and the goal of making another deep playoff run.

2011

The Indians entered the new football season with high expectations and a renewed sense of purpose following their heartbreaking playoff exit the previous year. After a dedicated offseason of hard work and preparation, the team was poised to make a serious run at a state championship. The 2011 squad featured an exceptionally large and experienced senior class, with 20 seniors - possibly the largest in school history - providing leadership, depth, and determination. The buzz around the team was evident even before the season began. *Dave Campbell's Texas Football* magazine ranked Ganado as the #1 team in the state, while the Associated Press placed them at #2, just behind Canadian. With such recognition came immense pressure, as the Indians now had a target on their back - every opponent would be aiming to knock off the top-ranked team. Head coach Jimmy Thompson was unfazed by the rankings and remained laser-focused on one goal: winning a state championship, a mission that began the moment their 2010 season ended with a tough loss to Goldthwaite.

Ganado's offensive firepower was anchored by two of the top players in the district - senior running back Josh Labay and senior quarterback Trey Thedford. Labay, who had rushed for 1,576 yards and 28 touchdowns the previous season, was a consistent offensive threat and a standout safety on defense. Thedford, a dual-threat quarterback, contributed 268 passing yards and 358 rushing yards while also recording six interceptions as a safety, proving his versatility on both sides of the ball. The Indians' revamped wishbone offense featured a multi-back rotation. Senior Tyler Gorman, who moved from the offensive line to the backfield, joined senior Derrick Hlavaty, promising sophomore Clay Vesely, and talented freshman Kaleb Leal to provide a diverse and powerful ground attack. Seniors Xavier Salazar and Kollin Smith added depth at receiver, offering passing options when needed. Ganado's offensive line was a massive and dominant unit, built to control the line of scrimmage. Returning starters Anthony Parks and Denton Lesak anchored the tackle positions, while juniors Kenny Kocian and Roman Leal, along with sophomore Will Malek, handled the guard spots. Anthony Landry returned at center, and sophomore Thomas Parks played at tight end, completing a physically imposing line expected to overwhelm opposing defenses. Defensively, the Indians were equally formidable. Gorman and senior Case Silliman held down the defensive end positions, while 300-pound Leal clogged the interior at defensive tackle. Senior Cade Cihal led the linebacker corps from the middle, supported by Kocian, Vesely, junior Kevin Gorman, and freshman Kaleb Leal. In the secondary, senior Cory Marroquin played cornerback, with Thedford and Labay patrolling the back end as experienced and dynamic safeties. With a deep, balanced, and battle-tested roster, Ganado entered the 2011 season fully committed to achieving one goal: reaching AT&T Stadium in Arlington on December 15 and bringing home a state championship. Every player, coach, and fan knew the path would be challenging, but the belief in this team's ability to make history had never been stronger.

The Indians began their highly anticipated 2011 football season with a dominant 32-7 home victory over Hallettsville, marking the first step in their quest for a state championship. The game was defined by the Indians' relentless defense, which recorded two safeties and controlled the tempo throughout. Defensive ends Tyler Gorman and Case Silliman led the charge, while cornerback Cory Marroquin added two interceptions to stifle Hallettsville's passing game. The tone of the game was set early in the first quarter when Gorman engulfed a Hallettsville player in the end zone, forcing a fumble that rolled out of bounds for the first safety and a 2-0 lead. In the second quarter, another Hallettsville miscue on a shotgun snap resulted in the ball being recovered in the end zone by the offense but quickly buried by defenders Brayden Andel, Clay Vesely, Kyle Sparkman, and Cutberto Ramos for a second safety, pushing the lead to 11-0. While

Hallettsville's defense made things difficult, limiting standout running back Josh Labay to just 87 rushing yards, Ganado found success in the passing game. Quarterback Trey Thedford threw for 75 yards and connected on touchdown passes to Xavier Salazar and Colin Smith. Thedford also rushed for a score, and Gorman added a powerful 25-yard touchdown run in the third quarter, sealing a strong season-opening win. In their second game, Ganado traveled to face Jackson County rival Industrial and encountered early adversity, falling behind 7-0 in the first quarter. The Indians responded in the second quarter when Labay scored on an 18-yard run, though a missed extra point left them trailing 7-6. On the following kickoff, Industrial appeared to return it for a touchdown, but a block-in-the-back penalty negated the score. The Ganado defense stepped up again, with Thedford making a diving interception in the end zone on a fourth down to halt the drive. On the very next offensive play, Labay broke free for an electrifying 80-yard touchdown run. Thedford added the two-point conversion, giving the Indians a 14-7 halftime lead. From there, Ganado controlled the second half, scoring three more times as Labay finished the night with an outstanding performance - 265 rushing yards and four touchdowns. The Indians improved to 2-0 with a 33-13 victory, showcasing both resilience and dominance against a tough opponent.

The Indians continued their impressive 2011 season with a challenging road game against East Bernard, who boasted a talented squad led by Texas A&M commit Ty Slanina at quarterback and a potent slot-T offense. The Indians struck first, with Labay rushing for a 6-yard touchdown to give Ganado a 7-0 lead in the first quarter. However, a fumble at the 9-yard line gave East Bernard a prime scoring opportunity, but the Indian defense stood strong, forcing a missed field goal attempt. On the very next play, Gorman broke loose for a 79-yard run to set up Labay's second touchdown, extending the Ganado lead to 14-0 with 9:48 left in the first half. East Bernard responded with a long run from Slanina, cutting the lead to 14-7 by halftime. In the second half, the game became more intense as Ganado committed two turnovers deep in East Bernard territory. The opposing team capitalized on those mistakes, scoring twice early in the fourth quarter to take a 21-14 lead. With the game on the line, the Indians embarked on a defining 17-play, 69-yard drive that consumed 8:47 of the clock. Labay capped the drive with a 1-yard touchdown, bringing Ganado within

21-20 with 2:59 left in the game. In a bold decision, the Indians chose to go for the two-point conversion instead of tying the game with an extra point. Labay answered the call, scoring the two-point conversion and giving Ganado a 22-21 lead. East Bernard had one final chance, but Ganado's defense stepped up when needed most. Thedford intercepted a pass on a fourth-down play, sealing the victory for the Indians. The win was a testament to the team's resilience and unity, as they responded to adversity and executed a game-winning drive. Labay was the star of the game, rushing for 200 yards on 46 carries and three touchdowns. The victory was even more significant considering that East Bernard would go on to win their district and reach the regional round of the playoffs, with a 3-year stretch of undefeated regular seasons, culminating in a state championship in 2012.

The Indians returned home and dominated Tidehaven 42-0, improving to 4-0. Ganado scored all 42 points in the first half, with Thedford throwing three touchdown passes and Labay rushing for two touchdowns. In their next game, the Indians faced the George Ranch JV team, a new school that would soon be playing varsity. Ganado handled the competition with ease, winning 41-7 and racking up 427 total yards, with Labay contributing 196 yards rushing and two touchdowns. The Indians' final non-district game came against Palacios, and though they were sluggish in the first half, the defense made key stops and the offense took control in the second half. After a 7-7 tie at halftime, Ganado scored 21 unanswered points, with Labay breaking free for an 85-yard touchdown run, Gorman adding a score, and Clay Vesely sprinting for a 51-yard touchdown. The Indians secured a 28-7 win, heading into district play with a perfect 6-0 record and solidified their position as the #1 ranked team in Class 1A.

Ganado opened district play on the road against Shiner, a team that had not lost a home district game since 2001. The Indians knew it would be a tough challenge, but they were ready to fight. Ganado struck first, with Labay rushing for a 2-yard touchdown and Brian Bubela adding the extra point to give the Indians a 7-0 lead with 1:51 left in the first quarter. However, Shiner responded with 21 unanswered points, capitalizing on two Ganado fumbles and an interception. Caleb Curtis, who rushed for 166 yards on 32 carries, put Shiner ahead 21-7 with a 20-yard touchdown run, leaving the Indians trailing by 14 points with 10:22 remaining in the game. Despite the deficit and the hostile environment, the Indians mounted a rally in the fourth quarter. After a strong 37-yard kickoff return by Labay, Thedford ran in a 12-yard touchdown, and Labay converted the two-point attempt, narrowing the lead to 21-15 with 9:17 left. The Ganado defense responded by forcing Shiner to punt, and the offense took advantage. Labay broke loose for a 65-yard touchdown run, his longest of the game, and Bubela's extra point gave Ganado a 22-21 lead with 5:37 remaining. Shiner had one final chance, starting at their own 9-yard line and driving to the Ganado 20-yard line with 14 seconds left. However, due to a strong south wind, Shiner opted against attempting a potential game-winning field goal and chose to go for the win. The defense held strong, and Curtis was tackled inbounds at the Ganado 18-yard line as time expired. Ganado held on for a thrilling victory, marking the first time in 10 years that Shiner had lost a home district game. The win improved Ganado's record to 7-0, and the Indians showed great composure throughout the game, making the key plays in the fourth quarter to secure the victory. Labay was a standout, rushing for 189 yards and scoring two touchdowns.

Ganado returned home and delivered a commanding 56-14 victory over neighboring Louise. Louise, shorthanded with a limited number of players, initially took an early 14-7 lead in the first quarter. After a strong opening kickoff return gave Louise good field position, they scored to lead 7-0. Josh Labay quickly tied the game at 7-7, but Louise answered with a return touchdown on the ensuing kickoff to go ahead 14-7. However, it was all Ganado from that point forward as the Indians racked up 481 yards of offense and scored on 8 of their 10 possessions. Labay was a standout, rushing for 227 yards and scoring four touchdowns. The game was marred by a tragic accident when Louise quarterback Angel Garza suffered a severe leg injury that required EMS assistance to remove him from the field. In a touching act of sportsmanship, Logan Tupa, a local elementary student who had won the game ball raffle, chose to donate the ball to Garza. The Ganado football team then presented the game ball to Louise at midfield, exemplifying class and empathy. With the win, Ganado improved to 8-0 and headed into their bye week with only two regular season games remaining - one on the road against Yorktown and another at home against Flatonia. Against Yorktown, Ganado exploded to a 35-0 lead in the first quarter, before Yorktown had even earned a first down, and went on to win 55-19 to improve to 9-0. Labay had a stellar performance, rushing for 241 yards, scoring six rushing touchdowns, and even throwing a touchdown pass to quarterback Thedford. Labay's outstanding play earned him the *Built Ford Tough Player of the Week* award. The following day, the Ganado Pride of the Tribe Marching Band also had a remarkable achievement, placing third at the UIL Area contest and qualifying for state for the second consecutive year. In their final regular season game against Flatonia, Ganado dominated with a 42-0 victory, amassing 494 total yards of offense while holding Flatonia to just 74 yards. The victory marked back-to-back undefeated regular seasons for Ganado. Labay rushed for 277 yards and scored four touchdowns, setting a new regular season rushing record with 2,016 yards, surpassing the previous record of 1,846 yards set by Tim Neumann in 2002. The record-breaking run came on a 38-yard touchdown in the second quarter. In addition, Cade Cihal set the regular season record for tackles with 140, surpassing the previous record of 138. With the regular season concluded, Ganado was poised for the playoffs, determined to continue their mission. The team's ultimate goal was clear: to keep winning and secure that elusive state championship. As district champions, the Indians enjoyed a bye in the first round, setting the stage for the next chapter in their journey toward the gold.

Ganado faced Goldthwaite in Elgin for the Area playoffs, determined to seek revenge after their season had ended the previous year at the hands of the defending state finalists. The Indians came out with a vengeance, dominating the game from start to finish. Ganado scored on their opening possession, marching 85 yards in 16 plays, with Labay running for a 10-yard touchdown to give the Indians a 6-0 lead with 1:32 left in the first quarter. Labay had an outstanding performance, rushing for 198 yards on 38 carries and scoring all four of Ganado's touchdowns. Gorman added 63 yards, while Trey Thedford contributed 78 yards, and only needed one pass attempt during the game. The offense completely controlled the line of scrimmage, accumulating a total of 348 rushing yards and 21 first downs. Defensively, Ganado was equally impressive, holding Goldthwaite to just 113 total yards and only 7 first downs throughout the game. The Indians shut out Goldthwaite with a dominant 28-0 win, playing at a championship caliber level. With the victory, Ganado improved to 11-0 and continued their march toward the ultimate goal.

For the fourth consecutive season, the Indians were playing playoff football on Thanksgiving weekend, and this regional playoff game was set to be a fierce battle against the undefeated Mason Punchers. Mason, averaging 54.6 points per game, was led by their senior running back David Mora, who had rushed for 1,807 yards and 39 touchdowns going into the game. The matchup was touted as "the state championship game," with many believing that the winner would go on to win the state title. This was similar to what would happen 13 years later in 2024, when Ganado again found themselves in a major playoff game with the winner likely advancing to the state championship. Ganado, averaging 36.4 points per game, featured star running back Josh Labay, and both teams had big, physical offensive lines. The game took place at New Braunfels Canyon Stadium on red artificial turf. Mason received the ball first, and on their opening drive, Mora scored a 5-yard touchdown run, giving Mason a 7-0 lead with 6:11 left in the first quarter. Little did anyone know at the time, this would be the only score of the game. After that, the Ganado defense stepped up and played exceptionally well, shutting down Mason for the remainder of the game. Although Ganado moved into the red zone several times, they couldn't capitalize on the opportunities and failed to make the big play when it mattered most. It was a hard-hitting, physical football game, with both teams giving their all. Ganado actually outperformed Mason in several areas, edging them 15 to 14 in first downs and accumulating 268 total yards compared to Mason's 194. Out of Mason's 14 first downs, nearly half came on their 13-play, 92-yard opening drive, with Mora accounting for 51 of those yards. Mora finished the night with 113 yards, but was hampered by an ankle injury in the third quarter and only had one more carry the rest of the game. His final carry, an 8-yard rush, was crucial for a first down with 3:51 remaining, draining two minutes off the clock and leaving the Indians with little time to respond. With just 1:54 left, Ganado attempted to drive 94 yards to tie the game. Thedford connected with Xavier Salazar for a 39-yard gain, and a personal foul penalty on Mason helped shorten the distance. However, on a critical fourth-and-16 with less than a minute left, Labay was stopped on a run to the left, turning the ball over on downs for the fourth time in the second half. Mason took possession and ran out the clock, ending the game with a 7-0 victory and sending the Indians home for the second consecutive year in the same round of the playoffs. Despite the loss, Ganado played an incredibly tough and competitive game, but Mason's defense and timely plays, along with the clock management, sealed the Indians' fate.

In his final game, Josh Labay rushed for 103 yards, finishing his senior season with an impressive 2,317 yards and 32 touchdowns. He also set the career rushing record at Ganado, amassing 5,799 total yards. Labay was honored as the *Victoria Advocate Offensive Player of the Year* and became the school's all-time leading rusher. Several of his teammates also earned recognition, with Tyler Gorman, Case Silliman, Cade Cihal, and Trey Thedford receiving first-team defense honors from the Advocate. In addition to their athletic achievements, three of these seniors - Thedford, Silliman, and Brian Bubela - along with Chance Poulton, earned the prestigious rank of Eagle Scout, a rare and impressive accomplishment. Their Eagle Scout Court of Honor ceremony took place during the season, I took special pride in this achievement, as I myself earned the rank in 1998. This was a significant accomplishment for the school, especially given how many members of the Ganado football community had earned the honor over the years. The team's loss in the playoffs was a difficult one, but the players knew they had given their best effort. Many people believed this team had the potential to win the state championship, as Mason, the team that defeated Ganado, went on to win the state title just three weeks later. This loss raised the question of whether Ganado would ever win a state championship, as it had been 15 years since their first semifinal appearance in 1996, and there had been several near-misses in the years since. This particular group of players, especially the senior class, was highly regarded, and many of them went on to achieve great things. Trey Thedford, the quarterback for the back-to-back 10-0 undefeated regular seasons in 2010 and 2011, later became part of the coaching staff at Ganado and helped secure the long-awaited state championship ring in 2024 as an assistant coach. The senior class of 2011 set numerous records and accomplishments that will be remembered for years, and they remain a source of pride for the school and community. Five of the seniors went on to play college football: Thedford at Mary Hardin-Baylor, Silliman and Cihal at Texas Lutheran, Landry at Blinn College and later Tarleton State, and Gorman at Bethany College in Kansas. Their accomplishments both on and off the field are a testament to their hard work, dedication, and character.

2012

Heading into the 2012 season, the Indians faced the challenge of replacing a significant core of talent after losing 20 seniors, many of whom were all-state caliber players. Despite concerns about inexperience, the next group of athletes quickly grew into their new roles, aided by a few key returners from the back-to-back undefeated seasons. At running back, junior Clay Vesely stepped into the lead role, joined by sophomore Kameron Smith, sophomore Kaleb Leal, and senior Kenny Kocian, who transitioned from the offensive line to the backfield to provide added depth. Junior Benny Garcia, a transfer from Palacios, was expected to contribute as well, though he was recovering from a knee injury. The quarterback position was filled by junior Ray Salazar, who took over from two-year starter Trey Thedford. In the tailback and receiver rotation, senior Zach Andel added speed and versatility, alongside Smith, senior Kyle Sparkman, sophomore Jonathan Martinez, and junior Taylor Thedford. At tight end, senior Michael Garcia - Benny Garcia's brother and also a Palacios transfer - impressed coaches with his size (240 pounds), mobility, and receiving ability. He shared tight end duties with junior Thomas Parks, while senior Kevin Gorman and junior Adrian Martinez served as backups. On the offensive line, juniors Will Malek and Dustin Arriaga anchored the right side at tackle and guard, respectively. The center position rotated between junior Nick Skoruppa and senior Ryan Arriaga. Junior twins Manuel and Salvador Almeda handled the left side of the line, while junior Brayden Andel, known for his speed as an 800-meter relay runner, provided flexibility and quickness up front. Defensively, Michael Garcia and Brayden Andel started at defensive end, rotating with Parks and Martinez. Senior Roman Leal and junior Sammy Cortez brought strength to the interior line at tackle, switching out with juniors Hunter Keszler and Billy Jones. Kocian led the linebacker corps from the middle, supported on the outside by Salazar, Kaleb Leal, and Gorman. In the secondary, Martinez and Sparkman covered at cornerback, while Vesely and Smith played at safety. Thedford, Zach Andel, and Jones also rotated in at defensive back positions. Though the team featured many new faces in critical positions, their mindset remained focused on hard work, team development, and the pursuit of a playoff berth. The 2012 Indians were determined to maintain the program's winning tradition and continue building success through dedication and resilience.

The Indians opened their 2012 football season with a challenging road game against Hallettsville, where missed early scoring opportunities cost them dearly. Despite advancing into Hallettsville territory three times in the first quarter - reaching the 36-, 15-, and 22-yard lines - the Indians came up empty. Hallettsville capitalized on their fifth play from scrimmage early in the second quarter, as Dalton Herrington took a short pass from quarterback Nate Kowalik and turned it into a 58-yard touchdown, followed by a successful two-point conversion for an 8-0 lead. Ganado answered with a touchdown run by Clay Vesely, but Hallettsville extended their lead before halftime with a Kowalik rushing touchdown, going into the break ahead 14-7. In the third quarter, Hallettsville's Teidrick Smith broke free for two long touchdown runs of 40 and 63 yards, putting the Brahmas up 28-7. Ganado fought back with a five-yard touchdown by Kaleb Leal to cut the lead to 28-14. However, Hallettsville sealed the game with another Smith touchdown - this time from 11 yards out - on a drive extended by a Ganado penalty. The Indians dropped the season opener 35-14, their first opening loss since 2007. Despite the defeat, the team showed potential, compiling 267 yards of total offense, with Vesely rushing for 106 yards on 31 carries and Kameron Smith recording 58 receiving yards on four catches.

The following week, in the home opener against Industrial, Ganado bounced back in dominant fashion. Smith opened the scoring with a 63-yard touchdown reception from quarterback Ray Salazar. Although Industrial responded with a touchdown by Evan Gregg and an extra point by Mason Davis to take a 7-6 lead, Ganado regained control when Vesely scored in the second quarter. Although the extra point was blocked and returned for two points, giving Industrial a brief highlight, the Indians led 14-9 at halftime. The second half belonged entirely to Ganado. Kenny Kocian bulldozed into the end zone for an 8-yard score, Vesely added a 65-yard touchdown run, Kaleb Leal contributed a 25-yard rushing score, and Kocian capped off the night with a 53-yard run. The Indians secured a dominant 40-9 victory over their rivals, improving to 1-1 on the season. Vesely starred with 240 rushing yards and two touchdowns. In Week 3, Ganado traveled to Van Vleck for their first meeting since 2005. The Indians built a 14-0 lead early and opened the second half with a kickoff return touchdown by Jonathan Martinez, extending the lead to 21-0. Although the team struggled with ball security, losing three fumbles in the third quarter, the defense held strong and kept Van Vleck out of the end zone. Billy Jones finished off the game with his second touchdown, leading all rushers with 98 yards. Despite some sloppy execution, the Indians earned a workmanlike 28-0 shutout win, their second straight victory, improving their record to 2-1. Ganado returned home for a homecoming matchup against Tidehaven and delivered another dominant performance. The Indians raced to a 35-0 halftime lead and cruised to a 48-6 final. The offense racked up 384 yards, while the defense was suffocating - holding Tidehaven to -8 yards rushing and only 110 yards passing. The defense also collected two interceptions, including a pick-six by Salazar in the second quarter. With the win, Ganado improved to 3-1. Next, the Indians traveled to Flatonia for a showdown with a former district rival. Vesely opened the scoring with a 25-yard touchdown run in the first quarter. Flatonia responded with a 58-yard touchdown pass from Will Bruns to Gus Venegas to tie it at 7-7. Salazar then connected with Smith for a 28-yard touchdown pass to reclaim the lead. A Flatonia fumble to start the second half set up a Kaleb Leal touchdown, making it 20-7. Flatonia narrowed the margin to 20-14 late in the third, but Vesely broke loose on a 58-yard touchdown run early in the fourth to extend the lead to 26-14. The Indians' defense held strong on a fourth-down stop, and the offense ran out the clock to seal the victory, improving to 4-1. Back home, the Indians faced longtime rival Louise in the "Battle of Mustang Creek." Ganado dominated from start to finish, earning a 54-0 shutout - its second of the season. The offense featured both quarterbacks, Salazar and Vesely, and totaled 405 yards (190 passing, 215 rushing). Vesely accounted for 155 passing yards and 94 rushing yards, contributing two touchdowns through the air and two on the ground. With a 5-1 record heading into a bye week before the district opener against Yorktown, the Indians had rebounded impressively from their opening loss. Riding a five-game winning streak, Ganado was developing into a well-rounded team with improving execution, a balanced offensive attack, and a stout defense.

The Indians opened district play with a powerful rushing performance, compiling 307 yards on the ground en route to a 21-0 shutout victory over Yorktown - marking their third shutout of the season. Although the team appeared slightly sluggish in the first half, likely showing some rust after a bye week, they regained their intensity and control as the game progressed. Vesely led the way with 175 rushing yards, and sealed the win with a short two-yard touchdown run in the fourth quarter. The following week, the Indians traveled to face Kenedy and showed no signs of slowing down. Ganado exploded for 21 points in the first quarter and never looked back, dominating in a 41-0 win. It was their third consecutive shutout, fourth overall for the season, and extended their winning streak to seven games, improving their overall record to 7-1 and district record to 2-0. However, the victory came with a potentially significant setback. Vesely, the team's leading rusher, left the game with an injury after gaining 82 yards on just 9 carries. His status became a major concern as the Indians prepared for a pivotal district showdown against perennial powerhouse Shiner.

In their final home game of the 2012 season, the Indians hosted longtime rival Shiner in a highly anticipated showdown that likely would determine the District 15-1A championship. This matchup had become a tradition of sorts, as the winner of the Ganado-Shiner contest had gone on to claim the district title in each of the previous four seasons. Shiner had won the meetings in 2008 and 2009, while Ganado had come out on top in 2010 and 2011. However, this year, the Indians faced a major setback entering the game without their standout running back, Clay Vesely, due to injury. Shiner took advantage of the situation early, jumping out to a 13-0 lead with two second-quarter touchdowns. Ganado responded after capitalizing on a Shiner turnover, when Smith hauled in a 29-yard touchdown pass from Salazar. Martinez added the extra point, cutting the deficit to 13-7 with 2:42 left in the first half. But Shiner answered in dramatic fashion on the next drive, as Evel Jones broke free for a 68-yard touchdown run and then converted the two-point play himself, pushing the halftime score to 21-7. That explosive run shifted momentum and proved to be a pivotal moment in the game. In the second half, Ganado's defense came out strong, forcing a Shiner punt on their opening possession. On Ganado's ensuing drive,

Billy Jones electrified the crowd with a 78-yard run down to the one-yard line, setting up a short touchdown run by Kocian. However, the two-point conversion attempt failed, and the Indians still trailed 21-13. With just under six minutes remaining in the fourth quarter, Shiner's Jacob Stafford scored his second touchdown of the night on a 13-yard run, extending the lead to 28-13. Refusing to back down, Ganado answered quickly as Salazar punched in a one-yard quarterback keeper for a touchdown. Unfortunately, another missed two-point conversion left the score at 28-19. The Indians attempted an onside kick, but Shiner recovered and ran out the clock to secure the win and the district championship. Despite the 28-19 loss, the Indians showed grit and determination, especially without their offensive leader. Billy Jones stepped up in a big way, rushing for 181 yards, while Evel Jones led Shiner with 177 yards on just 9 carries, including the game's momentum-swinging touchdown. Though the outcome favored Shiner, Ganado's effort and resilience stood out in a hard-fought contest between two longtime rivals.

Entering their final regular season game with a 7-2 record, the Indians had already secured a spot in the playoffs, but their exact seeding was still undecided. The outcome of their road matchup against Three Rivers would determine whether they entered the postseason as the second or third seed. Just two weeks earlier, the Indians had handled a long road trip to Kenedy with strong play. However, the even longer bus ride to Three Rivers - who had moved down from Class 2A to 1A in the February realignment - seemed to take a toll. Ganado struggled from the start in what Coach Thompson later described as "horrible" play, possibly the team's worst performance of the season. Three Rivers ran a disciplined slot-T offense and repeatedly gashed the Ganado defense, which had no answer throughout the night. The Bulldogs jumped out to a 14-0 lead in the first quarter before the Indians rallied in the second with a Vesely rushing touchdown and a scoring pass from Salazar to Thomas Parks to tie the game at 14-14. However, with just 14 seconds remaining in the first half, Ganado surrendered another touchdown and went into halftime trailing 21-14 - marking the second straight game in which they gave up a crucial score just before the break. Regrouping after halftime, the Indians came out strong. Benny Garcia scored a touchdown, and Vesely added the two-point conversion to give Ganado its first lead of the night at 22-21. Three Rivers quickly responded with a short touchdown run, though the Indians prevented the two-point try, keeping the score at 27-22. Late in the third quarter, Billy Jones found the end zone to return the lead to Ganado at 28-27 as the period ended. In the fourth quarter, Ganado put together a promising drive but turned the ball over on downs deep in Three Rivers territory. The Bulldogs took advantage, piecing together a long drive and scoring on a short touchdown run with 6:37 left. This time, they converted the two-point attempt, making it 35-28. On the ensuing possession, Ganado fumbled the ball away, and Three Rivers was able to run out the clock to secure the win. The defeat dropped Ganado to 7-3 on the season and solidified them as the third seed entering the playoffs. It also marked their second straight loss, both of which featured back-breaking touchdowns allowed just before halftime - a detail Coach Thompson emphasized in his postgame remarks. Despite limping into the postseason with back-to-back losses, the Indians had a reputation for elevating their play in the playoffs. With a determined group and a tradition of rising to the occasion in November, the Indians still had plenty of fight left as they looked to turn things around when it mattered most.

After four consecutive seasons of earning a bi-district bye, the Ganado Indians found themselves playing in a bi-district playoff game in 2012, taking on Ben Bolt at Mathis. The Indians entered the contest with renewed energy and intensity, quickly asserting control by jumping out to a 21-0 lead in the second quarter. By the time Benny Garcia returned the second-half kickoff 65 yards for a touchdown, Ganado had built a commanding 34-6 lead. Despite a high-scoring second half from both teams, the outcome was never in doubt, and the Indians cruised to a 55-35 victory. Vesely led the way with a strong performance, rushing for 113 yards and scoring three touchdowns. It was also a special night for the Garcia brothers - Bobby, Benny, and Michael - as each scored a touchdown. Bobby found the end zone in the second quarter on a rushing play, Benny made his mark with the kickoff return touchdown, and Michael scored on a third-quarter reception that extended Ganado's lead to 41-12. With the win, the Indians advanced to the Area round and continued a proud tradition of playing on Thanksgiving weekend for the fifth straight year. In the Area round, Ganado faced Weimar at Traylor Stadium in Rosenberg. The Indians opened the game with an impressive 20-play, 10-minute drive, capped by a one-yard touchdown run from Vesely to take a 7-0 lead late in the first quarter. Weimar responded with a touchdown of their own but missed the two-point conversion, leaving Ganado ahead 7-6. On Ganado's next possession, the Indians were on the move again but were stopped on a crucial fourth-down play. Weimar capitalized on the turnover and scored, although a key deflection by Vesely stopped another two-point attempt, making the score 12-7 at halftime. Weimar opened the second half with a touchdown drive, then extended their lead to 26-7 following a Ganado fumble. But the Indians did not go quietly. Early in the fourth quarter, the defense came up with a huge stop on a fourth-and-one play. That momentum carried into the next drive as Salazar scored a touchdown, cutting the deficit to 26-14 with 7:03 remaining. Ganado then recovered an onside kick, and Vesely broke off a long touchdown run to narrow the gap further to 26-21 with 4:48 left, igniting hopes of a dramatic comeback. However, Weimar answered with another scoring drive and then made a critical stop on Ganado's fourth-and-one attempt to put the game away. The Indians fell 34-21, ending their season with an 8-4 record.

Despite the loss, Coach Thompson praised the team for its effort, noting that while the offense played well enough to stay in the game, key defensive stops were missed and turnovers in the second half proved costly. This 2012 squad entered the season as a young and largely inexperienced team, but they grew through the challenges and upheld the Ganado tradition by making the playoffs for the fifth consecutive year. With much of the roster returning and valuable experience gained, expectations were high heading into the 2013 season.

2013

As the 2012–2013 school year came to a close, Ganado ISD marked the end of an era with the retirement of long-time teacher and coach David Grewe. Coach Grewe dedicated 36 years of service to Ganado, beginning his career in 1977. He primarily taught junior high science, but his impact was far-reaching through his extensive coaching roles across multiple sports, including football, basketball, and golf. Coach Grewe made a significant mark in golf, leading numerous students to success at the state level. Over the course of his career, he coached athletes to 15 state appearances, including individual qualifiers from both boys' and girls' teams, and two girls' teams that reached the state tournament. In football, Grewe served as a consistent presence on the high school staff and was the head junior varsity football coach beginning in 1995, when Monte Althaus and Andy Bridges joined the program. During that time, he coached in 43 playoff games, including four state semifinal appearances. Prior to his JV role, he spent many years coaching junior high football, often working alongside Coach Bill Silliman. Coach Grewe's retirement marked the conclusion of a remarkable career filled with dedication, success, and deep commitment to the students and athletes of Ganado. He left behind a lasting legacy and will be greatly missed by the school and community.

During the 2013 offseason, the Indians football program added two significant members to its coaching staff, further raising expectations for a team already brimming with experience and returning talent. Rick Ragsdale joined as the new offensive coordinator, coming from Mason, where he had coached against Ganado in a highly anticipated 2011 playoff game often referred to as the "real state championship." Mason won that tight defensive battle 7-0 and went on to claim the state title. Jim Bird came on board as the new defensive coordinator, bringing his own championship pedigree. Bird was the quarterback and linebacker for Groveton during their 1996 state semifinal victory over Ganado at the Astrodome, and he was named the Class 2A Defensive Player of the Year that season. These two additions joined head coach Jimmy Thompson, who was entering his fourth season at the helm for Ganado. Thompson brought his own championship experience, having led Garrison to a state title in 2003. With such a high-caliber coaching staff in place, the Indians were poised for success and carried lofty expectations into the 2013 season.

Ganado returned 11 seniors and a strong core of experienced players. Senior Ray Salazar resumed his role at quarterback, while senior running back Clay Vesely returned after rushing for 1,405 yards the previous year. The offensive line was one of the team's biggest strengths, both literally and figuratively, anchored by seniors Will Malek, Braydan Andel, and twin brothers Salvador and Manuel Almeda. Malek and Andel were all-state selections as juniors. Senior Thomas Parks transitioned from tight end to offensive tackle, while Manuel Almeda played center and his brother Salvador lined up at guard. Andel and Malek returned to their positions at guard and tackle, respectively. Junior Austin Alford stepped in at tight end. This unit would eventually earn the nickname "Fat Boys," not just for their size but for the camaraderie and fun they brought to the team dynamic. Ganado also featured a deep and talented group of skill position players. In addition to Vesely, the backfield included senior Billy Jones and the Garcia brothers - senior Benny and sophomore Bobby. The receiving corps was led by senior Taylor Thedford and juniors Kameron Smith and Jonathan Martinez. On defense, Coach Bird installed a 2-7 scheme, which placed defensive tackles head-up over the opposing guards. Malek and the Almeda twins returned as key players on the interior line, with Andel and Parks manning the defensive ends. The linebacker group included top sophomore prospect Brandon Lister, along with veterans Salazar, Jones, and junior Cody Plant. In the secondary, returning players included Vesely, Smith, Thedford, and Martinez, giving the Indians experience and depth across all levels of the defense. With a talented senior class, experienced returning starters, and a seasoned coaching staff with championship backgrounds, the 2013 Ganado Indians entered the season with high hopes and the potential to make a deep playoff run.

The Indians opened their 2013 football season at home against a strong Hallettsville team, but were forced to play without star running back Clay Vesely, who suffered a dislocated shoulder in a scrimmage. Despite playing competitively in the first half, Ganado was overwhelmed in the third quarter as Hallettsville scored 28 unanswered points. Dalton Herrington led the charge with three touchdowns - returning the second-half kickoff, rushing for one, and catching a pass for another. Ganado avoided a shutout with a late fourth-quarter touchdown pass from Ray Salazar to Kameron Smith, but ultimately suffered a 43-6 loss to begin the season. The Indians bounced back the following week in Vanderbilt against their Jackson County rivals, Industrial, with Vesely returning to the lineup and making an immediate impact. On Ganado's first offensive play, Vesely ran 65 yards for a touchdown. Then, on Industrial's first play, a deflected pass landed in Vesely's hands, and he returned it 52 yards for another score. He later added a 75-yard touchdown run in the second quarter and finished the game with 222 rushing yards. Ganado earned a dominant 34-7 victory to even their record at 1-1. Returning home for homecoming, Ganado hosted Van Vleck in a hard-fought contest. After trailing 7-6 at halftime, the Indians responded in the second half with two more touchdowns from Vesely, securing a 20-13 win and improving to 2-1. Despite the victory, Ganado struggled with ball security, fumbling four times, dropping a key touchdown pass, and committing costly penalties. Tensions rose at halftime when Coach Thompson was ejected after an altercation with officials. Assistant coaches Rick Ragsdale and Jim Bird led the team in the second half. In Week 4, the Indians traveled to El Maton to face Tidehaven under threatening weather conditions. Ganado struck first on a 76-yard touchdown run by Vesely, and Thomas Parks added the extra point. The game was marred by sloppy play, including five fumbles by Ganado, but the defense rose to the occasion with key stops. Tidehaven tied the game 7-7 in the third quarter, but late in the fourth, Salazar connected with Smith on a crucial pass. After a long drive, a holding penalty nullified a touchdown run by Billy Jones, but Parks came through with a 25-yard field goal with 2:15 left, lifting Ganado to a 10-7 win and a 3-1 record. Back at home, Ganado faced Flatonia in a game where turnovers once again proved costly. Vesely opened the scoring with a 28-yard touchdown run, and after Flatonia tied it, Jones put Ganado back on top to start the second half. However, Flatonia capitalized on Ganado's mistakes, tying the game and then taking the lead off turnovers. The Indians fell 24-14, dropping to 3-2 and extending a concerning turnover streak to three consecutive weeks. In their final non-district game, the Indians traveled to Louise and returned to dominant form with a 55-0 shutout victory. Vesely rushed for three touchdowns, Salazar added two rushing scores and threw an 89-yard touchdown pass to Smith, and sophomore Brandon Lister added two rushing touchdowns in the fourth quarter. The win brought Ganado's record to 4-2 heading into the bye week, restoring momentum and confidence just in time for the start of district play.

The momentum from Ganado's dominant performance against Louise carried over into their district opener at Yorktown, where the Indians secured a commanding 56-21 victory. Ganado raced to a 34-0 lead at halftime, and despite Yorktown scoring all 21 of their points in the third quarter, the Indians maintained control throughout the game. Vesely had an impressive performance, rushing for 156 yards and a touchdown, while also adding a 61-yard receiving touchdown. Jones contributed with 122 rushing yards and two touchdowns. The defense was also a key factor, with Cody Plant returning an interception for a 32-yard touchdown in the first quarter and Garrett McCann running back a blocked extra point 106 yards for a touchdown in the third quarter. One of the memorable moments of the game came when the officials asked Ganado's "Pride of the Tribe" marching band to quiet down, but the band continued playing louder, much to the amusement of the fans. On another note, the band would later march in the state contest for the third time since 2009. After the big district-opening win over Yorktown, the Indians returned home to face Kenedy. Despite a tight 6-6 tie in the first quarter, Ganado exploded in the second half, finishing with a 50-6 blowout victory. The Indians rushed for 552 yards on 61 carries, with Vesely leading the charge with 230 yards and two touchdowns. Salazar also had a standout performance, rushing for 115 yards and scoring three touchdowns. At this point in the season, the Indians had found their rhythm, working through early-season struggles, and were playing at a high level as they prepared for a critical district showdown at Shiner for the district championship.

Ganado entered their district championship showdown against Shiner on a high note, having scored over 50 points in three consecutive games. Shiner, after a 1-2 start to the season, was also playing some of their best football. On Ganado's opening possession, Salazar ran a read option, initially seeming to aim for the first down, but instead broke free and sprinted 55 yards for a touchdown. However, Parks' extra point attempt was blocked, and Ganado led 6-0 early in the first quarter. Both teams played solid defense throughout the first half, but with just two minutes remaining before halftime, Shiner's Marcus Coleman ran for a 28-yard touchdown, and Hunter Mraz kicked the extra point to give Shiner a 7-6 lead at the break. After Shiner was forced to punt on their first possession of the second half, Ganado seized control, using their strong running game to dominate the clock. Jones punched in a three-yard touchdown, and Vesely ran in the two-point conversion to put Ganado ahead 14-7 with 3:54 left in the third quarter. On Shiner's next possession, Coleman fumbled the ball, and McCann recovered it, giving Ganado a short field. Salazar ran a quarterback keeper to the ten-yard line, and Jones took it in from the one-yard line. Parks' extra point attempt was blocked again, but Ganado now led 20-7 with just 12 seconds remaining in the third quarter. The rest of the game was controlled by Ganado, who used a ball-control offense to seal a 20-7 victory over Shiner, claiming the district championship. This win would be Ganado's last victory over Shiner until 2023, exactly 10 years later on the same field. To close out the regular season, Ganado dominated Three Rivers 38-15 on senior night. Salazar scored two touchdowns and threw a touchdown pass to Vesely, who also added two touchdown runs. With their strong performance throughout district play, Ganado entered the playoffs on a high note, playing at a very high level and in prime position for postseason success.

Ganado entered the playoffs as district champions and, after receiving a bye in the bi-district round, began their postseason journey in the Area round against Brackettville at Three Rivers. On the morning of the game, a cold blue norther blew in, bringing strong north winds that made the weather even colder. However, the cold did not affect the Indians, who came out with high energy and quickly built a 20-0 lead early in the second quarter. Brackettville managed to score two touchdowns in a second-quarter scoring surge, but Ganado went into halftime with a comfortable 34-14 lead. The only scoring in the second half came from a 31-yard field goal by Parks, and the Indians won the game 37-14. Vesely had a standout performance, rushing for 145 yards and scoring three touchdowns. Additionally, Ganado's defense intercepted four Brackettville passes, helping secure the victory. Next up for Ganado was a regional playoff matchup against Thorndale at Rutledge Stadium in Converse. This marked the sixth consecutive year Ganado was playing football on Thanksgiving weekend, continuing a proud tradition. The Indians were hoping to advance past the regional round for the first time since 2009, after three straight exits at this stage. Thorndale got off to a strong start, aided by a big kickoff return, but Ganado responded well. Vesely scored from one yard out to tie the game at 7-7, and Parks kicked a 34-yard field goal to give Ganado a 10-7 lead in the second quarter. After a Thorndale fumble, Vesely took the ball into the end zone to extend Ganado's lead to 17-7 with 3:45 left in the first half. However, a fumble by Ganado on their last possession of the half, allowed Thorndale to score, narrowing the lead to 17-14 at halftime. Ganado received the ball to start the second half, hoping to build on their lead, but another costly fumble gave Thorndale a chance to score, and they took a 21-17 lead. Unfortunately for the Indians, that would be the last scoring of the game, as they were unable to mount another drive, and Thorndale held on for a 21-17 victory. Despite the loss, Vesely had a strong performance, scoring both of Ganado's touchdowns and rushing for 145 yards. The two turnovers, however, proved to be costly, as they directly led to Thorndale's scores.

Ganado finished the season with a 9-3 record. The season was filled with highs and lows, but it was ultimately a successful campaign. The team overcame injuries and early-season struggles to dominate through district play, win a district championship, and earn a playoff victory. What was particularly frustrating, however, was watching Shiner, whom Ganado had defeated just a month earlier in the district championship, advance further into the playoffs. Shiner pulled off a dramatic upset in the semifinals against previous state finalist Mart, eventually making it to the state championship before losing to Stamford. The thought of what could have been lingered, as many wondered how close Ganado had come to achieving their own state aspirations. Though the Indians were eliminated in the regional round, this season left lasting memories and served as a reminder of the potential of the program. It would be another six years before Ganado returned to the playoffs in 2019, after enduring some growing pains. Will Malek, one of the key players for Ganado during the season, went on to play at Hardin-Simmons University in Abilene, further showcasing the talent of the team. Despite the bittersweet end, this season stood as one to remember.

Chapter 8

Growing Pains

2014

During the Christmas break, Jimmy Thompson decided to resign from his position as athletic director and head football coach at Ganado ISD. Though it was a difficult decision, he chose to step down in order to be closer to his mother, whose health had declined, and he accepted the head coaching job at Mount Pleasant. During his four-year tenure at Ganado, Thompson achieved significant success, compiling a 39-9 record, making the playoffs each year, and winning three district championships. Following his departure, Ganado promoted defensive coordinator Jim Bird to the role of athletic director and head football coach. Bird, a former high school quarterback and linebacker at Groveton, notably played in the 1996 semifinal game at the Astrodome in which Groveton defeated Ganado 14-6. His father, also named Jim Bird, led China Spring to a state championship in 1978 and served as defensive coordinator at Groveton during his son's playing days. The younger Bird continued his football career at Mary Hardin-Baylor, later returning as an assistant coach at his alma mater, and also coached at Waller and Groveton. Now at the helm in Ganado, Bird was eager to implement his own system and prepare a new group of players to replace the large senior class set to graduate in the spring, ensuring the team would be ready for the upcoming fall season.

In February, during the biannual UIL realignment, a significant change was made with the introduction of Class 6A, now representing the largest school classifications in Texas. This new class essentially reclassified the former Class 5A schools, causing schools across the state to shift up one classification level based on enrollment. As a result, Ganado, which had competed as a 1A school from 2008 to 2013, returned to Class 2A - now the smallest division for 11-man football, as Class 1A became the designation for six-man teams. Ganado was placed in what was quickly dubbed the toughest 2A district in Texas, earning the nickname "The Little SEC," a nod to the strength of the Southeastern Conference in college football. This highly competitive district included Ganado, Refugio, Shiner, Schulenburg, Flatonia, and Weimar. Notably, Refugio and Schulenburg had recently dropped down a classification, and the group of Refugio, Shiner, Schulenburg, and Flatonia had collectively made 16 state championship appearances and won 8 titles. The coaching pedigree in the district was equally impressive, with Weimar's David Husmann, Refugio's Jason Herring, and Shiner's Steven Cerny combining for nine state final appearances and five state championships. In terms of recent performance, the entire district was strong, with all six teams playing a combined total of 20 playoff games the previous season and winning 14 of them. Refugio and Shiner even advanced to the state finals. Although it was undeniably a challenging district, Ganado was ready to embrace the competition.

In August, the Ganado football team adopted the mantra "Go to Work," a phrase Coach Bird said the players echoed at the start of every practice. This season's squad was notably young, with many players moving up from the junior varsity ranks and needing to fill key roles. The varsity roster included only 23 players, but several experienced returners provided leadership and talent. Senior Austin Alford, an all-district selection at tight end and defensive end, transitioned to offensive tackle. Junior Jacob Foltyn, a first-team all-district defensive back, would also start at running back. Sophomore Garrett McCann, who was named freshman newcomer of the year and earned honorable mention all-state honors, was slated to start both at running back and in the defensive secondary. Senior Kody Plant, previously a first-team all-district linebacker, moved to defensive tackle and would also start at center. Senior Kameron Smith returned as a first-team all-district receiver and defensive back. Additional returning contributors included juniors Brandon Lister and Bobby Garcia at linebacker, and senior quarterback Jonathan Martinez, who was returning from an ACL injury that sidelined him for most of the previous season. Other notable players included senior offensive linemen Garrett Estrada and Cameron Martinez; juniors Lukas Herring and Ross Fowler on the offensive line, with Fowler also playing linebacker; Mark Macha at tight end and defensive end; and junior Caleb Thedford at receiver and defensive back. Key sophomore prospects included defensive tackle Malcom Chaisson, linebacker Christian Palacios, and Matt Bridges, who would contribute at receiver and defensive back. The coaching staff welcomed a new addition in Ganado alum and 2006 graduate Drew Bridges, who joined the team alongside his father Andy. They would coach under offensive coordinator Rick Ragsdale. Despite their youth and small roster, the team was confident in its ability to rise to the challenge. Coach Bird emphasized that the intangible strengths of this group - particularly their strong work ethic, mental and physical toughness, and eagerness to prove themselves - were qualities that wouldn't show up on paper but would define their season.

The Indians opened their football season on the road in Altair against Rice Consolidated. Midway through the third quarter, the Indians appeared to be in control, leading 19-0 behind two touchdowns from Garrett McCann and another from quarterback Jonathan Martinez. However, Rice finally scored in the closing seconds of the third quarter and went on to score 28 unanswered points, including 20 in the fourth quarter, to complete a dramatic comeback and defeat Ganado 28-19. Despite playing hard, Ganado was outmatched in depth by the larger 3A school, making it a tough but valuable learning experience. The following week, Ganado traveled to Wallis to face Brazos. On the first play from scrimmage, Kameron Smith took a sweep from the slot and raced 63 yards for a touchdown. McCann added another score late in the first quarter, giving the Indians a 14-0 lead. However, Brazos fought back, closing the gap to 14-12 by halftime with a touchdown pass from Chris Demny to Dillon Gonzales just before the break. The Indians extended their lead to 21-12 in the fourth quarter with another McCann touchdown, but Brazos responded with a fluke 60-yard touchdown when receiver John Vasquez wrestled a near-interception away from McCann and took it to the end zone, making it 21-19. Despite multiple defensive stops, including Smith's interception, and a missed opportunity on a dropped pass to a wide-open Dalton Service, Ganado surrendered the game-winning touchdown to Demny with 53 seconds left, losing a close battle 25-21. The game was played in extreme heat and humidity, and although Ganado gave full effort, turnovers and missed chances proved costly. At 0-2, the Indians returned home for their home opener against rival Industrial. Ganado exploded to a 28-0 lead in the first quarter and cruised to a dominant 43-12 victory. Martinez threw for 198 yards and two long touchdown passes to Smith, who finished with 131 yards on just three receptions. The win marked Coach Bird's first as head coach, capped off with a celebratory Gatorade bath from the players. Now 1-2, Ganado stayed home for their homecoming game against a tough Goliad squad featuring 18 seniors, a standout quarterback in Nate Kowalik, and significantly more size and depth as a 3A Division I school. The

Indians fought hard and trailed just 7-6 after a 54-yard touchdown pass from Martinez to Smith, but Goliad pulled away with 20 second-quarter points and four touchdown passes from Kowalik en route to a 47-12 victory. Ganado wrapped up non-district play on the road against Van Vleck. After leading 21-14 at halftime and extending the lead to 24-14 with a 33-yard field goal by Martinez in the third quarter, the Indians were unable to hold on, allowing 20 unanswered points in the second half to fall 34-24. Ganado finished non-district play with a 1-4 record. Despite the tough start, the Indians faced a grueling non-district schedule, playing exclusively against larger Class 3A opponents, including three 3A Division I schools - Rice Consolidated, Industrial, and Goliad. With only 23 varsity players and a young roster, Ganado gained valuable experience and showed resilience throughout. The team looked forward to the challenge of district play in "The Little SEC" after a much-needed bye week, battle-tested and determined to improve.

Ganado opened district play with a road matchup against Flatonia, a fellow regional finalist from the previous season. Flatonia had also defeated Ganado in a non-district contest the year before. The game began with Flatonia taking a 7-0 lead in the first quarter, capitalizing on a miscue from Ganado - a bad snap on a punt that gave the Bulldogs excellent field position. The Indians responded in the second quarter with a touchdown run by Martinez, though a missed extra point left them trailing 7-6 at halftime. Unlike earlier in the season where second halves had been a struggle, the Indians showed growth and resilience, dominating the second half against an opponent of similar size and classification. Ganado scored 22 unanswered points, with two touchdown runs from McCann and another from Brandon Lister, building a commanding 28-7 lead late in the fourth quarter. Flatonia managed a late score with 21 seconds remaining, but the Indians secured a 28-14 win and began district play 1-0 with a strong defensive showing. The following week, Ganado hosted defending state finalist Shiner in a historic rivalry where, between 2008 and 2013, the winner often went on to claim the district title. Ganado started strong, battling to a 0-0 tie after the first quarter. However, Shiner made key adjustments and took control in the second quarter, scoring 21 unanswered points. Ganado's lone touchdown came from a short run by Martinez, set up by a 54-yard kickoff return from McCann. The rest of the game was all Shiner, as they dominated on the ground with 419 rushing yards, including standout Tyler Patek's 195 yards and two long touchdown runs. Ganado's offense struggled, managing just 94 total yards and seven first downs in a 35-7 loss.

Things didn't get any easier for the Indians, as they next traveled to face top-ranked Refugio, another defending state finalist and a perennial powerhouse under head coach Jason Herring. Known for their high-powered passing attack, Refugio featured new quarterback Jaylon Mascorro, who had stepped in after record-setting quarterback Travis Quintanilla graduated. Despite being outmatched in size, talent, and depth, Ganado came out fearless and delivered an early shock. After recovering a fumble on Refugio's opening possession, Ganado struck first with a 29-yard touchdown pass from Martinez to Matt Bridges. A blocked extra point by Bobby Garcia helped preserve a 7-6 lead, and another big play followed as McCann broke loose for 66 yards, pushing the Indians deep into Refugio territory. However, the promising drive stalled, and Refugio quickly took over. The Bobcats exploded with 34 points in the second quarter to take a 40-7 halftime lead and added another 20 in the third quarter, ultimately cruising to a 67-7 win. Mascorro threw for 343 yards and four touchdowns, while McCann led the Indians with 109 rushing yards. Though outplayed, Ganado showed heart and grit in the face of overwhelming odds. Now sitting at 1-2 in district play with two games remaining, Ganado needed to win both to extend its playoff streak. The next test came on the road at Weimar on Halloween night. Weimar jumped out to a 20-2 halftime lead, with Ganado's only score coming on a blocked extra point return by Smith. In the second half, the Indians mounted a comeback behind two McCann touchdowns, narrowing the deficit to 20-17. However, Weimar sealed the game with a late touchdown in the final two minutes to secure a 28-17 win, leaving Ganado with a 1-3 district record and in a precarious position heading into the final week of the regular season.

As the final week of district play approached, the season unfolded much as expected, with Refugio and Shiner securing the top two spots in the standings. Meanwhile, Ganado, Schulenburg, and Weimar were all vying for the third and final playoff berth. For Ganado, the playoff path was clear but difficult - they needed not only to defeat Schulenburg in their regular-season finale, but to win by at least 18 points to secure a postseason berth. The high-stakes matchup took place at home on Senior Night, where seven seniors - Kameron Smith, Jonathan Martinez, Arturo Almeda, Garrett Estrada, Cameron

Martinez, Cody Plant, and Austin Alford - were honored for their dedication and contributions to the program. The game itself was tightly contested from start to finish. Schulenburg took a 14-7 lead into halftime and appeared to be in control after adding field goals in the third and fourth quarters, extending their lead to 20-7 with just under seven minutes remaining. The playoffs seemed out of reach, but as they had all season, the Indians refused to quit. Smith sparked the comeback with a 62-yard touchdown reception from Martinez, and a successful two-point conversion to Caleb Thedford cut the deficit to 20-15 with six minutes left. Ganado then recovered the ensuing onside kick but was unable to capitalize offensively, turning the ball over to Schulenburg. The Indian defense responded with a critical stop, forcing a punt. Smith fielded the kick at his own three-yard line and electrified the home crowd with a 97-yard punt return touchdown, giving Ganado a 21-20 lead. Martinez again found Thedford for the two-point conversion, putting the Indians ahead 23-20 with just over three minutes remaining. McCann sealed the win with an interception on Schulenburg's next possession, completing the comeback. Although Ganado ultimately fell short of the 18-point margin needed to qualify for the playoffs, the 23-20 win was a proud and emotional moment for the team. Their six-year playoff streak came to an end with a final record of 3-7, but that record did not reflect the true character and effort of the team. Throughout the season, the Indians were outnumbered and often outmatched athletically, especially against larger schools, but they consistently demonstrated toughness, heart, and determination. The seven seniors went out with a memorable final performance, and many juniors and sophomores had stepped up over the course of the year, laying a strong foundation for the future of the program.

2015

After the 2014-2015 school year ended and summer began, the excitement for the upcoming football season grew. However, on June 23, head coach Jim Bird was offered the position of athletic director and head football coach at Bangs ISD, prompting him to leave Ganado. Along with Bird, assistant coaches Rick Ragsdale, Rocky Vaclavick, and Richard Gunnels also departed. Ragsdale had been the baseball coach, Vaclavick coached track, and Gunnels led the powerlifting program. Additionally, John Armstrong, another coach on the staff, took a position at Austwell-Tivoli, leaving Ganado ISD without any head coaches. Bird met with the athletes the following day to inform them of his departure, and it was announced that superintendent John Hardwick and coach/principal Andy Bridges would work quickly to find a new head coach as the season was fast approaching. The vacancy was filled on June 30 during a special board meeting, when Keith Wright was hired as the new athletic director and head football coach. Wright, who had retired the previous four years, was no stranger to Ganado, having previously served as the athletic director and head football coach from 2001 to 2003. During his prior tenure, he led the team to a 32-8 record, with an undefeated home record. Wright brought a wealth of experience to the table, boasting a career record of 155-74 over 20 seasons, including a state championship with Farmersville in 2007. One of Wright's first hires was former Ganado graduate Johny Lesak, a 2005 alum who had played under Wright in his earlier years at Ganado, as the new defensive coordinator. Wright also brought in several new coaches, including Tim Hughes, Paul Pliler, Tim Harrison, Kris Cavazos, and Brock Larson, a 1997 Ganado graduate. Principal Andy Bridges, who had been coaching alongside Wright, also joined the staff. Wright implemented the I-formation as the primary offensive set, a system he had used successfully in his previous stint at Ganado.

The team, although smaller in numbers with only about 25 varsity players, had a solid returning core. The seniors, including Mark Macha (tight end-defensive end), Bobby Garcia (running back-linebacker), Caleb Thedford (receiver-defensive back), Ross Fowler (offensive guard-linebacker), Austin Eastlick (offensive tackle-defensive line), Lukas Herring (offensive tackle), Brandon Lister (fullback-linebacker), Jacob Foltyn (running back-defensive back), Dalton Service (receiver), Israel Cruz (defensive back), and Christian Palacios (linebacker), provided strong leadership. Top juniors included Garrett McCann (running back-linebacker), Matt Bridges (receiver), and Malcom Chaisson (defensive tackle). Junior Michael Douglas Maresh, who was related to assistant coach Larson, was set to start at quarterback. This team was eager to succeed and willing to put in the work to win. An added advantage for Ganado was the UIL's decision to expand the playoffs to four teams per district, which increased the team's chances of making the postseason. Last year, Ganado had been part of a three-way tie for third place in the district, known as "The Little SEC," with Weimar and Schulenburg, but was left out of the playoffs due to tiebreaker points. With the expanded playoff format, the Indians were hopeful for a more successful season.

Ganado opened the season at home against Rice Consolidated, where Coach Wright, returning for his second stint at Ganado, had an undefeated record in home games from his previous tenure. The stadium was filled with a large crowd as the season kicked off. Rice Consolidated jumped to a 14-0 lead in the second quarter, but the Indians fought back. Matt Bridges made a big play, returning an interception 65 yards to the Rice 15-yard line. On the next play, Michael Douglas Maresh connected with Caleb Thedford for a 15-yard touchdown pass, cutting the lead to 14-6 at halftime. The Indians kept battling, but in the second half, they struggled to convert, missing a field goal attempt from Jorge Campuzano, and Rice added two more touchdowns to take a 28-6 lead. Ganado closed out the scoring with a 30-yard touchdown run by Matthew Sterling, but Rice took the game 28-14, leaving the Indians with a 0-1 record to start the season. The following week, Ganado returned home to face Brazos, and the Indians dominated the game, winning 54-20 to even their record at 1-1. This marked Coach Wright's first victory in his second tenure. Ganado ran for 447 yards, with Sterling leading the way, rushing for 248 yards and three touchdowns. Garrett McCann also contributed with 104 yards and two touchdowns. The team's performance mirrored the strong, ground-based offense Wright had used during his previous time at Ganado. In their next game, Ganado defeated Industrial 26-7 at Cobra Field in Vanderbilt, marking their last win over Industrial to date. The field conditions were challenging due to recent rainfall, and the players, dressed in white jerseys, were covered in mud by the end of the game. Despite only having eight first downs, Ganado controlled the game, rushing for 176 yards. The defense dominated, limiting Industrial to just one first down and 26 total yards of offense. The only score Ganado allowed was a kickoff return touchdown after their own first-quarter score. The following week, Ganado faced a tough Goliad team on the road. Unfortunately, the Indians were without seven key players, and the lack of depth proved costly. Goliad won the game 39-7, with Ganado's only score coming from a 30-yard interception return by Thedford in the second quarter. With a 2-2 record, the Indians hoped to bounce back in their homecoming game against Van Vleck. However, the weather had other plans. Just before kickoff, lightning and an approaching thunderstorm forced the game to be postponed. Fans were evacuated to the parking lot, and it was announced that the game would be rescheduled for the following evening. Despite the delay, the homecoming festivities took place that night, and the game was played the next evening. After a tight 7-7 tie at halftime, the Indians pulled away in the second half to win 26-7. The victory brought the Indians' record to 3-2, and for the first time that season, the team was healthy and had all their players on the field. With a bye week ahead of district play, the team was optimistic about their chances of making a playoff run.

Ganado opened their district campaign at home against Flatonia. Despite Flatonia's winless record from the previous season, they had always been a tough team to face. The Indians seemed to have control in the first half, leading 14-0 thanks to two touchdown runs by McCann. However, the second half saw a dramatic shift. Flatonia scored on a 60-yard fumble return by Casen Novak, cutting the lead to 14-6. Novak would strike again late in the third quarter, and with a successful two-point conversion, the game was tied 14-14. Ganado had a chance to win the game late in the fourth quarter, but their drive stalled inside the red zone due to a fumble. After forcing Flatonia to punt, Ganado muffed the punt return, giving Flatonia good field position. They capitalized with a 20-yard field goal and went on to win 17-14, scoring 17 unanswered points in the second half. This tough loss put the Indians in an early hole in district play. Next, Ganado faced #4 Shiner on the road, who had just defeated Refugio the week before. Shiner jumped to a 21-0 lead at halftime and extended it to 28-0 in the third quarter on Dadrian Taylor's third touchdown of the night, as he rushed for 132 yards. Ganado struggled offensively, managing only five first downs and 150 total yards. Their lone score came in the fourth quarter when Brandon Lister returned a fumble for a 42-yard touchdown, but the final score was 28-7 in favor of Shiner. Despite the loss, the Indians played hard, but at 0-2 in district, their challenges continued. The following week, Ganado hosted #10 Refugio. Although the Indians trailed 14-7 at halftime, Refugio exploded in the second half, scoring 28 points to win 42-7. Ganado tied the game at 7-7 in the second quarter when Matt Bridges threw a 23-yard touchdown pass to Thedford. Refugio's offense, led by quarterback Jaylon Mascorro, who passed for 329 yards and five touchdowns, proved too much for the Indians. Refugio would go on to make it to the state finals that year, ultimately falling to Canadian. In their final home game of the season against Weimar, Ganado needed to win by 10 points and defeat Schulenburg in the last game to have a chance at the playoffs. Unfortunately, they were unable to get anything going and lost 33-0, falling to 0-4 in district, which eliminated their playoff hopes. In the season finale at Schulenburg, the game was all about pride. The Indians had faced numerous injuries throughout the season, with five key players sidelined, including seniors Brandon Lister and Austin Eastlick. Schulenburg led 14-0 at halftime, but Ganado fought back in the second half, tying the game 14-14 in the third quarter. However, Schulenburg scored the last touchdown of the game in the fourth quarter to win 21-14. The Indians finished the season 3-7, going 0-5 in district play, marking their first winless district campaign since 2006. Despite the tough season, filled with injuries and a smaller roster, the team never quit and gave their best effort in every game. For the second consecutive year, Ganado missed the playoffs, marking the first back-to-back playoff misses since 2006 and 2007.

2016

Under Coach Wright's leadership, the team had a full year of preparation focusing on strengthening the squad and improving depth. However, the team was only able to field a roster of 17 players for the upcoming season, with more than half of the roster composed of nine seniors. These seniors were the most experienced players returning, but due to the small roster size, many of them had to play both offense and defense. This posed a risk, especially if injuries, similar to those from the previous season, occurred, as it would significantly impact the team. Key returning players included senior receiver-defensive back Cameron Lambert, senior running back Matthew Sterling, senior quarterback Michael-Douglas Maresh, senior receiver-defensive back Matt Bridges, senior running back-linebacker Garrett McCann, senior offensive lineman-defensive lineman Michael Malek, senior defensive lineman Malcom Chaisson, senior linebacker Christian Palacios, and junior center Ben Ramsey. The district remained challenging, with Shiner and Refugio as the front-runners, the latter having advanced to the state finals in the previous year as the defending 2A Division 1 state finalist. Weimar also returned with a strong team. Notably, Schulenburg had moved up to 3A Division 2, while Flatonia dropped to Division 2, making way for Kenedy and Yorktown, who both moved up to Division 1 after making the playoffs in Division 2 the previous year.

Ganado opened the season with a dominant 47-8 win over Louise in the "Battle of Mustang Creek," marking their first season opener victory since 2011. The Indians amassed 581 total yards, including 379 rushing yards. Matthew Sterling led the charge with 187 rushing yards and a touchdown, while Garrett McCann added 102 yards and two touchdowns. Quarterback Michael-Douglas Maresh threw for 202 yards and two touchdowns, while also rushing for one touchdown, contributing to a balanced offensive effort. The defense also played well, forcing turnovers, and the Indians started the season 1-0. The following week, the Indians traveled to Palacios, but the game was interrupted by thunderstorms. Despite a strong start, including a 65-yard touchdown run by Sterling on the first play from scrimmage, lightning forced a 30-minute delay before the game was ultimately canceled. The game was ruled a no contest and did not count on either team's record. Returning home, the Indians faced former district rival Schulenburg, a physical team with a powerful backfield. Schulenburg led 21-10 at halftime, with Ganado's only scores coming from a 61-yard touchdown run by McCann and a 24-yard field goal by Oscar Almeda. In the second half, the Indians fought back, with Maresh passing for two touchdowns, one to Matt Bridges and one to McCann. With just over eight minutes left, Ganado trailed 28-23 and had a chance to win, but after failing on a fourth-down pass and receiving a penalty to extend their drive, the Indians were unable to score. Schulenburg ran out the clock, securing a 28-23 victory, and Ganado's record moved to 1-1. The next week, the Indians traveled to Danbury, where they struggled in the first half, trailing 6-0. However, they came alive in the second half. Maresh scored a touchdown to give Ganado a 7-6 lead, and a key interception by Cameron Lambert helped set up a 12-yard touchdown run by McCann. McCann later added a 57-yard touchdown run to seal a 21-6 win. The victory spoiled Danbury's homecoming and improved Ganado's record to 2-1. Next up, Ganado played Snook on homecoming night and won 27-6. Maresh threw for three touchdowns, connecting with Bridges, Sterling, and McCann, and also ran for a score. Sterling led the ground game with 137 yards. The win brought the Indians to a 3-1 record, closing out non-district play before a bye week and preparing for their district opener against state-ranked Refugio.

Ganado faced a tough challenge against the #3-ranked Refugio, as the Indians only had 19 players suited up, compared to Refugio's 38.

Refugio, the defending state finalist, had only one loss, which was to Class 4A Navarro, a top-ranked team. The game quickly became a mismatch, with Refugio dominating from the start. They led 41-0 at halftime, and the second half was played with a running clock. Refugio went on to win 62-0 and would later capture the 2A Division 1 state title, defeating Crawford. Despite the lopsided score, the Indians fought hard and never gave up. The following week, Ganado rebounded with a 37-0 victory over Kenedy, evening their district record at 1-1. Matthew Sterling had a standout performance, rushing for 233 yards, including two long touchdown runs of 98 and 63 yards. The defense also played well, shutting out Kenedy and even scoring a safety on an intentional grounding penalty in the end zone. This win marked Ganado's first district victory in two years, providing a boost of momentum as they looked to make a playoff push. With three games remaining, Ganado needed to win just one to secure a playoff spot. The next game was against Weimar, where the Indians struggled with inconsistency, penalties, and turnovers, ultimately losing 27-8. Weimar's size and speed proved to be too much, but the Indians played hard, and a fumble recovery touchdown by Aaron Lenhart in the final minute of the game avoided the shutout. The loss meant that Ganado needed to win one of their next two games, either against Shiner or Yorktown, to make the playoffs. In their final home game against Shiner, Ganado honored nine seniors, including key players such as Sterling, Maresh, and McCann. The Indians battled hard and scored two touchdowns in the first half - one from a Sterling run in the first quarter and another from a Maresh pass to Logan Hurt in the second quarter. However, Shiner's offense was too strong, as they scored 21 points in both the first and second quarters to take a 42-14 lead at halftime. Shiner added two more touchdowns in the second half, securing a 55-14 victory. Despite the defeat, the Indians played with heart.

In a must-win situation, Ganado faced Yorktown in the season finale, where the winner would secure the fourth seed in the playoffs, and the loser's season would end. The Indians came out strong, scoring on their opening possession with a 13-yard touchdown run from McCann. However, the extra point was missed, and Ganado held a narrow 6-0 lead. Yorktown responded with a touchdown and took a 7-6 lead by the end of the first quarter. Ganado regained the lead early in the second quarter with a one-yard touchdown run from Maresh, though the two-point conversion attempt failed, leaving the Indians up 12-7.

Yorktown answered with another touchdown, and they held a slim 14-12 lead at halftime. In the second half, Ganado continued to fight, driving the ball down the field but missing a short field goal. On the very next play, Yorktown broke free for a 90-yard touchdown, sparking a run of three consecutive touchdowns that gave Yorktown a commanding 34-12 lead. Sterling added a touchdown for Ganado, cutting the deficit to 34-20 at the end of the third quarter. However, Yorktown scored two more touchdowns in the fourth quarter, ultimately winning 48-20 and clinching the final playoff spot, ending Ganado's season. Despite the loss, the Indians showed great effort throughout the game, especially in the first half, but were unable to recover after falling behind in the third quarter. Coach Wright expressed his pride in the team's performance, commending their resilience and determination. He highlighted that the team never quit, and they followed the coaches' instructions all season long. Ganado finished the season with a 4-5 record. The JV team had a strong season as well, with many freshmen moving up to the varsity in the middle of district play, gaining valuable experience. The Indians would be a young team in 2017, but as always, they were committed to working hard and giving their best.

2017

At the end of the 2016-2017 school year, Andy and Jeanne Bridges retired after long and impactful careers at Ganado ISD. Both had started their careers at the school in 1995, with Jeanne serving as a high school math teacher and Andy as an assistant football coach and the baseball coach. In 2004, Andy transitioned to an assistant high school principal role before eventually becoming the principal while also returning to coaching in 2009 until his retirement. The Bridges family saw all four of their children graduate from Ganado ISD, and their contributions to the district left a lasting impact. They were well respected and would be greatly missed by the community.

In August, Coach Wright began his third year back at Ganado. When he was initially hired in 2001, he took over a program that was a state championship contender. Now, 16 years later, he was working to rebuild the program and bring it back to that level. The 2017 team was very young, consisting of 15 sophomores, many of whom had moved up from the JV team the year before and had some experience, but still lacked maturity. The team also included nine juniors and only four seniors. Key returning seniors included offensive lineman Ben Ramsey and running back-linebacker Toby Martinez. Sophomore Ethan Guerra, who played running back and defensive back, was expected to contribute significantly, as was junior Logan Hurt, who would take the snaps as quarterback. Junior Miguel Hernandez would also contribute to the line, while other sophomores like tight end-linebacker Gabriel Aguilar, tight end-defensive end Adrian Mata, and running back-linebacker Ryan Williams would play key roles. While the team was young, Coach Wright and the coaching staff were hopeful that by the end of the season, these players would have gained valuable experience, setting the stage for future success. The foundation laid by this young team would be crucial for the program's growth in the years to come.

As the start of school and football workouts were about to begin, everything came to a standstill due to the arrival of Hurricane Harvey. On August 25, the powerful Category 4 storm made landfall near Rockport and Port Aransas, causing severe devastation along its direct path. The storm then moved inland, severely impacting areas like Refugio, a district rival, which took the full brunt of the storm. Harvey stalled near Cuero, bringing historic rainfall and flooding to Houston, and it remained over the area for nearly a week before finally moving out. During this time, the focus shifted from football to helping those in need. The state of Texas, along with the assistance of Louisiana, came together in a remarkable display of unity and support. Ganado held strong during this crisis, with residents coming together to check on one another and assist those affected by the storm. The community donated food, water, clothing, and blankets to help those in need, and the Ganado High School gym even served as a shelter for evacuees. Many students and football players actively participated in helping out, showing immense dedication and compassion during the difficult time. Eventually, the recovery efforts allowed school and football to resume. However, the first game, originally scheduled at Louise on September 1, was canceled due to the aftermath of the storm, as was the case for many other games that first week. When the second scheduled game against Palacios took place on September 8, it was not a regular game but a scrimmage, as the school also held its Fall kickoff event that evening.

As things began to return to normal after Hurricane Harvey, the Indians traveled to Schulenburg on September 15 for their first game of the season. The team gave a strong effort but ultimately suffered a 40-7 defeat. Quarterback Logan Hurt struggled in the second half, throwing three interceptions, two of which led to touchdowns for Schulenburg. Ganado avoided a shutout when Hurt connected with Ethan Guerra for a short touchdown pass with just two seconds remaining. The team also played without starting center Ben Ramsey, who was sidelined with a high ankle sprain and would return in the following weeks. Ganado looked to bounce back in their home opener and homecoming game against Danbury. The game started with a good crowd in attendance. Danbury took an early lead, scoring on their opening possession with a 28-yard option play by their quarterback. They missed the extra point, leading 6-0. Ganado responded quickly, with Toby Ortiz scoring a 46-yard touchdown to cap a 68-yard drive. Fernando Rubio's successful extra point gave Ganado a 7-6 lead. Just before halftime, Danbury thought they had scored again, but a penalty negated the touchdown. Later, a Ganado defender blocked a field goal attempt, allowing the Indians to take a 7-6 lead into the locker room. However, the game would take a drastic turn in the second half, marking the start of a difficult stretch for the team. On Ganado's first play after halftime, they fumbled, and a Danbury player returned the ball 42 yards for a touchdown, giving Danbury a 14-7 lead. The Indians' struggles continued as they threw an interception on the next possession, and Danbury capitalized with another touchdown to extend their lead to 22-7. Danbury further increased their lead in the fourth quarter, scoring on a 62-yard drive to make it 28-7. Ganado put together a strong drive later in the game, but a fake punt attempt came up short, and Danbury ran out the clock, securing a 28-7 victory. This marked Danbury's first win over Ganado since 1989, and the loss was particularly hard for the team, as turnovers and a lack of physicality in the second half played a key role in the outcome.

Despite the team's hard-fought effort, some fans expressed frustration, with a few unfairly criticizing the players and coaches after the game. This reaction was disheartening, especially when witnessing a fan loudly expressing their displeasure in the parking lot. It was a reminder that not all fans understood the challenges of coaching and developing a young team. In a shocking turn of events, Coach Wright resigned for personal reasons on Sunday evening following the loss. His decision to leave midseason left many questions unanswered, but it was clear that Wright had deep respect for the Ganado community, having been welcomed and loved by many. He met with the team before his departure, wishing them well. Defensive coordinator Johny Lesak, who had played for Wright from 2001 to 2003, was named the interim head coach for the remainder of the season. Lesak took on the role with the understanding that, as Wright had always said, one must be prepared for when they are called upon, and now it was his turn to lead the team.

After the loss to Danbury and the coaching change, the Indians traveled to Louise for a makeup game, as the season opener had been canceled due to the aftermath of Hurricane Harvey. The Indians responded well to the adversity and delivered a solid performance, securing their first win of the season with a 34-6 victory. The win was especially meaningful as it marked Coach Lesak's debut as the interim head coach and athletic director. Ortiz was the standout player, scoring three touchdowns, all in the second quarter, which gave Ganado a commanding 20-0 lead at halftime. In the third quarter, Hurt and Guerra each scored to extend the lead to 34-0. Louise managed to score a touchdown in the final minute to avoid a shutout. Defensively, Ganado played an outstanding game, swarming to the football, forcing turnovers, and consistently tackling for negative yardage. This performance not only marked a significant confidence boost for the team but also set the stage for the upcoming district competition. With a bye week ahead, the Indians had time to regroup and prepare for the challenges to come.

The Indians hosted #6 Refugio in their district opener. Refugio, the defending state champions, were playing under challenging circumstances due to the devastation caused by Hurricane Harvey, which had damaged their stadium. As a result, the team had to play all their games on the road. In addition, during Refugio's second game of the season, a player suffered a broken neck and was in the recovery process. In an act of sportsmanship, Ganado presented Refugio with a check to support recovery efforts and well wishes for the injured player prior to the game. On the field, Refugio dominated the game. Quarterback Jared Kelly threw for five touchdown passes and 300 yards. However, it was the Refugio defense that truly controlled the game, holding Ganado to just two first downs and 17 total yards, including only four net rushing yards on 27 attempts, many of which came from negative yardage. Refugio went on to reach the state final for the third consecutive year, although they ultimately lost to Mart in the championship. The Indians quickly rebounded the following week with a strong 36-6 road victory over Kenedy. Sophomore Cameron Bates had a standout performance, scoring four rushing touchdowns. This game marked a positive sign for the future as Ganado's young players, particularly the sophomores, stepped up and made significant contributions, showing growth throughout the season. With a 1-1 district record, Ganado still had a chance to make the playoffs, but their next opponent, Weimar, proved to be a tough challenge. Despite Weimar's 1-5 record, they were a strong team with size, talent, and speed. Ganado fought hard but was defeated 42-13, with Ryan Williams and Hurt scoring the team's touchdowns. The following week, the Indians faced Shiner, a very strong team that quickly gained a 27-0 lead in the first quarter. Shiner dominated the game, winning 48-0. They held Ganado to just four first downs and rushed for 359 yards, completely overpowering the Indians. Shiner would go on to face Refugio for the district title, which Refugio claimed with a 35-0 victory. Despite the tough losses, Ganado showed determination and effort throughout the season, with several young players stepping up and gaining valuable experience. In their season finale, the Indians faced Yorktown at home with a playoff spot on the line. The team needed to win by at least 18 points to force a three-way tie for the playoff berth with Yorktown and Weimar. Yorktown quickly jumped out to a 20-0 lead in the first quarter, but Ganado fought back in the second quarter, scoring 21 points to close the gap to 28-21 at halftime. Guerra put the Indians on the board first, and after a Yorktown fumble, Hurt connected with Louis Olvera on a 46-yard touchdown pass, bringing the score to 20-14. Yorktown added another score, but with just five seconds left in the first half, Hurt threw a short touchdown pass to Ortiz, keeping the game close. In the second half, Ganado came out strong, with Angel Rubio returning the opening kickoff 82 yards for a touchdown, cutting Yorktown's lead to 28-26 after a failed two-point conversion. However, Yorktown responded with 20 more points, pulling away to win 48-27 and clinch a playoff spot, along with Weimar. Despite the loss, Ganado displayed incredible heart and determination, playing hard until the final whistle.

The Indians finished the season with a 2-6 record. The team had faced numerous challenges, including a delayed start to the school year due to Hurricane Harvey, a mid-season coaching change, and the struggles of a young team with mostly underclassmen. While they were often compared to a JV team against varsity-level opponents, particularly due to their youth, the sophomores showed growth and development throughout the season. The four seniors - Jacob Martinez, Toby Ortiz, Fernando Pacheco, and Ben Ramsey - played their final game, leaving behind a legacy of perseverance. Interim head coach Johny Lesak stepped in after the resignation of Coach Keith Wright in September and led the team through a difficult season. Despite the challenges, Ganado demonstrated resilience, and the future looked promising as the team gained valuable experience. In early December, it was announced that Ganado would be moving up to a new classification, 3A, with the upcoming UIL realignment in February. The details of their new district would be revealed later, but this change marked an exciting new chapter for the program.

Chapter 9

New Coach, New System, and a New Beginning

2018

Significant changes were underway for Ganado, and they were happening quickly, bringing a wave of new developments. On February 1, two major events took place. First, the biannual UIL realignment was announced, and as anticipated, Ganado moved up from Class 2A to Class 3A by a margin of seven students. This placed them in District 14-3A Division 2 for the 2018–2019 football seasons. The new district was extremely competitive, featuring former rivals from earlier years such as East Bernard, Tidehaven, and Van Vleck - all of whom had advanced to the regional round the previous season. Van Vleck, having dropped down from 3A Division 1, added to the district's difficulty. Additional teams in the district included Schulenburg, Bloomington, and Danbury. That same evening, another major change occurred when the Ganado Board of Trustees selected Brent Bennett as the new athletic director and head football coach, replacing interim coach Johny Lesak. Bennett was chosen from a pool of 95 applicants. His coaching career began in 2009 at Navasota, and he later served as offensive coordinator at Buffalo (2011–2012), Cameron Yoe (2013), Abilene Cooper (2014), and most recently Bay City since 2015. At Cameron Yoe, he was part of a program that won the state championship. Bennett came in with a strong vision, aiming to push student-athletes to perform at their highest level and restore the athletic program's past success. Ganado had not reached the football playoffs since 2013, and the players were eager to return to postseason competition. In addition to changes in leadership and competition, the school district was also undergoing physical transformation. A brand-new school was under construction, and a new football stadium was being built with artificial turf. The stadium and field were expected to be completed just in time for the start of the upcoming football season, marking a fresh and hopeful new era for Ganado athletics.

The 2018 season marked the beginning of a new era for Ganado football, ushered in by Coach Bennett and his newly assembled coaching staff. With this new leadership came a dramatic shift in offensive philosophy. The traditional, hard-nosed, run-heavy approach was replaced with a modern spread offense. Instead of lining up under center, the team would now operate primarily out of a shotgun formation, often with four wide receivers and either one or no running backs in the backfield. This system was a significant change for the young team, which returned the majority of its roster after losing only four seniors the previous year. Although the transition was challenging early on, the team gradually adapted, and the foundation laid in 2018 was expected to benefit the program in the years to come. A key figure in this offensive transformation was 24-year-old Josh Ervin, who was hired as the offensive coordinator. A 2012 Bay City graduate and former quarterback, Ervin played college football at the University of St. Mary in Leavenworth, Kansas. Before joining Ganado, he coached quarterbacks and served as the head softball coach at Bay City. Joining him on the staff were fellow Bay City coach Andrew McFaddin, Colby Andrews, Mark Freeman - a 1989 Ganado graduate - and defensive coordinator Chris Van Cleave.

Returning to lead the offense on the field was senior quarterback Logan Hurt, who threw for 521 yards and five touchdowns the previous season. Junior running back Ethan Guerra, who rushed for 550 yards and five touchdowns, was expected to be the main weapon in the backfield. At receiver, the team featured juniors Louis Olvera, Gavin Sanchez, and Cameron Bates, along with standout freshman Riley Hurt, Logan's younger brother. Their sibling connection at quarterback and receiver was reminiscent of the 1998 brother duo of Heath and Matthew Bures. Up front, the offensive line brought back key contributors including seniors Miguel Hernandez and Colton Lindsey at tackle, juniors Dean Ramsey and Alex Campuzano at guard, and sophomore Christopher Gobellan at center. Defensively, senior Vincent Aguilar and junior Gabe Aguilar anchored the interior line, while junior Adrian Mata and sophomore Larson Workman held down the end positions. The linebacker unit consisted of juniors Colton Teague, Bates, and Ryan Williams. In the secondary, Sanchez and sophomore Erik Alvarez played cornerback, while Olvera and Guerra returned as the safeties. Although the team faced early struggles during scrimmages while adjusting to the new system, they remained united and committed to one another. Week after week, they continued to improve and compete, laying the groundwork for a promising future under the new regime.

On August 31, the Indians ushered in a new chapter of their football program with the debut of their new stadium and artificial turf field, kicking off the season with a highly anticipated homecoming game against their longtime rivals, the Louise Hornets, in the "Battle of Mustang Creek." The game began as a defensive battle, with neither team scoring in the first quarter. Louise eventually struck first in the second quarter when quarterback Colin Gonzales connected with Kristian Munoz for a 30-yard touchdown pass. After a missed extra point, the Hornets led 6-0. Following a quick Ganado three-and-out, Louise extended their lead with an 18-yard touchdown run by Gonzales, though they again failed on the extra point, making the score 12-0. Ganado responded just before halftime with a determined drive, capped off by a two-yard touchdown run by Ethan Guerra, narrowing the deficit to 12-6 at the break. The Indians took their first lead of the night in the third quarter when quarterback Logan Hurt found Louis Olvera for a 21-yard touchdown pass, putting Ganado ahead 13-12. However, the momentum shifted again in the fourth quarter after Hurt threw a costly interception deep in Ganado territory that was returned for a touchdown, giving Louise an 18-13 lead. Late in the game, with Louise trying to run out the clock, a tipped pass was intercepted by Gavin Sanchez, setting up Ganado with great field position. On the very next play, Logan Hurt connected with his freshman brother, Riley Hurt, for a 38-yard touchdown pass. On the two-point conversion attempt, with all receivers covered, Logan scrambled into the end zone himself, giving Ganado a 21-18 lead. Another interception by Olvera gave the Indians a chance to seal the game, but unable to advance the ball and pinned deep in their own territory, Ganado took an intentional safety, reducing their lead to just 21-20. Following the safety and ensuing free kick, Louise had one last opportunity, starting from the Ganado 40-yard line with only 30 seconds left. On fourth down, senior Vincent Aguilar delivered a game-sealing sack, securing a thrilling 21-20 victory for Ganado. It was their first win in the new stadium and a successful debut for Coach Bennett. Despite a rocky start, the team showed resilience and determination. Logan Hurt finished with 192 passing yards in the new offensive system.

The Indians hit the road for the next three games, beginning with a trip to Wallis to face Brazos in a high-scoring contest that resembled a Wild

West shootout. Brazos jumped out to a 7-0 lead, but Ganado quickly answered, though a missed extra point left them trailing 7-6. Brazos surged ahead again, eventually leading 22-6 in the second quarter before Ganado narrowed the gap to 22-14 with a touchdown and successful two-point conversion. However, Brazos continued to pile on points and led 36-21 at halftime. The second half saw more scoring, but the Indians could not catch up, and Brazos handed Ganado its first loss of the season with a 49-27 final. Despite the defeat, there were major bright spots for Ganado, particularly in the passing game. Logan Hurt threw for an impressive 363 yards and two touchdowns, breaking a 26-year-old single-game school passing record previously held by Billy Benavides from 1992. Sanchez led the receivers with 93 yards on five catches, while Cameron Bates added 84 yards on eight receptions. Though the season was still young, these performances hinted at the promising future of Ganado's new-look offense. The following week, due to a major rain event forecasted across South Texas, most football games were rescheduled from Friday to Thursday night, including Ganado's matchup against Odem. The Indians traveled south for the game, which was heavily impacted by turnovers. Both teams combined for seven total turnovers, but Ganado was responsible for four of them. These mistakes proved costly, as Odem built a commanding 26-0 lead by halftime. Ganado managed to get on the scoreboard late in the third quarter when quarterback Logan Hurt connected with Guerra for an 18-yard touchdown pass, cutting the deficit to 26-6. However, Odem responded with two more touchdown passes in the fourth quarter, ultimately defeating the Indians 40-6. Now sitting at 1-2 on the season, the Indians continued to show grit despite their struggles, playing hard and learning together as a young team. Logan Hurt contributed with 61 rushing yards and threw for 99 yards, but was intercepted four times. Freshman Riley Hurt led the receivers with 59 yards on four catches.

Looking to bounce back, a determined Ganado team traveled to face the undefeated Palacios Sharks, who entered the game at 3-0. The Indians struck first in the opening quarter with an 8-yard touchdown run by Guerra, taking a 7-0 lead. After a Ganado turnover, Palacios threatened to score with a drive deep into Indian territory, but on a critical fourth-and-two from the Ganado 3-yard line, the Indians' defense made a huge stop, forcing a turnover on downs. The first half remained a defensive battle, with Ganado missing a field goal attempt by Giovanny Avalos, and the Indians carried a 7-0 lead into halftime.

Palacios opened the second half with a 64-yard touchdown drive, capped by an 11-yard quarterback keeper, but missed the extra point, allowing Ganado to maintain a narrow 7-6 lead. On the very next play from scrimmage, Guerra broke loose for a 65-yard touchdown run, extending the Indians' lead to 14-6 in the third quarter. Palacios had another chance late in the game when they reached the Ganado 21-yard line, but instead of attempting a field goal, they opted for a short punt. Midway through the fourth quarter, while trying to run out the clock, Ganado suffered a setback when Logan Hurt fumbled and Palacios returned it 55 yards for a touchdown. However, the Indians' defense once again rose to the occasion, stopping the crucial two-point conversion attempt and preserving a 14-12 lead. Ganado regained possession, secured a key first down, and successfully ran out the clock to clinch a hard-fought 14-12 victory. The win improved the Indians' record to 2-2 and gave them momentum heading into a much-needed bye week before beginning play in the highly competitive District 14-3A Division 2.

The Indians made their 3A district debut in dominant fashion with a commanding 52-6 victory over Bloomington at home. Despite a narrow 10-6 lead at halftime, the Indians exploded in the third quarter, scoring 28 unanswered points to break the game wide open. The scoring spree began on Ganado's second play of the second half when quarterback Logan Hurt connected with his younger brother, freshman Riley Hurt, for a 66-yard touchdown pass to extend the lead to 17-6. Following a Bloomington fumble, Ganado capitalized with a 33-yard touchdown run by Guerra, pushing the lead to 24-6. On the next Bloomington possession, the Indians blocked a punt and took over at the 13-yard line, where Logan Hurt immediately found Olvera for another touchdown, increasing the margin to 31-6. The third-quarter onslaught continued when Colton Teague returned a fumble 25 yards for a touchdown, making it 38-6. In the fourth quarter, Logan Hurt and Riley Hurt connected again, this time on a 68-yard touchdown pass - Logan's second of the game. Earlier, Hurt had scored on a 52-yard run in the second quarter, and Guerra later added a 9-yard touchdown run to close out the scoring. Ganado had responded to an early 6-0 deficit by scoring 52 unanswered points in a complete team performance on both sides of the ball. The dominant win marked an ideal start to district play, with the Indians improving to 1-0 in District 14-3A Division 2. The following week, Ganado faced a long road trip to take on Danbury, and once again, the Indians showed resilience in a game of two very different halves. Ganado started slowly and trailed 14-0 in the first quarter before finally getting on the scoreboard with four minutes remaining in the second quarter, cutting the deficit to 14-7 at halftime. In the third quarter, the Indians recovered a Danbury fumble at the 10-yard line and converted it into a touchdown, tying the game at 14-14. On the next possession, Guerra broke a 39-yard run to the Danbury 5-yard line, and although the offense stalled, Avalos nailed a field goal to give Ganado its first lead of the game at 17-14. Danbury quickly responded with a touchdown and successful two-point conversion to regain the lead at 22-17. However, that would be their final score of the game. The Ganado defense tightened up and shut down Danbury for the remainder of the contest, while the offense surged forward. The Indians scored 22 unanswered points, sealing the victory when Adrian Mata intercepted a Danbury pass and returned it for a touchdown. The 39-22 win improved Ganado to 2-0 in district play and showcased their ability to overcome adversity and dominate the second half.

Ganado entered a challenging three-week stretch against the toughest opponents in District 14-3A Division 2, beginning with a home game against district favorite East Bernard. East Bernard, boasting a 6-1 overall record and a 3-0 district mark, had already defeated Van Vleck and Tidehaven. Known for their strong tradition, including six district titles in the previous seven years and a 2012 state championship, East Bernard was a powerhouse. The matchup featured two contrasting styles: Ganado's spread passing attack versus East Bernard's run-heavy Slot-T offense. East Bernard quickly asserted its dominance, scoring just 25 seconds into the game and building a commanding 35-6 halftime lead. Ganado's only first-half highlight came when Sanchez returned a fumble 21 yards for a touchdown, briefly closing the gap to 7-6 after a missed extra point. In the third quarter, East Bernard extended their lead to 42-6 before Ganado showed some signs of life. A defensive play by Larson Workman led to an interception by Teague near the East Bernard 30-yard line, and Guerra finished the short drive with a touchdown run to make it 42-13. East Bernard added another score in the fourth quarter, while Ganado responded with a field goal from Avalos and a late touchdown in the final seconds, but ultimately fell 48-23. East Bernard's dominance was clear, as they rushed for 354 yards and would go on to win the district championship and advance to the state semifinals, narrowly losing to eventual state champion Newton. For Ganado, it was a wake-up call and a reminder of what it would take to compete at a higher level. The following week, Ganado faced another state-ranked opponent in No. 11 Van Vleck, a team that had narrowly lost to East Bernard earlier in district play. The Indians traveled to Van Vleck, but the result was one of the most lopsided losses in school history. Van Vleck dominated every phase of the game, building a 35-0 halftime lead and scoring 35 more points in the second half never letting off the gas, including a controversial two-point conversion attempt in the final minute to reach 70 points. Their star running back, De'mitri Monroe, ran for 256 yards and four touchdowns, while quarterback Cameron Hudson added 174 passing yards, contributing to Van Vleck's 559 total rushing yards. The 70-0 defeat was a tough blow, but despite the devastation, the Indians remained resilient and still had a chance to make the playoffs if they could win one of their final two games. Ganado returned home for their last home game of the season against Tidehaven, determined to bounce back. They started strong, but Tidehaven built a 14-0 lead by the second quarter. Guerra responded with a short touchdown run to make it 14-7. However, Guerra suffered a significant collision before halftime and did not return, which proved to be a major loss for Ganado. With limited offensive options in the second half, the Indians struggled, and Tidehaven pulled away to win 34-7. Despite the loss, Ganado continued to play hard and showed heart. Heading into the final week of the regular season, Ganado and Schulenburg were tied at 2-3 in district play, battling for the fourth and final playoff spot. Unfortunately for Ganado, Guerra remained sidelined due to his injury. The Indians traveled to Schulenburg, but the offense struggled without their key running back. Schulenburg led 14-0 at halftime and extended the lead to 20-0 in the third quarter. Ganado scored their only touchdown of the game in the third, but Schulenburg added another in the fourth, sealing a 27-7 victory and clinching the final playoff berth. Ganado's season ended with a district record of 2-4, narrowly missing the playoffs. Despite facing several setbacks, including injuries and tough losses to top-ranked opponents, the young team showed growth, resilience, and potential for future success.

The Ganado Indians were denied a playoff berth in 2018, marking the fifth consecutive season since 2014 that the team failed to reach the postseason. In four of those five seasons, Ganado entered the final game with a chance to secure a playoff spot, only to fall short each time. Under first-year head coach Brent Bennett, the Indians concluded the season with a 4-6 overall record. While the team did not achieve its ultimate goal, the year was marked by growth, perseverance, and adaptation to a new offensive system. The Indians worked hard throughout the season, showing resilience and determination while adjusting to a completely new style of play. Senior quarterback Logan Hurt led the way, passing for 1,693 yards and nine touchdowns, breaking the school's single-season passing record previously held by Jamie Bures since 1995. Hurt also finished as the leading passer in the district. His younger brother, freshman Riley Hurt, emerged as the team's top receiver and the district's leading receiver, recording 608 yards on 43 receptions with five touchdowns. On the defensive side, Colton Teague earned all-district honors for his strong play. Despite the disappointment of missing the playoffs, the team graduated only eight seniors, including Logan Hurt, and would return a core group of experienced players. Many of the returning athletes had two full years of varsity experience, and the incoming senior class promised to be strong. With a solid foundation and valuable lessons learned in 2018, the future looked bright for Ganado football, and expectations were high heading into the 2019 season.

Chapter 10

The Playoff Tradition Returns: The Third Run

2019

In Coach Bennett's second year at the helm, the Indians entered the season determined to end a five-year playoff drought, fueled by a strong offseason and commitment to mastering a new system. Despite their efforts, they faced a challenging path in a tough district, where *Dave Campbell's Texas Football Magazine* predicted a fifth-place finish for them. The district was expected to be led by East Bernard, followed by regional finalist Tidehaven, Van Vleck, and Schulenburg, all posing significant competition. The Indians returned a core of experienced players, particularly a strong senior class, though the team faced uncertainty at the quarterback position following the graduation of Logan Hurt. That role was ultimately filled by a talented freshman, Kyle Bures-Guerrero. Offensively, the team was poised for success, with senior running back Ethan Guerra and a fully returning receiving corps consisting of seniors Gavin Sanchez, Louis Olvera, Cameron Bates, and standout sophomore Riley Hurt. The offensive line was anchored by seniors Dean Ramsey (center) and Alex Campuzano (tackle), with juniors Larson Workman (tackle), Julian Martinez (guard), and sophomore Jose Ramos (guard) completing the unit. Defensively, the Indians showed significant improvement under new defensive coordinator Luke Barganier. Also joining the staff was 1996 Ganado alumnus Jason Chambless, who coached the linebackers. The defensive line was bolstered by senior Colton Teague, who shifted from linebacker to tackle, and Workman, who moved to the other tackle spot. Sophomores Logan Riojas and Dylan Alvarez held down the end positions. At linebacker, returning seniors Ryan Williams and Bates were joined by Guerra, who transitioned from safety. The secondary featured senior Luke Prove and sophomore Manny Calderon at cornerback, with Olvera and junior Erik Alvarez covering the safety roles. With a combination of returning talent, new leadership, and a solid offseason of preparation, the Indians appeared poised to defy expectations and compete for one of the four coveted playoff spots, aiming to restore the program's winning tradition.

The Indians began their season on the road at Louise, where they had narrowly won the previous year by just one point, 21-20. This time, however, the outcome was drastically different. A much-improved Ganado team dominated from start to finish, delivering a decisive 71-6 victory. Freshman quarterback Kyle Bures-Guerrero played with remarkable poise, passing for 126 yards and two touchdowns - one each to Gavin Sanchez and Erik Alvarez - while also leading the team in rushing with 187 yards and two touchdowns. Senior running back Ethan Guerra added three touchdowns in the first half, helping the Indians to a commanding 20-0 lead in the second quarter and finishing the game with 149 rushing yards. The defense was equally dominant, forcing six turnovers - five fumble recoveries and an interception - and capped the scoring when Manuel Calderon returned a blocked punt for a touchdown. Following their dominant season opener, the Indians returned home for a three-game homestand, beginning with Brazos, who sought revenge for last year's 49-27 defeat. Instead, Ganado delivered another lopsided performance, winning 49-6. The Indians led 28-0 at halftime and controlled the game throughout. Bures-Guerrero once again led the offense, throwing for 199 yards and a touchdown to Riley Hurt, while rushing for 114 yards and three more scores. Guerra contributed 80 rushing yards and three touchdowns of his own, showcasing the team's balanced and explosive offense. With a 2-0 record, Ganado faced their toughest test so far in unbeaten Odem. The first half was a defensive battle, ending in a 0-0 tie after Ganado squandered two scoring opportunities due to turnovers, including one inside the red zone. However, the Indians came out energized in the second half. A strong kickoff return by Luke Prove set up a quick strike, as Bures-Guerrero connected with Hurt for a 38-yard touchdown. The defense held Odem again, and the offense capitalized with a crucial fourth-down conversion that led to a 40-yard field goal by Giovanny Avalos, extending the lead to 10-0. Guerra added a short rushing touchdown, and Bures-Guerrero later found Sanchez for a 77-yard touchdown to make it 23-0. Odem's final drive was halted by a fumble recovered by the Indians, who then ran out the clock to secure their first shutout of the season and improve to 3-0. Bures-Guerrero finished the Odem game with 190 passing yards and 46 rushing yards. Guerra led the ground game with 52 yards, while Sanchez led all receivers with 94 yards on four catches, followed by Hurt with 70 yards on four receptions. Through three games, the Indians had shown remarkable improvement, playing as a cohesive unit and proving that their offseason dedication was paying off as they established themselves as a team to watch.

In their final non-district game, the Indians faced a tough challenge in the undefeated 3-0 Palacios Sharks, a team performing at a high level similar to Ganado. The matchup featured a compelling showdown between two standout freshman quarterbacks - Ganado's Kyle Bures-Guerrero and Palacios' Anthony White - both making impressive varsity debuts. Adding to the stakes, this game also marked Ganado's homecoming, with memories still fresh from their narrow 14-12 win over Palacios the previous year on the Sharks' homecoming night. This time, Palacios hoped to return the favor and spoil the celebration in Ganado. The Indians struck first in the opening quarter with a 38-yard field goal by Avalos. However, the second quarter proved disastrous for Ganado as Palacios capitalized on three interceptions thrown by Bures-Guerrero, converting them into two touchdowns and taking a 14-3 lead into halftime. Despite the setback, the Indians came out determined in the second half. On the opening drive of the third quarter, Bures-Guerrero connected with Olvera for a 24-yard touchdown, but a failed two-point conversion left them trailing 14-9. Palacios answered with a 10-yard touchdown run by Gary Haynes, who rushed for 142 yards in the game, pushing their lead to 21-9. Still undeterred, Ganado responded with a seven-yard touchdown run from Bures-Guerrero, but again failed on the two-point attempt, narrowing the gap to 21-15 by the end of the third quarter. The Indians defense delivered in the fourth quarter with a key stop, giving the offense another chance. With just over a minute remaining, Bures-Guerrero scored on a one-yard run to tie the game 21-21, but Avalos missed the extra point, sending the game into overtime. In the first overtime, Bures-Guerrero found Olvera for a 23-yard touchdown, and Avalos converted the extra point to give Ganado a 28-21 lead. Palacios quickly answered as Haynes scored again and tied the game at 28-28, forcing a second overtime. Palacios took the lead in the second extra period when White threw a three-yard touchdown pass to Camron Polk and added the extra point to go up 35-28. Facing a must-score situation, Ganado rose to the occasion as Bures-Guerrero again connected with Olvera, this time on a 20-yard touchdown pass. However, the Indians' extra point attempt was blocked, and Palacios held on for a thrilling 35-34 double-overtime win - its first victory over Ganado since 1985. Despite the heartbreaking loss, the game was a standout performance for both quarterbacks. White threw for 213 yards and two touchdowns while rushing for another 45 yards and a score. Polk led Palacios in receiving with 85 yards on five catches. Bures-Guerrero had his best passing performance of the season with 240 yards and three touchdown passes, though his three interceptions in the second quarter proved costly. Olvera was a consistent playmaker, leading Ganado with 89 receiving yards on seven catches. Though Ganado dropped to 3-1, the team showed remarkable resilience and determination, never giving up despite multiple setbacks. This hard-fought game, filled with adversity and lessons, served as a valuable builder heading into the bye week. The Indians emerged more prepared and battle-tested as they looked ahead to the start of district play and a determined push for the playoffs.

Ganado opened district play on the road against Bloomington and faced an early setback when Bures-Guerrero threw an errant pass that was intercepted and returned 20 yards for a touchdown, giving Bloomington an early 6-0 lead. However, that would be the last time Bloomington scored, as the rest of the game was completely controlled by the Indians. Ganado responded with 64 unanswered points, dominating in every phase of the game to secure a commanding 64-6 victory. By halftime, the Indians had built a 50-6 lead and never looked back. Bures-Guerrero rushed for three touchdowns, while Guerra led all rushers with 107 yards and added three rushing scores of his own. The Indians carried their momentum into the following week at home against Danbury, playing on a cold and blustery night after a strong fall front rolled in that morning. Despite the weather, Ganado continued to dominate. Bures-Guerrero surpassed 100 yards in both passing and rushing, finishing with 140 yards in each category. He threw for two touchdowns and added three more on the ground, including a highlight-reel 67-yard run. The defense remained stout, contributing two safeties in another lopsided win as Ganado rolled to a 58-6 victory. With the two dominant wins, Ganado began district play at 2-0 - the same position they were in at this point last season. However, with tougher opponents on the horizon, the Indians knew the real tests were still to come. Confident and prepared, they were ready to meet those challenges head-on.

In a much-anticipated district showdown, the Indians traveled to face undefeated East Bernard, a perennial powerhouse and the team widely viewed as the one to beat in the race for the district title. Fully prepared and confident, the Indians entered the game determined to challenge East Bernard and knew that the outcome would ultimately come down to execution on both sides of the ball. Ganado's defense set the tone early, forcing a three-and-out on East Bernard's opening possession. On the ensuing punt, Colton Teague blocked the kick and Ryan Williams recovered, giving the Indians excellent field position. However, the offense was unable to convert and missed a field goal attempt. The defense came up big again on East Bernard's next drive, with Noah Thedford intercepting a pass and once again setting up Ganado in favorable territory. Despite these opportunities, the offense could not find the end zone, and the first quarter ended in a scoreless 0-0 tie. The defensive battle continued into the second quarter, but East Bernard eventually broke through with a touchdown. Just before halftime, a long punt return set up another score, giving East Bernard a 13-0 lead at the break. Ganado responded to start the second half, as Bures-Guerrero connected with Hurt for a touchdown, narrowing the gap to 13-7. East Bernard answered with a third-quarter score to extend the lead to 20-7. In the fourth quarter, Bures-Guerrero again found Hurt in the end zone, capping a strong receiving night for Hurt, who finished with 99 yards on seven receptions. The Indians cut the deficit to 20-14, but East Bernard sealed the game with another touchdown to make the final score 27-14. The matchup was physical from start to finish, with the Indians' defense playing exceptionally well against East Bernard's challenging slot-T offense. Ultimately, the missed scoring opportunities in the first quarter - particularly failing to capitalize on two early turnovers - proved to be the difference. Despite the loss, Ganado proved they could compete with one of the top teams in the region, and the possibility of a playoff rematch remained in the back of their minds. The game served as a valuable learning experience and showed that the Indians were capable of playing at a high level against elite competition.

With their playoff hopes on the line, the Indians returned home for a critical district matchup against Van Vleck, knowing that a victory would clinch a postseason berth and end a five-year playoff drought. Van Vleck entered the game winless in district play at 0-4, and Ganado came out with intensity and purpose, eager to make a statement after last year's lopsided 70-0 loss to the same team. The Indians opened the game with a missed field goal on their first possession but quickly regrouped. After regaining possession, Bures-Guerrero connected with Guerra for a 13-yard touchdown pass, a drive set up by a key 31-yard reception by Teague. That score gave Ganado a 7-0 lead, which they extended in the second quarter when Bures-Guerrero scored on a seven-yard touchdown run, putting the Indians up 14-0. Just before halftime, Van Vleck threatened to score with a deep pass that placed them at the Ganado one-yard line. However, the Indians' defense delivered a game-defining goal-line stand. Van Vleck was stuffed on first down, then pushed back by a 15-yard penalty, and after two incomplete passes, turned the ball over on downs. Ganado carried its 14-0 lead into the locker room with momentum and confidence. In the second half, the Indians took complete control. Bures-Guerrero threw touchdown passes to Teague and Cameron Bates in the third quarter and added another rushing touchdown in the fourth to make it 35-0. Van Vleck managed to score late in the game, but it was far too late to change the outcome. The Indians secured a dominant 35-8 victory. Bures-Guerrero had a stellar performance, throwing for 126 yards and three touchdowns while also leading the team in rushing with 147 yards and two rushing touchdowns. This win was especially meaningful, not only avenging last year's devastating defeat but also eliminating Van Vleck from playoff contention and securing Ganado's first playoff appearance since 2013. With the victory, Ganado improved to 6-2 overall and 3-1 in district play. Though East Bernard had already secured the district title, the Indians still had two important games remaining against playoff-bound teams Tidehaven and Schulenburg, which would determine final district seeding. After the game, Coach Bennett praised the team's all-around effort and resilience, emphasizing how far they had come. With their playoff berth secured, Ganado now had their sights set on closing out the season strong.

On the evening of October 29, tragedy struck the Ganado community with the heartbreaking loss of 12-year-old LaMarquis Lee, a sixth-grade student who was killed in an automobile accident near his home while returning from youth football practice. The accident occurred just days before his team's bantam league Super Bowl, leaving the entire school and town in mourning. In a touching tribute, the Ganado student body wore orange - LaMarquis' favorite color - on the Friday of that week to honor his memory. That morning's pep rally was deeply emotional, as the school came together to remember a beloved classmate. LaMarquis' bantam league team honored him by wearing his number, 89, on their uniforms during their Super Bowl game against Tidehaven. Though Tidehaven won the game 26-6, they showed incredible sportsmanship by naming LaMarquis the game's MVP and presenting an engraved trophy to his team, who then gave it to LaMarquis' family. Funeral services were held the following Monday at the football stadium, with teachers and classmates remembering him fondly. LaMarquis was a well-liked, respected student, and his presence remained with the team throughout the rest of the season - he was never forgotten. That same Friday night, the varsity Indians played a critical district game against Tidehaven, but the emotional toll of the week weighed heavily on the team. Without key defensive lineman Colton Teague, who was sidelined due to injury, Ganado struggled to contain Tidehaven's rushing attack and fell 45-28. Though the Indians fought hard, the adversity and emotional strain proved too much to overcome.

In the regular season finale, Ganado returned home to face Schulenburg in a game that would determine playoff seeding. A win would give the Indians the third seed; a loss would drop them to fourth. Both teams traded touchdowns in a competitive, high-scoring contest. After the score was tied 28-28 late in the third quarter, Schulenburg took its first lead of the game on a field goal to go up 31-28. However, the fourth quarter belonged entirely to Ganado. Facing a crucial fourth-and-one, Bures-Guerrero broke free for a 39-yard touchdown run, putting Ganado ahead 35-31. The Indians' defense then stepped up with a key fumble recovery, and the offense capitalized, scoring two more touchdowns to pull away for a 49-31 victory and clinch the third seed heading into the playoffs. Bures-Guerrero had another outstanding performance, passing for 148 yards and a touchdown to Hurt, who totaled 105 receiving yards on three catches. Bures-Guerrero also led the ground attack with 91 rushing yards and four touchdowns. Guerra added 89 yards and two scores of his own. With this emotional and hard-fought win, the Indians closed the regular season with resilience and renewed focus, ready to carry their momentum - and the spirit of LaMarquis Lee - with them into the playoffs.

The Indians began their playoff journey in the bi-district round with a matchup against Brady on a cold night in Manor - a perfect setting for Texas high school playoff football. Brady struck first, taking an early

7-0 lead, but the Indians responded immediately as Hurt electrified the crowd with a 72-yard kickoff return for a touchdown to tie the game at 7-7. Ganado continued its offensive momentum with rushing touchdowns by Bures-Guerrero and Guerra, ending the first quarter with a commanding 21-7 lead. In the second quarter, however, the Indians missed two key scoring opportunities - one drive ended with an interception, and another stalled on a failed fourth-down conversion. Brady capitalized late in the half, connecting on a 55-yard touchdown pass with just over a minute remaining, cutting Ganado's lead to 21-13 at halftime and keeping the game within reach. The second half was all Ganado. The Indians exploded for 21 unanswered points in the third quarter. Guerra started the surge with a five-yard touchdown run, followed by two more scores from Bures-Guerrero on runs of 18 and 6 yards, giving the Indians a commanding 42-13 lead heading into the fourth quarter. Brady managed to add two touchdowns in the final period to close the gap to 42-25, but Bures-Guerrero sealed the victory with a 50-yard touchdown run, making the final score 49-25 and sending Ganado into the Area round of the playoffs. Ganado dominated on the ground, rushing for a staggering 443 yards. Bures-Guerrero delivered a career-best performance, rushing for 278 yards on 29 carries and scoring three touchdowns - his highest rushing total of his high school career. Guerra also contributed significantly, rushing for 165 yards and adding two touchdowns. With the impressive win, the Indians advanced confidently in the playoffs, showcasing a powerful ground game and resilient team effort.

In the Area round of the playoffs, the Ganado Indians faced Corpus Christi London in La Vernia, and the game began in rough fashion for the Indians. On their very first offensive play, Bures-Guerrero was intercepted. Though the defense held strong to prevent a score, disaster struck again just two plays into the next drive when Bures-Guerrero threw another interception - this time returned for a touchdown by London, giving them an early 7-0 lead. Ganado responded in the second quarter with a field goal from Avalos to cut the deficit to 7-3. Then, just before halftime, on a crucial fourth-and-20, Bures-Guerrero found Hurt for a 28-yard touchdown pass. Although the extra point was missed, the Indians took a narrow 9-7 lead into the locker room. London regained the lead in the third quarter with a field goal to make it 10-9, and for much of the second half, the game remained a defensive battle. Then came a dramatic final two minutes. With just 1:35

remaining in the game, Guerra punched in a six-yard touchdown to give the Indians a 15-10 lead in what looked to be the game-winning score. However, on the ensuing kickoff, London's Donyae Castaneda returned it 80 yards for a touchdown, swinging the momentum back and giving London a 16-15 lead. Ganado, now with just 1:28 on the clock, mounted what would become a season-saving drive. The Indians orchestrated a determined 10-play, 74-yard march down the field. With first-and-goal and only seconds remaining, Bures-Guerrero called his own number and powered into the end zone from one yard out, scoring with just 8 seconds left to deliver a thrilling 23-16 victory. Despite the early mistakes, Bures-Guerrero showed incredible resilience and poise for a freshman. He passed for 180 yards, including the pivotal touchdown to Hurt just before halftime. Hurt finished with 64 receiving yards on three catches, Olvera added 59 yards on four receptions, and Bates contributed 38 yards on four receptions - all playing key roles in the clutch drives. This victory was a true testament to teamwork and perseverance. The Indians overcame adversity, stayed composed under pressure, and played as a united team to earn their spot in the next round of the playoffs. At this point in the season, Ganado was clicking on all cylinders and proving they had what it took to compete deep into the postseason.

On Thanksgiving weekend, the Ganado Indians faced their biggest playoff challenge yet, taking on a strong Poth team in the regional semifinals. Poth entered the matchup riding an 11-game winning streak and had just defeated Tidehaven 23-7. They had a very good defense that allowed only nine points per game, Poth was widely expected to win. But the Indians, fueled by belief in themselves and a resilient spirit, were ready to prove everyone wrong. The game took place on Black Friday at 2:00 p.m. at Gobbler Stadium in Cuero under damp, foggy, and dreary weather conditions. The opening quarter was a defensive battle as both teams tested each other. Ganado struck first when Bures-Guerrero connected with Hurt for a 25-yard touchdown pass on third-and-12, giving the Indians a 7-0 lead. Ganado's defense remained strong, even blocking a punt in the second quarter to set up a first-and-goal at the Poth two-yard line. However, Poth's defense held, and Ganado missed the ensuing field goal. The halftime score remained 7-0 in favor of the Indians. Poth came out strong in the second half, tying the game 7-7 with a touchdown on their opening drive. Things appeared to shift in their favor when they intercepted Bures-Guerrero on Ganado's first possession of the half and quickly turned it into a 23-yard touchdown pass to take a 14-7 lead. Though two big kickoff returns by Bates were called back due to penalties, the Indians stayed composed. Bures-Guerrero broke off a crucial 47-yard run and later scored from seven yards out to tie the game at 14-14 by the end of the third quarter. With momentum swinging back to Ganado, Bures-Guerrero scored again in the fourth quarter to put the Indians ahead 21-14. The defense then tightened up, shutting down Poth's offense. On the next offensive series, Bures-Guerrero found Hurt at the Poth 39-yard line, and Hurt weaved through defenders for an electrifying 63-yard touchdown, extending Ganado's lead to 28-14. Poth had one last chance to rally, but their drive ended with a clutch interception by Olvera, sealing the game. The Indians' 28-14 victory stunned many outside of Ganado but affirmed what the team and coaches always believed - they could compete with and beat anyone. This was a game dominated by Ganado outside of a brief third-quarter setback. Bures-Guerrero had an outstanding performance, throwing for 183 yards and two touchdowns and rushing for 121 yards and two more scores. Hurt also shined, recording 128 receiving yards on seven catches and scoring twice. From a 4-6 record the previous season to now advancing to the fourth round of the playoffs and being among the final eight teams in the state, this win was a testament to the players' hard work, belief, and the guidance of an exceptional coaching staff. Ganado was not just surviving the playoffs - they were thriving.

East Bernard was the next opponent for Ganado in the quarterfinals. They had previously defeated Ganado 27-14 on October 18 and were the district champions, making them a formidable challenge once again. As expected, Ganado entered the game as the underdogs, but Coach Bennett assured that the team would be prepared and ready to compete. The game was played at Freedom Field in Alvin, a new stadium opened just the year before in 2018, which hosts Manvel High School and the new Alvin ISD schools, Shadow Creek and Iowa Colony. The impressive venue impressed both the team and fans as they arrived. Ganado entered the game with confidence, remembering their solid performance against East Bernard in the district matchup and knowing they were just two wins away from reaching the state championship. However, from the opening kickoff, things did not go well. The ball was touched and rolled into the end zone, where Bates recovered it but was tackled at the three-yard line. After a quick three-and-out and only one net yard gained, the subsequent punt snap went over the punter's head into the back of the end zone, resulting in a safety and giving East Bernard an early 2-0 lead. Following the safety kick, East Bernard quickly capitalized, scoring on a 55-yard play on only their second snap. They then extended their lead with a 30-yard touchdown run, jumping out to a commanding 16-0 lead in the first quarter. Ganado eventually settled down and mounted a promising drive that reached the red zone, highlighted by a 31-yard pass from Bures-Guerrero to Olvera. Although the drive stalled, Avalos successfully kicked a 27-yard field goal, bringing the score to 16-3. East Bernard responded with a long, time-consuming drive that carried into the second quarter and ended with another touchdown, extending their lead to 23-3. Ganado then made a big play on special teams when Ryan Williams blocked an East Bernard punt, recovering the ball at the four-yard line. From there, Bures-Guerrero scored a touchdown, narrowing the gap to 23-10. However, East Bernard answered quickly with a 70-yard touchdown run, increasing their lead to 30-10 by halftime. Neither team scored in the second half. Despite three scoring opportunities in the second half, Ganado was unable to convert. The Indians advanced the ball to the East Bernard four-yard line and the 14-yard line, but one attempt ended in a turnover on downs and another with an interception. The second half began with a promising drive that also ended with an interception. With 3:27 left on the clock, East Bernard intercepted Bures-Guerrero for the third time and then used the ensuing possession to gain enough first downs to run out the clock, officially ending Ganado's remarkable season. While the Indians fought hard, East Bernard's early dominance and timely plays proved too much to overcome. Despite the loss, Ganado's playoff run was a testament to their resilience and growth throughout the season.

Ganado finished the season with an impressive 10-4 record, exceeding many expectations. Entering the year, the team was predicted to finish fifth in their district and not make the playoffs. However, they defied those predictions by defeating several teams they were not expected to beat. Throughout the season, the team worked hard, played with great effort until the final whistle, and never gave up. Despite facing adversity late in the season, they refused to back down and continued pushing forward. For the seniors, this season was remarkable and memorable, especially considering many had endured a difficult 2-7 season as sophomores two years earlier. The team showed tremendous growth, improving significantly from a 4-6 record the previous year to becoming a quarterfinalist team that advanced four rounds in the playoffs. The entire coaching staff did an excellent job preparing the players each week. Coach Bennett spoke about leaving a legacy, and that is exactly what this senior class accomplished. The team functioned as one big family, embodying the spirit of small-town football and demonstrating how the community of Ganado came together to support their team. Freshman quarterback Kyle Bures-Guerrero had an outstanding season, setting a bright path for his future. He was named the district's newcomer of the year after passing for 2,175 yards and 22 touchdowns, which was a single-season school record at the time. Additionally, he rushed for 1,483 yards and 25 touchdowns. Looking ahead, Ganado was expected to move back to Class 2A Division 1 the following year, with a promising future on the horizon. This season marked the beginning of a playoff run that continues to this day, with even greater achievements anticipated for the program.

2020

On February 3, as expected, Ganado moved down one classification from Class 3A, Division II, to Class 2A, Division I. However, the Indians were placed in a very challenging district. They reunited with their longtime rivals Shiner, who entered the 2020 season preseason ranked number one in the state and had narrowly lost to Refugio - last year's state champions - in the final seconds of the regional playoffs. Schulenburg also joined Ganado in the district after dropping from 3A. The district was rounded out by former rivals Flatonia and Weimar, both of whom had impressive records last season, finishing 11-2 and 10-2 respectively. Every school in the new District 13-2A, Division I had qualified for the playoffs the previous year. This district closely resembled the one Ganado competed in during the 2014 and 2015 seasons, with the exception of Refugio, and the Indians were prepared and eager for the challenge ahead.

In the second week of March, the world came to a sudden halt as the COVID-19 pandemic emerged, with no known cure at the time. The Houston Livestock Show and Rodeo was abruptly shut down midway through its annual event, and people were sent home. Schools closed nationwide, and many workers began working from home, with meetings and classes moving online via platforms like Zoom. Wearing masks became mandatory in public, popularizing the phrase "mask up." High school sports were also impacted, as the University Interscholastic League (UIL) halted all athletics that same week, interrupting the boys' basketball state tournament in San Antonio. Spring sports including golf, tennis, track and field, baseball, and softball were canceled mid-season, devastating many senior athletes who could not finish their final seasons. Uncertainty surrounded the 2020 football season until UIL approved its return in July. Class 4A and below began two-a-day workouts on August 3 and started games on the weekend of August 27-29, while Classes 5A and 6A began their seasons later, on September 24-25. If all went well, Classes 1A through 4A would crown state champions between December 16-19 at AT&T Stadium, with 5A and 6A champions decided in mid-January. Due to ongoing uncertainties, many schools, including Ganado, had to adjust their schedules. Ganado dropped non-district games against Palacios, East Bernard, and Refugio, replacing them with a game against Burton. The district schedule was also rearranged to include two bye weeks mid-season, reserved as potential makeup dates for any games postponed due to positive COVID-19 tests.

Ganado began the season ranked No. 8 in Class 2A Division I, following a successful campaign in 3A where they advanced to the quarterfinals. There was much promise, especially with sophomore Kyle Bures-Guerrero, who was one of eleven returning players. Other key contributors included senior Larson Workman, a Kansas commit, who would later transfer to Texas State, playing offensive tackle, and junior receiver Riley Hurt, who had 810 receiving yards and 10 touchdowns the previous year. After graduating three key receivers from the prior season, seniors Noah Thedford and Erik Alvarez, along with junior Logan Riojas, stepped up to fill those roles. On the offensive line, senior Julian Martinez returned to play tackle alongside Larson, while senior Jose Briones and junior Javier Rodriguez took the guard positions, and sophomore Michael Bubela played center. Defensively, the line featured experienced players such as Larson at tackle, with junior Dylan Alvarez and Riojas returning at end, and Rodriguez filling the other tackle spot. The linebacker group was young, replacing three graduated seniors with Thedford and juniors Nick Fitzgerald and Corbin Teague stepping in. In the secondary, junior Manny Calderon returned at cornerback alongside Hurt, while the safety positions were held by Erik Alvarez and Bures-Guerrero. Junior Giovanny Avalos returned as kicker for his third consecutive year. Despite the challenges occurring globally at the time, the team felt blessed to be able to return to practice. They worked hard through their workouts and responded well, showing great dedication and resilience.

The Indians opened their season against their Jackson County rival, Industrial, in Vanderbilt. This was the first time the two teams had faced each other since 2015, with Ganado having won the last six meetings. The last time Industrial defeated Ganado was in 2009, although the schools had met in scrimmages over the past two years. Industrial entered the game with a highly touted team after advancing to the regional playoffs last season. Despite the challenges posed by Covid-19, it finally felt real and good for the Indians to play football again, even with stadium attendance limited and ticket purchases moving online. Industrial set the tone immediately, as Matthew Davis scored on the opening play with a 69-yard touchdown run. Industrial missed the extra point, giving them an early 6-0 lead, which held until just before halftime when Davis scored again on a quarterback sneak with nine seconds left, extending the lead to 12-0. Both teams had scoring opportunities in the first half, with Ganado missing a key chance when a receiver dropped a pass in the end zone. In the second half, the Indians responded quickly as Kyle Bures-Guerrero scored on a seven-yard run, and Giovanny Avalos added the extra point to bring the score to 12-7. A 55-yard connection from Bures-Guerrero to Riley Hurt helped set up the score. However, Industrial took control from there, with Davis scoring two more touchdowns in the third quarter and throwing for another in the fourth. The game ended with a pick-six by Phenix Lopez, who intercepted a Bures-Guerrero pass and returned it 50 yards, sealing a 40-7 victory for Industrial. Davis had an impressive game with 165 rushing yards and four touchdowns. Despite the score, Ganado actually led in first downs 14 to 9 and played hard, with the team looking to grow from this opening game experience.

The Indians returned home the following week for their home opener against former district rival Tidehaven. Ganado started strong, scoring on their opening possession when Bures-Guerrero ran in a 23-yard touchdown, giving the Indians a 7-0 lead. Tidehaven fumbled the kickoff, giving Ganado another chance to score, but the defense held, and Ganado missed a 35-yard field goal. Tidehaven responded in the second quarter, with quarterback Logan Crow scoring on a four-yard run, and later connecting with Austin Smith on a 32-yard touchdown pass to take a 14-7 halftime lead. The third quarter was a defensive battle, but Noah Thedford scored on a blocked punt recovery in the end zone to tie the game 14-14. Tidehaven regained the lead with a three-yard touchdown run by Crow, though the extra point was missed, making the score 20-14. In the fourth quarter, Bures-Guerrero scored to give Ganado a one-point lead at 21-20 with under four minutes left. Tidehaven then drove down the field, and Crow threw a 36-yard pass to Kylan Sardinea, setting up Crow's game-winning three-yard touchdown run with 1:22 remaining. Ganado fell to 0-2 but left everything on the field and played hard until the final whistle. Next, Ganado hosted Hallettsville, which featured the highly regarded University of Texas commit running back Jonathan Brooks. Despite being limited by injuries, the Indians fought bravely. After falling behind 14-0 in the first quarter, Ganado got on the board with Bures-Guerrero's first touchdown pass of the season - a connection to Logan Riojas - closing the gap to 14-7. Bures-Guerrero passed for 127 yards in the game, but Hallettsville pulled away, scoring three more times in the second quarter to lead 35-7 at halftime. Hallettsville added two more touchdowns in the second half, winning 49-7. Jonathan Brooks finished with 145 yards and four touchdowns. Hallettsville went on to compete for the Class 3A Division I state title in December but lost to Jim Ned 29-28 in overtime. Despite starting the season 0-3 with two lopsided losses, the team's record did not define them. The Indians played hard and remained determined, continuing to work hard to improve amid the challenges they faced.

Due to schedule changes caused by Covid, the Indians began their district play in Weimar the following week, eager to secure their first win of the season. Bures-Guerrero set the tone early in the game by taking the snap on the first play of the team's second possession and rushing 94 yards for a touchdown, giving the Indians a 6-0 lead that they maintained throughout the game. On Weimar's next possession, Nick Fitzgerald intercepted the ball, leading to another Indian touchdown by Corbin Teague and extending the lead to 12-0. Although Weimar scored their only touchdown and a successful two-point conversion at the start of the second quarter to make it 12-8, Ganado responded strongly by scoring 20 more points before halftime, taking a 32-8 lead. The Indians added two more touchdowns in the second half to dominate Weimar 44-8 and secure their first win of the season, starting district play at 1-0. Bures-Guerrero had his best game of the season, rushing for 114 yards including the big touchdown run, and passing for 272 yards and five touchdowns to receivers Josiah Sterling, Hurt - who each caught two touchdowns - and Thedford. Following this win, the Indians hosted Burton in a non-district game the next week. This Burton team was not the strong playoff contender of past years and had declined somewhat this season. This game was also the first meeting between the teams since 2008 and 2009 when Burton was in the same district as Ganado. Ganado dominated from the start, winning decisively 65-7, with both offense and defense performing strongly. This win demonstrated the team was reaching the competitive level they aimed for. At the end of September, Ganado held a 2-3 record and was heading into a bye week. Coach Bennett emphasized that early season games in August and September do not define a team's legacy; instead, teams are remembered for their performances in November and December during the playoffs. The team's goal was to extend their season into those months. With only three district games remaining on the schedule - along with another bye week - the Indians prepared to finish the regular season strong before entering the playoffs.

The Indians hosted Schulenburg after coming off a bye week, and the game was a hard-fought battle that lasted until the very end. Ganado scored first when Bures-Guerrero ran for a 9-yard touchdown, followed by Avalos' successful extra point, giving the Indians a 7-0 lead with 4:17 remaining in the first quarter. A key play on that drive was a 31-yard pass from Bures-Guerrero to Hurt. Schulenburg responded by tying the game at 7-7 with 11:22 left in the first half. The score remained tied after three quarters, as both teams battled back and forth without scoring again until the dramatic fourth quarter. Early in the final quarter, Schulenburg attempted a 44-yard field goal, which was blocked and returned for a touchdown by Hurt. Avalos' extra point was good, putting Ganado back on top 14-7 less than a minute into the quarter. After forcing Schulenburg to punt on the next defensive stop, the Indians extended their lead with a 24-yard touchdown run by Bures-Guerrero. Avalos again converted the kick, making the score 21-7 with 8:12 left in the game. Schulenburg quickly responded with a touchdown, cutting the lead to 21-14, then recovered an onside kick and scored again to tie the game at 21-21 with 4:50 remaining. Schulenburg attempted their own onside kick, but Fitzgerald recovered it for Ganado, giving the Indians possession at Schulenburg's 45-yard line and a chance to score the winning points. Bures-Guerrero connected on a long pass to Hurt, setting up a first-and-goal, and then scored on a 4-yard run with 2:09 left, putting Ganado ahead 28-21. The Indians' defense held strong on Schulenburg's final possession, and Ganado ran out the clock to secure a 28-21 victory, improving their district record to 2-0. Bures-Guerrero had an impressive performance, rushing for 127 yards and scoring all of Ganado's offensive touchdowns. Though he passed for only 99 yards, his key completions to Hurt, who had 67 yards on three receptions, and Riojas, who contributed 32 yards on three catches, were crucial.

Next, the Indians faced their toughest opponent of the year on the road against the #1 ranked Shiner Comanches, which was a well-rounded squad led by the Brooks brothers, Dalton and Doug. Dalton Brooks returned the opening kickoff 90 yards for a touchdown, setting the tone early. He also caught a 68-yard touchdown pass, ran for a 32-yard touchdown, and intercepted a pass that led to a Zane Rhodes 58-yard touchdown. Shiner amassed 555 yards of total offense, with Dalton Brooks rushing for 100 yards, Doug Brooks gaining 176 yards and scoring three touchdowns, and Rhodes rushing for 131 yards. Shiner's offensive and defensive lines controlled the line of scrimmage, dominating Ganado, which managed to enter Shiner territory only twice and totaled just 120 yards of offense. Ganado did not achieve a rushing first down until 3:35 remained in the game and had a net rushing total of minus 26 yards before their final possession. Shiner convincingly won the game 57-0, taking sole possession of the district lead and securing the top seed going into the playoffs. Shiner would go on to win the district championship and capture the Class 2A Division I state title over Post, finishing the season with a perfect 14-0 record and marking the third state title in their school's history at that time.

Ganado, holding a 2-1 district record and 3-4 overall, used their next bye week to regroup and prepare for their game against Flatonia, with an opportunity to secure the second seed going into the playoffs. The Indians returned home for the final regular-season game against Flatonia, already having clinched a playoff berth, but the outcome of this game would determine second place and the district runner-up spot. The game started with strong defensive efforts from both teams, resulting in a scoreless first quarter. In the second quarter, Flatonia recovered a Ganado fumble at the 12-yard line, but Ganado's defense held firm when Riojas sacked the quarterback, forcing a fourth-and-20. Flatonia ultimately settled for a field goal, taking a 3-0 lead, which remained the score at halftime. In the second half, as both teams exchanged possessions, the momentum shifted when Erik Alvarez intercepted a pass and returned it to Flatonia's 9-yard line. Bures-Guerrero capitalized on the opportunity by scoring a touchdown, and Avalos' extra point put Ganado ahead 7-3 as the third quarter ended. Early in the fourth quarter, Bures-Guerrero connected with Riojas for a 5-yard touchdown pass, extending the Indians' lead to 14-3. Riojas then recovered a Flatonia fumble at the 27-yard line, setting up Bures-Guerrero to score again on the very next play, pushing the lead to 21-3. Teague added the final touchdown for Ganado, increasing the lead to 28-3. Flatonia scored a late touchdown against a prevent defense with just 15 seconds remaining, but Ganado held on to win 28-10, securing the district's second seed going into the playoffs. This victory was a complete team effort, showcasing composure during a tightly contested three quarters before pulling away. The Indians were confident and ready to make a strong playoff run.

The Indians opened the playoffs against Johnson City in the bi-district round at Bastrop Memorial Stadium on a Thursday night. This was the first-ever meeting between Ganado and Johnson City, with Ganado entering the game at 4-4 and Johnson City holding a 4-6 record. Ganado struck quickly, scoring just 15 seconds into the game, and the scoring frenzy continued throughout. Although Johnson City managed to cut the lead to 14-7 early on, that would be the closest they got for the rest of the game. Bures-Guerrero responded immediately with a 28-yard touchdown run, and Ganado followed with three more touchdowns to take a commanding 42-7 lead by halftime. The Indians came out strong in the second half, scoring two more touchdowns early to extend their lead to 55-7. Johnson City scored once more at the end of the third quarter, making the score 55-14, which remained the final score as Ganado controlled the clock in the fourth quarter and advanced to the next round. Johnson City's Cade Boyer led their offense with 203 passing yards and two touchdowns, but Ganado's Bures-Guerrero shined by rushing for 106 yards with two touchdowns and passing for 199 yards and three touchdowns. Thedford was Ganado's top receiver, catching three passes for 117 yards and a touchdown.

Next, the Indians faced Three Rivers in the Area round at Victoria's Memorial Stadium, again on a Thursday night. This was the first meeting between the two teams since Three Rivers was last in Ganado's district in 2013. Ganado dominated the game, winning 55-0. Three Rivers turned the ball over five times, and Ganado capitalized on each turnover by scoring a touchdown. Three Rivers' first four drives all resulted in turnovers, allowing Ganado to jump out to a 48-0 halftime lead. Larson Workman led the defensive front with two fumble recoveries, while Dylan Alvarez had another. One of those fumble recoveries was a 30-yard scoop-and-score by Thedford, who also recorded an interception, helping Ganado take a 21-0 lead early on. In the second half, Ganado focused on maintaining possession and running out the clock, with Teague rushing for 95 yards and scoring a touchdown. Bures-Guerrero capped the scoring with his fifth rushing touchdown of the night in the fourth quarter. He finished with 163 yards rushing and passed for 136 yards and a touchdown. Coach Bennett expressed great pride in the team's performance, calling it the most complete game they had played all year and suggested it might be as close to a "complete game" as one could ever play. He stated the team would go home to celebrate the win before preparing for the next challenge.

After dominating their first two playoff opponents and looking like the best team all season, the Indians faced a formidable challenge against Refugio. Originally scheduled to play Refugio in a non-district game, that matchup was canceled due to Covid-related schedule changes, making this their first playoff meeting since 2005, when Ganado narrowly won 7-6 in Port Lavaca. Historically, Ganado held a 3-1 playoff series lead over Refugio dating back to 1996. Refugio entered the game undefeated at 9-0 and ranked third in the state, as the defending Class 2A Division I state champions. The question was whether Ganado's playoff dominance would continue. The game took place at Victoria's Memorial Stadium, the same venue as the previous week, but this time Ganado was the visiting team. The game occurred the day after Thanksgiving, continuing a Ganado tradition of playing playoff football during the holiday. Unlike the previous week's dominant performance, this game proved much more challenging. The contest began with a 1 hour and 17-minute lightning delay, forcing fans to evacuate the stadium. When play resumed, the teams faced miserable weather conditions with constant rain and a cold front moving in.

Ganado started the game promisingly with a run by Bures-Guerrero, but the drive ended without points. Refugio quickly took control, dominating the game on the ground with 384 rushing yards, spread among nine different backs who all gained positive yardage. Eziyah Bland scored two rushing touchdowns on runs of 30 and 11 yards and returned the second-half kickoff 62 yards for another touchdown. Due to the weather, Refugio only attempted five passes, but Caleb Hesseltine connected with Jordan Kelly on a 56-yard flea-flicker touchdown. Refugio's defense also stifled Ganado's offense, preventing any touchdown scores. The Indians' only points came from a rare extra-point return by Josiah Sterling, making the score 18-2 early in the second quarter. Refugio added two more touchdowns before halftime, taking a 33-2 lead. A major setback for Ganado was losing quarterback Bures-Guerrero to a foot injury at the end of the first quarter, forcing junior Lane Benavides to take over for the remainder of the game. Ganado struggled offensively, gaining only 77 total yards on four first downs and committing three turnovers, including a 7-yard interception returned for a touchdown by Zavien Wills. Refugio cruised to a 54-2 victory and advanced to face Shiner in the quarterfinals. That much-anticipated game ended with Shiner winning 24-13 en route to claiming the state title, avenging a narrow loss to Refugio from the previous season.

The Indians' 2020 season came to an end with a final record of 6-5. Considering the many challenges throughout the year - including the Covid pandemic, a difficult 0-3 start, and early-season struggles - finishing second in the district and advancing three rounds deep into the playoffs was a job well done and marked another successful season for the team. The players showed dedication by coming to practice every day and giving their best effort in each game. Despite the obstacles, all state championship games at every level were played, making the football season a success under the circumstances. Although the seniors would be greatly missed, the team looked forward to having several talented players return to contribute toward another strong run in 2021. By early 2021, Covid vaccines became available to those who wished to be vaccinated. While the virus never completely disappeared, life gradually returned to normal over the following months and years. The 2021 season would feel more like the familiar, "normal" football season that everyone had been used to before the pandemic began.

2021

Throughout the offseason and as workouts began in August with the start of the new school year, things gradually returned to normal, resembling the pre-pandemic routine. This season, Ganado was able to play a full 10-game schedule, which had originally been planned for 2020 before the pandemic caused major disruptions. Coach Bennett was entering his fourth season leading the team, with a solid core of returning players ready to make another strong run. Lane Shands, who had joined the coaching staff the previous year, took over as defensive coordinator, a role previously held by assistant coach Luke Barganier over the past two seasons; Barganier remained on staff. Defending state champion Shiner, despite losing 22 seniors to graduation, still returned key players including the Brooks brothers and entered the season ranked #2. Another formidable opponent was region favorite and #1 ranked Refugio, who had eliminated Ganado from the playoffs the previous year; Ganado was set to face Refugio in their final non-district game. The non-district schedule also included tough matchups against Industrial, Hallettsville, and East Bernard, all ranked in the top 10 of their respective regions, providing Ganado with strong preparation for a challenging district and a hopeful deep playoff run.

Leading the Indians' offense was junior Kyle Bures-Guerrero, returning for his third year. In the previous season, he passed for 1,373 yards and 15 touchdowns while rushing for 908 yards and 17 touchdowns, making him a dual-threat capable of scoring whenever he had the ball. His top receiving target was senior Riley Hurt, returning for his fourth and final year, who had 605 receiving yards and six touchdowns the year before. Other returning receivers included senior Logan Riojas and senior Josiah Sterling, both bringing valuable experience, as well as juniors Clayton Webernick and Corbin Teague, the latter returning at running back. The offensive line was relatively young, featuring three sophomores starting: Vincent Barajas and Martin Ramirez at guard, and Logan Tupa at tackle. Senior Jose Ramos played the other tackle position, and junior Michael Bubela, the lone returning starter on the line, returned at center. Senior Giovanny Avalos also returned for his fourth and final year as the team's kicker. On defense, Riojas returned as an end on the line, having recorded 42 tackles and three sacks the previous season. He was joined by juniors Fabian Almeda at the other end and Adam Tristan and Bubela at tackle. Bures-Guerrero transitioned from safety to linebacker, while sophomore Dylan Holt and freshman Vince Sablatura filled the other linebacker roles. In the secondary, Hurt was the only returning player with experience at cornerback, paired with junior Jayden Gonzales at the other corner. Senior Lane Benavides and freshman Cain Hayden started at safety. Hayden, a promising athlete, also contributed as a key receiver on offense and was at the beginning of what would become an outstanding football career. The team was eager and excited to return to the field and see how the season would unfold.

Ganado opened the season hosting their Jackson County rival, Industrial, who was ranked #6 in the state. The Indians came out strong, eager to prove they could compete with the best. On the opening kickoff, Riley Hurt returned the ball from Ganado's 19-yard line to Industrial's 25-yard line, setting up excellent field position. On the very first play, Kyle Bures-Guerrero ran to the five-yard line, and two plays later, he scored, giving Ganado a quick 7-0 lead. Industrial then faced a penalty on their kickoff return near their own goal line, and the aggressive Ganado defense recovered a fumble. With less than two minutes left in the first quarter, Bures-Guerrero scored again, pushing Ganado's lead to 13-0 and putting the upset possibility in the air. Industrial's quarterback, Matthew Davis, helped cut the lead to 13-7 by converting a fourth-and-20 from the Ganado 28-yard line with a pass to Tate Karl and a touchdown run himself. Industrial scored again in the second quarter and succeeded on a two-point conversion to take their first lead of the game, 15-13. However, Ganado responded with a 13-yard touchdown pass from Bures-Guerrero to Hurt, reclaiming the lead at 20-15. Industrial quickly answered with a 74-yard touchdown run by Kaleb Figirova, going ahead 22-20 at halftime. Industrial opened the second half strong, with Davis connecting for a touchdown pass to Mason Roe, extending the lead to 29-20. After forcing a Ganado punt, Davis returned the punt 47 yards for a touchdown, increasing Industrial's lead to 36-20. Despite the deficit, Ganado showed resilience. Bures-Guerrero connected with Hurt on a 36-yard pass, setting up a four-yard touchdown run by Manny Calderon to narrow the gap to 36-26. The Ganado defense forced another punt, but a penalty on a defender gave Industrial a crucial first down. Two plays later, Clay Martin scored on a 44-yard touchdown run, pushing the lead to 43-26. Ganado answered once more with Bures-Guerrero finding Hurt again, making the score 43-32. Industrial controlled the remainder of the game, with Davis scoring a final 16-yard touchdown run to seal a 50-32 victory. Davis had a big night, rushing for 160 yards, while Bures-Guerrero carried Ganado with 177 yards rushing and two touchdowns, plus 70 passing yards and two touchdown passes to Hurt, who led in receiving with 72 yards on five receptions. Ganado played a competitive game against a higher-classification, state-ranked rival and longtime foe, improving greatly from the 40-7 loss to Industrial the previous year. Coach Bennett praised the team's performance, noting room for growth after mistakes in the first game.

The following week, Ganado traveled to El Maton to face Tidehaven. After trading punts early, Bures-Guerrero broke free for a 36-yard touchdown run on third-and-long, giving Ganado a 7-0 lead. He then connected with Logan Riojas on a 27-yard touchdown pass, extending the lead to 14-0 in the first quarter. However, Ganado suffered a setback as Hurt left the game with a gash on his chin requiring stitches and did not return. In the second quarter, Tidehaven mounted a seven-minute drive to Ganado's three-yard line, but penalties pushed them back, and a potential touchdown catch was dropped on fourth down. Tidehaven later intercepted a pass to halt Ganado's next drive. The half ended with Ganado leading 14-0. Tidehaven opened the second half with an onside kick recovery and scored on a three-yard run to cut the lead to 14-7. Ganado responded with a 27-yard touchdown run by Corbin Teague, making it 21-7. The third quarter saw Ganado intercept Tidehaven, but a missed field goal ended the drive. Tidehaven scored again in the fourth quarter, narrowing the gap to 21-14. Tidehaven then drove deep into Ganado territory late in the game, reaching the five-yard line with under three minutes remaining. However, Ganado's defense held firm on fourth-and-two. With 2:31 left, Bures-Guerrero connected with Ashton Strauss for a 76-yard gain, keeping hope alive. Ganado's field goal attempt was blocked, giving Tidehaven 54 seconds to score. Tidehaven gained 23 yards but ran out of time with no timeouts left, allowing Ganado to escape with a thrilling 21-14 victory and improving their record to 1-1.
Bures-Guerrero had a strong game passing for 219 yards, distributing the ball to six different receivers. Overall, Ganado showed they were playing solid football against tough competition early in the season.

Ganado faced another tough challenge on the road against Hallettsville, the defending 3A Division I state finalist. Although Hallettsville's star running back Jonathan Brooks had graduated and was now playing for the University of Texas, they still returned a strong core of players. Unfortunately, Ganado did not play well at all, falling behind significantly by halftime with a score of 35-0. In the first half, Ganado managed only three first downs, one net rushing yard, and 38 passing yards. Defensively, the Indians struggled badly as Hallettsville's offense sliced through them with ease. Hallettsville extended their lead to 42-0 early in the second half before Ganado finally scored in the fourth quarter on an 11-yard touchdown pass from Bures-Guerrero to Riojas. Hallettsville capped the game with a late field goal, securing a 45-7 victory over Ganado. The following week, Ganado regrouped and traveled to Palacios for their homecoming game. The Indians started strong, jumping to a 14-0 first-quarter lead on a Bures-Guerrero touchdown run and a 56-yard touchdown pass to Hurt. Palacios responded with two second-quarter touchdowns, helped by a blocked punt and a mishandled snap, tying the game 14-14 at halftime. Late in the first half, Ganado appeared to score again on a Bures-Guerrero run, but the ball was punched loose and recovered by Palacios on a touchback. Palacios attempted a 44-yard field goal before halftime, but it fell short. In the second half, Ganado added two more touchdowns to take a 27-14 lead. However, Palacios' athletic quarterback Anthony White broke free for a 43-yard touchdown run, narrowing the gap to 27-21. The game was exciting but marred by penalties, fumbles, and bad snaps from both teams. The Indians' defense stepped up in the final eight minutes, intercepting three passes to seal the win. Cain Hayden's interception led to a 13-yard touchdown pass from Bures-Guerrero to Hurt, extending the lead to 34-21. On the very next Palacios possession, Josiah Sterling intercepted a pass and returned it for a pick-six, pushing the score to 40-21. Finally, Clayton Webernick's interception ended any hope of a Palacios comeback, allowing Ganado to run out the clock and improve their record to 2-2. Despite the adversity throughout the game, Ganado remained composed and fought hard. The strong defensive stand in the fourth quarter was crucial, highlighted by the three key interceptions. Bures-Guerrero finished the game with 174 passing yards and two touchdowns to Hurt, who had a career-best performance with 146 receiving yards on eight catches.

Ganado faced a challenging three-game home stand, beginning with tough non-district opponents East Bernard and Refugio, before hosting Weimar for their district opener. Against East Bernard, Ganado started strong but was unable to score on their first two possessions, allowing East Bernard to take a 6-0 lead in the first quarter. East Bernard ran their traditional slot-T offense, but had adapted it to include a strong passing game. Their quarterback, Dallas Novicke, passed for 256 yards and four touchdowns, helping East Bernard build a commanding 28-0 lead. Just before halftime, Ganado finally made a breakthrough when Bures-Guerrero connected with Hayden for a 50-yard gain down to the one-yard line, and Bures-Guerrero scored on the next play, making the halftime score 28-7. In the second half, East Bernard extended their lead to 35-7, but Ganado responded with a spectacular 95-yard kickoff return for a touchdown by Hurt, cutting the deficit to 35-14. East Bernard then scored three more touchdowns, and with the game effectively decided at 56-14 late in the fourth quarter, backup quarterback Lane Benavides threw a 65-yard touchdown pass to Bures-Guerrero, who lined up at wide receiver, to close the scoring at 56-20. Defensively, Ganado struggled throughout the game, but the team was determined to learn from the loss. Next, Ganado hosted the state's #1 ranked team, Refugio, in a rematch of their playoff loss from the previous season. Refugio came out firing, scoring on their second play from scrimmage with quarterback Caleb Hesseltine connecting on a 59-yard touchdown pass to Jordan Kelly, quickly building a 22-0 lead in the first quarter. Ganado settled down and managed to score their only touchdown on a five-yard run by Bures-Guerrero, cutting the score to 22-7. However, Refugio responded immediately as Antwaan Gross returned the kickoff 81 yards for a touchdown, and Eziyah Bland followed with a 56-yard touchdown run, giving Refugio a 36-7 lead at halftime. In the second half, Refugio scored three more touchdowns, ultimately winning 57-7. Despite the lopsided score, Ganado showed signs of competitiveness throughout the game. They moved the ball effectively at times, had one touchdown called back due to a questionable penalty, forced Refugio to punt on their first second-half possession, and held them to three turnovers on downs in the first half. These positive moments suggested that Ganado might be able to challenge Refugio again in the playoffs. Finishing their tough non-district schedule with a 2-4 record, Ganado prepared to shift focus toward district play, aiming to make a strong impact in the upcoming games.

The Indians hosted Weimar in their district opener on homecoming night and delivered an impressive performance, defeating Weimar 55-7.

After a tough non-district schedule, Ganado came out strong as Corbin Teague scored early to give the Indians a 7-0 lead. Although Weimar managed to tie the game at 7-7, Ganado dominated the rest of the contest. Bures-Guerrero was nearly flawless in his passing, completing 23 of 25 attempts for 256 yards and throwing two touchdowns to Sterling and Benavides. Hurt led the receiving corps with 131 yards on 10 receptions. With only five teams in the district, one win was enough to clinch a playoff spot, but the Indians aimed to improve their district standing and compete for the title. After this victory, their overall record improved to 3-4, and following seven consecutive games, the team headed into a much-needed bye week to rest and prepare for the remaining three district games. After the bye week, the Indians traveled to face Schulenburg. On Ganado's first possession, Schulenburg forced a fourth-and-14, but Ganado gambled and Bures-Guerrero found Hurt for a 42-yard touchdown, putting Ganado ahead 7-0. Schulenburg responded with a similar fourth-down attempt on their first possession, but the pass was intercepted by Hurt, setting the tone for the game. Ganado dominated from that point forward, while Schulenburg struggled to gain momentum. Bures-Guerrero broke free for a 77-yard run and was tackled just shy of the goal line as the first quarter ended. Three plays later, he scored, extending Ganado's lead to 14-0 early in the second quarter. Freshman running back Vince Sablatura added a 21-yard touchdown run later in the half, putting Ganado up 21-0 at halftime. Schulenburg threatened early in the second half, reaching the Ganado 17-yard line but was stopped by a fumble recovery. Ganado capitalized on the turnover with a methodical drive that ended with Bures-Guerrero scoring on a fourth-and-goal run, increasing the lead to 28-0. The defense continued to impress, intercepting another Schulenburg pass and setting up Bures-Guerrero's 37-yard touchdown pass to Hurt, pushing the lead to 35-0. Although Schulenburg attempted to mount late drives in the fourth quarter, they were unsuccessful, and after failing on a fourth-and-five play, Ganado took over and ran out the clock in victory formation. This game marked one of Ganado's most complete performances of the season, with the defense playing exceptionally well after earlier struggles. Bures-Guerrero passed for 160 yards and two touchdowns, both to Hurt, who recorded 94 yards on seven catches. Bures-Guerrero also led the rushing attack with 150 yards and scored two rushing touchdowns, solidifying Ganado's dominant 35-0 win over Schulenburg.

Ganado was playing solid football, holding a 4-4 overall record and a perfect 2-0 mark in district play, heading into their final home game of the season against the top-ranked defending state champion Shiner. This game was critical, as it would decide the district title. Shiner proved to be as formidable as expected, dominating the Indians just as they had the previous year. Shiner took a commanding 42-0 lead by halftime and went on to secure a 49-7 victory. Their rushing attack was relentless, amassing 548 yards on 39 attempts, with Dalton Brooks leading the charge with 297 yards and five touchdowns. Ganado's lone touchdown came on a 22-yard pass from Bures-Guerrero to Hurt. Bures-Guerrero finished the game with 153 passing yards and 43 rushing yards but threw two costly interceptions, one of which was returned for a pick-six by Shiner's Eli Fric in the second quarter. With the win, Shiner preserved their undefeated record and clinched a share of the district title, securing the number one seed heading into the playoffs. Coach Bennett praised his team's effort despite the loss and expressed readiness to prepare for the upcoming playoff run.

The Indians then traveled to face Flatonia in the regular season finale, a critical matchup to determine the second seed for the playoffs. On a chilly night, the two teams battled fiercely for playoff positioning. Ganado struck first as Bures-Guerrero broke free for a 54-yard run to the Flatonia 10-yard line and scored on the very next play with a 9-yard touchdown run, giving Ganado a quick 7-0 lead. Flatonia responded and successfully converted a two-point attempt, taking an 8-7 advantage by the end of the first quarter. In the second quarter, Bures-Guerrero scored again on a 22-yard run, putting Ganado ahead 14-8. Flatonia answered immediately but missed the two-point conversion, leaving the halftime score tied at 14-14. In the third quarter, Ganado extended their lead to 21-14, but Flatonia countered with two touchdowns to take a 26-21 lead heading into the final quarter. The fourth quarter was full of drama as Ganado faced a critical fourth-and-nine situation and executed a fake punt successfully, with Bures-Guerrero racing 42 yards to set up a touchdown run from five yards out, giving the Indians a 27-26 lead after a failed two-point conversion. With just over a minute remaining, Flatonia mounted what seemed to be a game-winning drive and scored, taking a 33-27 lead. However, the Indians refused to quit. Bures-Guerrero connected with Hurt on a dramatic 50-yard touchdown pass - Hurt's only reception of the game - to retake the lead. Despite defensive struggles throughout the game, Ganado's defense made the crucial stops when it mattered, holding Flatonia on downs to secure a thrilling 33-32 victory and clinch the number two seed in the playoffs. Bures-Guerrero had a standout performance, rushing for 276 yards on 31 carries with four touchdowns - his second-best rushing output of his career. Flatonia quarterback Fidel Venegas also put up impressive numbers, rushing for 129 yards and three touchdowns while passing for 133 yards and one touchdown. Ganado secured a playoff berth for the third consecutive year and was poised to make a deep run. Although the team had experienced ups and downs throughout the season, they had shown resilience when it counted most and were ready to elevate their game as the playoffs began.

Ganado's first playoff opponent was Ozona, with the game played on a Thursday night at San Antonio's Comalander Stadium in the bi-district round. The Indians started strong when Ozona failed an onside kick on the opening kickoff, giving Ganado excellent field position. Just a minute into the game, Bures-Guerrero connected with Hurt on a 22-yard touchdown pass to put Ganado up 7-0. Ozona struggled on their first possession, gaining a net of minus eight yards, and Ganado quickly responded as Bures-Guerrero scored on a 24-yard run early in their second drive. After a missed extra point, Ganado led 13-0. The Indians' only setback came on the next possession when an interception was returned to the Ganado 14-yard line, allowing Ozona to score their first touchdown and narrow the gap to 13-6. Ganado then exploded in the second quarter, scoring 42 points to take a commanding 55-6 lead at halftime. The Indians continued their dominance and ultimately won 68-16, advancing to the next round. Bures-Guerrero had a spectacular game, passing for 321 yards and setting a school record with seven touchdown passes. Two receivers surpassed 100 yards receiving: Hurt with 124 yards on eight receptions and four touchdowns, and Sterling with 123 yards on nine receptions and three touchdowns. Webernick also caught a touchdown pass and had 37 yards on three receptions. The defense played well, intercepting four passes from Ozona. In the Area round, Ganado faced La Villa, a perennial playoff contender from South Texas. This game was held on a Thursday night at Cabaniss Stadium in Corpus Christi. La Villa made an early statement by scoring on their opening possession and leading 7-0 within the first minute. However, Ganado responded with a powerful offensive performance, scoring 60 unanswered points to take a 60-7 lead by the third quarter.

At halftime, Ganado held a 39-7 advantage. La Villa scored two late touchdowns in the fourth quarter after the outcome was decided, but Ganado dominated the game, winning 60-23 and advancing to the regional round for the third consecutive year. Bures-Guerrero continued his strong play, passing for 277 yards and four touchdowns. Hurt caught three of those touchdown passes and was the game's leading receiver with 137 yards on seven receptions. Hayden caught the remaining touchdown pass. Bures-Guerrero also contributed on the ground, rushing for 59 yards and scoring three rushing touchdowns.

For the second consecutive year, the Indians faced Refugio in the regional round of the playoffs, with the game played the day after Thanksgiving at Sandcrab Stadium in Port Lavaca - the same location where Ganado last defeated Refugio in a playoff game, winning 7-6 back in 2005. To be the best, Ganado knew they had to beat the best. Earlier in the season, on October 1, Refugio had defeated Ganado decisively, 57-7, in the final non-district game for both teams. Despite that heavy loss, Ganado had performed some positive plays and prepared diligently for this rematch. The game night was cold, and things quickly went downhill for Ganado. The Indians fumbled the opening kickoff inside their own 20-yard line, but the defense held strong and prevented Refugio from scoring immediately. Unfortunately, on just the fourth play of the game, Bures-Guerrero was injured while playing defense and did not return for the rest of the game. Senior Lane Benavides stepped in to play quarterback for the remainder of the contest. Ganado's offense struggled to gain momentum on their first possession, while the defense again stood firm and forced Refugio into a fourth-and-five situation. However, Refugio's freshman quarterback Kelan Brown responded by connecting with Antwaan Gross on a 43-yard touchdown pass, giving Refugio a 7-0 lead. On the next Refugio drive, they nearly scored again but were stopped when Hurt intercepted a pass at the goal line. Despite this defensive effort, Refugio dominated the remainder of the half, leading 34-0 at halftime. Early in the third quarter, Refugio extended their lead to 40-0. Ganado's Hurt responded with a highlight play, returning the kickoff 80 yards for the Indians' only score of the night. Refugio went on to secure a 54-7 victory. For Refugio, Brown passed for 215 yards and five touchdown passes, while Lane Benavides did his best in relief, passing for 149 yards in his final game as a senior. Ganado was held to just 162 total yards for the game. For the second year in a row, the Indians' season ended with a loss to Refugio. The following week featured the highly anticipated quarterfinal matchup between Refugio and Shiner at Victoria's Memorial Stadium. The game drew a crowd of approximately 11,000 fans, including University of Texas football coach Steve Sarkisian. Shiner dominated the contest, winning decisively 55-14. Shiner went on to repeat as state champions by defeating Hawley 47-12 in the state final, earning their fourth title in school history. They completed an undefeated 16-0 season, matching their perfect records from 1986 and 2004 when they won their first two state championships. For the second consecutive year, the Class 2A Division I state champion came from Ganado's district.

Ganado finished the 2021 season with a 7-6 record. Although the season had its ups and downs, the Indians consistently responded and played hard in every game. Senior Riley Hurt concluded his outstanding career as the school's all-time leader in receiving, accumulating 3,038 total receiving yards. He also set a school record for receiving yards in a single season by finishing his senior year with 1,015 yards. While there was talent returning for another run the following season, significant changes were on the horizon. Just two weeks after the Indians' season ended and before the Christmas holidays, Coach Bennett resigned from his position as athletic director and head football coach. During his tenure at Ganado, Bennett compiled an overall record of 27-21 and led the team to three consecutive playoff appearances. Before his departure, he addressed the team and expressed pride in the success achieved in the relatively short time he was there. With his resignation, Ganado began the search for a new athletic director and head football coach. Additionally, with the upcoming biannual realignment, many changes and developments were expected in the near future.

2022

On January 26, Josh Ervin was officially promoted to athletic director and head football coach at Ganado, a decision unanimously approved by the board of trustees during a special-called meeting. The timing made the occasion even more special, as it coincided with Ervin's 28th birthday. Ervin had served as Ganado's offensive coordinator for four seasons since 2018 under head coach Brent Bennett, who had resigned in December and was named the new athletic director and head coach at George West the day before Ervin's promotion. Ervin, being relatively young, was seen as someone who can easily relate to the players. His motivation for applying stemmed from the commitment he had already made to the Ganado football program. He emphasized his strong relationships with the players, his understanding of the program's growth, and his desire to continue building on its foundation. Ervin expressed confidence in the work ethic and potential of the team and was determined to help the players reach that potential. Offensively, Ervin planned to maintain the spread formation with a few adjustments. One of the changes he hoped to implement is the introduction of a sixth-grade athletic period, aiming to develop athletes from an earlier stage. While some program-wide changes are expected, the football program's core foundation will remain intact, with modifications made where necessary. Ervin's immediate priorities included assembling his coaching staff and preparing for the upcoming University Interscholastic League (UIL) realignment. Most of the current staff was expected to stay, but he would need to hire a new defensive coordinator to replace Lane Shands, who served in that role during the 2020 and 2021 seasons.

On February 3, the UIL announced the new district alignments, placing Ganado in District 15-2A Division I. The new district included powerhouse programs like Shiner and Refugio, both of which had met in the quarterfinals the previous two seasons, with Shiner emerging victorious en route to back-to-back state championships. The district also featured Bloomington, Kenedy, Skidmore-Tynan, and Three Rivers, while former district opponents Flatonia, Schulenburg, and Weimar were no longer in Ganado's district. The strength of the new district was seen as a challenge that would push Ganado to elevate its performance. The Indians were scheduled to open district play at home against Shiner and conclude the regular season on the road at Refugio.

By August, after a dedicated and productive offseason, the Indians were fully prepared to make another strong run as the football season began. The team welcomed three new coaches, including defensive coordinator Jason Chambless, a 1996 Ganado graduate who had previously served in the same role under Brent Bennett in 2019, helping lead the team to the quarterfinals in Class 3A. Also joining the staff were Trey Thedford, a 2012 Ganado graduate and former quarterback for the Indians, and Jason Cann, who would also take over as the school's new baseball coach. Improving the defense was a major focus, especially after a difficult previous season in which the Indians gave up 426 total points - an average of 32.8 points per game - one of the worst defensive performances in school history. The team allowed 50 or more points in four games and suffered heavy losses to Refugio twice, as well as to traditionally strong programs like Shiner, Hallettsville, and East Bernard. With new leadership and a renewed emphasis on a defense-first mentality, expectations were high for significant improvement on that side of the ball. In addition to physical readiness, the coaching staff worked on instilling a competitive mindset, teaching players to believe in their ability to win no matter the opponent's classification or ranking. At the core of the team was senior quarterback Kyle Bures-Guerrero, a three-year letterman returning for his fourth season as the Indians' starter. In the previous season, he had passed for 2,034 yards, rushed for 1,034, and scored a total of 46 touchdowns, leading the team to its third consecutive appearance in the third round of the playoffs. The Indians returned nine starters on both offense and defense, providing a strong foundation for continued success. On offense, Bures-Guerrero led a unit that included senior wide receiver Ashton Strauss and sophomore Cain Hayden, along with sophomore Luke Bures and freshman Landon Hicks starting at the other receiver spots. Senior Corbin Teague transitioned to tight end in running formations after spending the past two seasons in the backfield, while junior Dylan Holt assumed the starting running back role. The offensive line featured returning senior center Michael Bubela, junior guards Martin Ramirez and Vincent Barajas, and senior tackles Adam Tristan and Coltyn Chambless. Defensively, Bures-Guerrero also contributed at defensive end alongside senior Fabien Almeda. Tristan returned at tackle with Teague filling in at the other tackle spot. Holt returned at linebacker, joined by senior Clayton Webernick and Hicks. The secondary was young but filled with speed and potential. Sophomore Cain Hayden was the only returning starter at safety, while sophomore Bryce Ullman, a talented athlete who missed his freshman year due to a broken collarbone, started at the other safety spot and also served as the backup quarterback. At cornerback, Bures and freshman Austen Pena, both fast and promising athletes, rounded out the defensive backfield. With a talented and experienced roster, a new head coach, and a revitalized coaching staff, the team entered the season with high expectations. *Dave Campbell's Texas Football Magazine* projected Ganado to finish third in the district behind powerhouses Shiner and Refugio, who were ranked #1 and #3 in the state respectively. With all the pieces in place, the Indians were ready to compete and make their mark.

The Indians opened the 2022 football season with a strong performance on the road against Van Vleck, securing a 39–14 victory in Head Coach Josh Ervin's debut. The Indians started fast, jumping out to a 13–0 lead in the first quarter with a touchdown pass from Kyle Bures-Guerrero to Clayton Webernick and a short touchdown run by Dylan Holt, set up by a 40-yard pass to Cain Hayden. However, Van Vleck cut into the lead with a pick-six, making the score 13–8 by the end of the first quarter. Ganado responded in the second quarter with another touchdown pass from Bures-Guerrero to Hayden, extending the lead to 19–8. Van Vleck showed signs of life, scoring their first offensive touchdown after a big pass play, narrowing the gap to 19–14. Ganado threatened to score again before halftime but a fumble ended the drive, and the Indians went into the break with a five-point lead. The Indians dominated the second half both offensively and defensively. After a Van Vleck three-and-out to start the third quarter and a poor punt, Ganado capitalized immediately with a Bures-Guerrero touchdown run, increasing the lead to 25–14. Another defensive stop and another special team miscue by Van Vleck gave Ganado excellent field position, though this time they were stopped on downs. However, the Indians quickly regained possession after yet another defensive stand and bad punt, and Bures-Guerrero added another rushing touchdown to make it 33–14. Despite another fumble stalling a Ganado drive, the defense again held firm, and Holt scored his second touchdown to seal the 39–14 win. This victory was especially meaningful given the context - Ganado had lost 70–0 the last time they played at Van Vleck in 2018, which was Coach Ervin's first year at Ganado as offensive coordinator. The defense showed massive improvement compared to the previous season, while the offense displayed strong execution despite a few fumbles. Bures-Guerrero passed for 145 yards and two touchdowns and rushed for 76 yards and two scores. Holt led the team with 96 rushing yards and two touchdowns as Ganado rushed for 182 total yards.

The following week, Ganado hosted Palacios for their home opener, featuring a quarterback matchup between seniors Bures-Guerrero and Palacios' Anthony White - players who had faced off as freshmen in a classic 2019 game that Palacios won in double overtime. This time, Ganado dominated. Bures-Guerrero opened the scoring with an 8-yard touchdown run. Palacios nearly responded with a kickoff return touchdown, but it was called back due to a penalty. In the second quarter, Bures-Guerrero connected with Hayden on a 51-yard touchdown pass, and then followed up with a 90-yard touchdown run after starting a drive from Ganado's own 10-yard line, giving the Indians a 20–0 lead. Palacios finally scored on a 13-yard run by White to make it 20–7 at halftime. Ganado controlled the second half completely, scoring four more touchdowns - two on runs by Vince Sablatura, one on another Bures-Guerrero run, and one on a 34-yard pass to a wide-open Joe Rodriquez. The Indians won decisively, 49–7, improving to 2–0 on the season. Bures-Guerrero had a standout night, throwing for 233 yards and two touchdowns and rushing for 140 yards and three more scores. Hayden caught five passes for 90 yards and a touchdown, while Ashton Strauss added 62 receiving yards on three catches. Despite some areas still needing improvement, Ganado's performance in the first two games showed promise and highlighted the team's high potential under new leadership.

Next up, the Indians hosted East Bernard in an emotional and high-stakes matchup. For the senior class, the game carried special significance, as East Bernard had eliminated Ganado from the playoffs in 2019 when they were freshmen. Adding to the tension, East Bernard had won the last four meetings between the teams, including a lopsided 56–20 win the previous year. The last Ganado victory over East Bernard dated back to 2011. Ganado struck first with a one-yard touchdown run by Sablatura. East Bernard responded with a big 73-yard run by Alex Henriquez, though a missed extra point kept Ganado ahead, 7–6. Just before halftime, a turnover deep in Ganado's own territory gave East Bernard a short field, and they capitalized with a 10-yard touchdown pass from Clayton Fajkus to Maddox Crist, taking a 12–7 halftime lead after a failed two-point try. Ganado regained the lead early in the second half when Bures-Guerrero broke free on a fourth-and-one play for a 47-yard touchdown run, making it 14–12. East Bernard answered with a long drive that stalled inside the 10-yard line, resulting in a 21-yard field goal by Christian Ruiz to take a 15–14 lead. Ganado responded with a balanced offensive drive highlighted by a 39-yard pass from Bures-Guerrero to Landon Hicks, culminating in a six-yard touchdown run by Bures-Guerrero and a 21–15 lead heading into the fourth quarter. East Bernard once again responded with a methodical, five-minute drive, capped by a one-yard

Fajkus touchdown run to take a 22–21 lead with just over eight minutes remaining. But Ganado refused to fold. Bures-Guerrero scrambled for a 27-yard gain to keep the next drive alive and eventually connected with Hayden for a nine-yard touchdown pass, putting the Indians ahead 27–22 with just over two minutes left. East Bernard mounted one last threat, with Crist catching two more passes, including a key fourth-and-eight conversion to the Ganado 8-yard line. However, on fourth-and-goal, Luke Bures delivered a crucial defensive stop, breaking up a pass intended for Crist to seal the win. The crowd erupted as Ganado entered victory formation and finally earned a long-awaited 27–22 triumph over East Bernard. Coach Ervin praised the team's resilience and ability to overcome adversity. Statistically, East Bernard quarterback Fajkus threw for 189 yards, with Crist tallying 149 receiving yards and a touchdown. Bures-Guerrero completed 10 of 12 passes for 92 yards and a touchdown, while rushing for 182 yards and two scores.

Ganado carried that momentum into its final non-district game with a dominant 40–0 shutout at Danbury. The Indians quickly established control, converting two fourth-down plays into touchdowns in the first quarter - an eight-yard pass from Bures-Guerrero to Hayden and a five-yard Bures-Guerrero run - to take a 14–0 lead. Danbury struggled with fumbles and bad snaps, which Ganado capitalized on. Sablatura broke loose for a 51-yard touchdown run, and Bures-Guerrero connected with Ashton Strauss on a spectacular 20-yard touchdown catch, giving Ganado a 26–0 lead at the half. In the third quarter, Bures-Guerrero and Strauss connected again on a 28-yard touchdown pass after converting another fourth down, extending the lead to 33–0. Danbury nearly scored in the fourth quarter, but Bures-Guerrero made a hustle play, chasing down the ball carrier and forcing a fumble that Ganado recovered. Sablatura followed with two long runs, setting up another Bures-Guerrero rushing touchdown to finish the scoring. Bures-Guerrero finished the game with 160 passing yards and three touchdowns, along with 31 rushing yards and two scores. Sablatura led the ground game with 117 yards and a touchdown. Seven different receivers caught passes, demonstrating the team's offensive depth and balance. The shutout marked Ganado's first of the season and a clear sign of the defense's growth. With a 4–0 record and confidence building, Ganado wrapped up their non-district schedule and turned its attention to the biggest challenge yet: the district opener against two-time defending state champion Shiner.

The Indians opened district play at home against the fourth-ranked Shiner Comanches, who came in with a 3–1 record. Although Shiner had graduated their standout Doug Brooks - now playing at Texas A&M-Kingsville - his younger brother Dalton Brooks, a senior and Texas A&M commit, remained a dominant force on a veteran-led team. For Ganado, the game represented a chance to measure themselves against elite competition and take a step toward the next level. However, the night ultimately belonged to Shiner in a 50–12 rout. Ganado tried to set the tone early with an onside kick, but Shiner recovered and immediately asserted control. The Comanches opened with a methodical 66-yard, 12-play drive capped by a six-yard touchdown run from Brooks. On their next three offensive plays, Shiner scored three more touchdowns - first a 54-yard pass from quarterback Ryan Peterson to Brooks, then a 72-yard Brooks run, and finally, after a series of Ganado miscues including two bad snaps and a safety, a 52-yard touchdown run by Brooks. That scoring burst gave Shiner a commanding 30–0 lead late in the first half. Ganado finally responded just before halftime with their most promising drive of the night. Starting at their own 25-yard line, the Indians moved the ball with effective passing and finished the drive with a touchdown pass from Bures-Guerrero to Hicks from 24 yards out with just nine seconds remaining, cutting the deficit to 30–6 at the break. The Indians carried that momentum into the second half, beginning with a 38-yard run by Sablatura to the Shiner 41-yard line. Austen Pena followed with a key reception that moved the ball inside the 10, giving Ganado a first-and-goal. However, the drive stalled after a controversial no-call on a facemask penalty, and the Indians turned the ball over on downs. Despite recovering a Shiner fumble shortly after, Ganado again failed to capitalize, missing a wide-open pass in the end zone. Shiner responded as they had all night - decisively. Brooks added a 69-yard touchdown run, bringing his total to five touchdowns, and extending the lead to 37–6. Ganado managed to score again in the fourth quarter on a fourth-down pass from Bures-Guerrero to Hicks, their second connection of the game, making it 37–12. Shiner added two more scores in the final minutes from backups Trace Bishop and Carson Schuette, finishing the game with a dominant 50–12 victory. Statistically, Brooks was unstoppable, rushing for 276 yards and four touchdowns, and adding a receiving touchdown. Bures-Guerrero threw for 115 yards and two touchdowns, both to Hicks, who finished with 38 yards on three catches. The loss dropped Ganado to 4–1 overall and 0–1 in district, marking their seventh straight defeat to Shiner since 2014 - all by wide margins. Coach Josh Ervin expressed his disappointment after the game, acknowledging that the team had come in expecting to compete and win. Still, he pointed to the positives - such as the offensive flashes late in the first half and early in the third quarter - as building blocks. He emphasized the need to learn from the mistakes, focus on what went well, study the film, and get back to work for the remainder of the season.

After a tough district-opening loss to Shiner, the Indians bounced back in dominant fashion with back-to-back wins over Kenedy and Bloomington, improving their overall record to 6–1 and their district mark to 2–1. Ganado traveled to Kenedy determined to respond, and they did just that with a strong 42–14 victory. Despite Kenedy's commitment to their slot-T power running game - which gained 359 yards on 56 attempts - the Indians made key defensive stops when it mattered most. Kenedy attempted only four passes and completed none. On offense, Ganado was explosive and efficient. Bures-Guerrero led the charge, rushing for 201 yards and four touchdowns, while also throwing for 147 yards and two fourth-quarter touchdown passes - one to Bures and the other to Strauss. Holt added 106 yards on the ground, helping Ganado rack up 323 rushing yards on just 29 attempts. The win evened Ganado's district record at 1–1 heading into a bye week. Following the bye, the Indians returned home for a Homecoming showdown against Bloomington, and the team came out firing on all cylinders. With extra motivation on defense, Ganado delivered a thoroughly dominant performance, shutting out Bloomington 58–0. The Indians controlled the line of scrimmage, recorded seven sacks, and held the Bobcats to just 36 total yards of offense - including a staggering -53 rushing yards, credited by the numerous tackles for loss. The defense also forced three turnovers with two interceptions and a fumble recovery. Offensively, Ganado wasted no time, jumping out to a 24–0 lead in the first quarter and never looking back. Bures-Guerrero once again led the way, throwing for 177 yards and two touchdowns, both to Hayden, who finished with four catches for 51 yards. Bures-Guerrero also rushed for 114 yards and found the end zone five times on the ground, putting together another standout performance.

With three games remaining in the regular season, Ganado's record stood at 6–1 overall and 2–1 in district play. The Indians were building momentum and inching closer to clinching a playoff berth.

The Indians suffered a tough 24–22 district loss on the road at Three Rivers, in a game filled with missed opportunities, turnovers, and adversity. Despite a strong effort to rally late, the Indians fell to 6–2 overall and 2–2 in district play. The game started with promise for Ganado, as Hayden intercepted a pass on Three Rivers' third play, setting the Indians up at the opponent's 34-yard line. However, the Indians fumbled the ball away and Three Rivers capitalized with a six-yard touchdown run to take an early 6–0 lead. On the ensuing possession, Bures-Guerrero ripped off a long run into Three Rivers territory, but a tipped pass was intercepted, halting the drive. Three Rivers responded again, converting a key fourth down and scoring on a one-yard run by quarterback Caden Soliz early in the second quarter for a 12–0 lead. After Hayden returned the kickoff to the Three Rivers 22-yard line, the Indians were again stopped and turned the ball over on downs. Three Rivers took advantage once more, aided by a third-down conversion and a personal foul penalty. Soliz found Derek Lancaster in the corner of the end zone for a 15-yard touchdown pass, stretching the lead to 18–0. Finally, Ganado's offense broke through, as Bures-Guerrero connected with Hayden on a big third-down pass, setting up a five-yard rushing touchdown by Bures-Guerrero to make it 18–7. Ganado's defense held on the next series, giving the offense another opportunity before halftime. Bures-Guerrero led a promising drive to the 11-yard line but threw his second interception of the half near the goal line, ending the threat and sending the game into halftime with Three Rivers up 18–7. The second half saw both teams trading defensive stops and punts. Three Rivers recovered a Ganado fumble but were denied when Bryce Ullman intercepted a pass in the end zone. Later, Ganado closed the gap as Bures-Guerrero connected with Hicks for a 25-yard touchdown, and Hayden added the two-point conversion, making it 18–15 early in the fourth quarter. However, Three Rivers nearly returned the ensuing kickoff for a touchdown, setting up a short field. Despite a penalty pushing them back, Soliz punched in his second rushing touchdown from three yards out, extending the lead to 24–15. The Indians answered once again, as Bures-Guerrero connected with Hayden and Holt to move into scoring range. On third down, he found Hicks on a slant, and the freshman bounced off defenders for his second touchdown of the night, bringing Ganado within two points at 24–22 with 2:24 left. The Indians attempted an onside kick, but Three Rivers recovered and ran out the clock to seal the win. Soliz led Three Rivers with 159 passing yards and two touchdowns, while also rushing for 69 yards and two scores. Lancaster and Amaro combined for 159 receiving yards and both touchdown catches. For Ganado, Bures-Guerrero passed for 155 yards and two touchdowns but was hurt by two interceptions. He also rushed for 89 yards and a touchdown. Hicks led the team in receiving with 62 yards and two touchdowns. Despite the slow start and early mistakes, the Indians showed resilience and fight, nearly pulling off the comeback. Coach Ervin acknowledged the missed opportunities and pointed to penalties, turnovers, and controversial calls as hurdles the team must learn to overcome. He emphasized the need for better preparation and taking each game one step at a time.

After a tough loss to Three Rivers, the Ganado Indians quickly regrouped, refocused during practice, and delivered a dominant performance in their final home game of the regular season, shutting out Skidmore-Tynan 70–0 on Senior Night. The Indians came out with intensity and purpose, completely controlling the game from start to finish. Bures-Guerrero, playing his final game on his home field, was outstanding, throwing for 233 yards and five touchdowns while rushing for 109 yards and two additional scores. Hayden had a big night receiving, catching all three of his targets for 66 yards and three touchdowns. Holt led in receiving yards with 83 on three catches and added both a rushing and receiving touchdown, rushing for 52 yards. After a relatively slow start, the Indians erupted for 30 points in the second quarter to take a commanding 42–0 lead into halftime. The defense held strong throughout, notching its third shutout of the season, and the victory officially clinched Ganado's fourth straight playoff berth.

The Indians wrapped up the regular season on the road against district champion Refugio in a game moved to Thursday night due to impending severe weather that Friday. Refugio, ranked among the best in the state, dominated early, jumping out to a 28–0 lead in the first quarter and extending it to 35–7 by halftime. Ganado's lone first-half score came on a five-yard touchdown run by Bures-Guerrero. Refugio added 17 more points in the third quarter, pulling away with a 52–6 lead before resting their starters. Despite the lopsided score, the Indians continued to battle, refusing to quit. Bures-Guerrero ignited the team with a 75-yard touchdown run late in the third quarter and added two more scores in the fourth, finishing with 100 rushing yards and all four of Ganado's touchdowns, along with 115 yards passing. Refugio's sophomore running back Jordan King led their offense with 135 rushing yards and four touchdowns, while quarterback Kelan Brown added 200 passing yards and a score. The game ended in a 52–26 loss for Ganado, but the effort and heart displayed by the Indians were clear, especially in the second half. The team entered the playoffs as the fourth seed in a tough district that included champion Refugio, runner-up Shiner, and third-place Three Rivers. The strong finish against Refugio, even against their backups, showed that Ganado still had fight left - and left open the possibility of a postseason rematch.

The Indians opened the playoffs with a commanding performance against district champion La Villa, a team they had defeated 60–23 in the area round the previous year. Playing as a fourth seed, Ganado entered the Thursday night matchup in Taft as underdogs on paper, but the game quickly proved to be a mismatch. The Indians exploded to a 21–0 lead in the first quarter and followed that up with 34 unanswered points in the second quarter to take a staggering 55–0 lead into halftime. By the final whistle, Ganado had secured a dominant 68–6 victory to advance to the next round. Bures-Guerrero led the offensive onslaught, passing for 182 yards and two touchdowns while rushing for 144 yards and four touchdowns. Backup quarterback Bryce Ullman also saw action, going a perfect 3-for-3 for 70 yards, including a 56-yard touchdown pass to Luke Bures. Bures led all receivers with 106 yards on five catches. It was a complete team effort, showcasing both the starting unit's power and the depth of the roster. The Indians were not just satisfied with one playoff win - they were hungry for more.

In the Area round the following Thursday, Ganado faced Thorndale at Bastrop Memorial Stadium. The last meeting between the two teams had been in the regional playoffs back in 2013, where Thorndale narrowly won 21–17. This time, however, the result was entirely different, as Ganado dominated from start to finish in a 66–12 blowout. Ganado once again set the tone early with a 21–0 lead in the first quarter and extended that advantage to 28–0 at halftime. While Thorndale managed to score two touchdowns in the third quarter, the game was never in doubt. Bures-Guerrero turned in another stellar performance, throwing for 215 yards and three touchdowns while adding 165 yards rushing and four more scores. Hicks had a huge night receiving, hauling in 11 receptions for 115 yards and all four of the team's touchdown catches - three from Bures-Guerrero and one from Ullman, who again was flawless off the bench, going 3-for-3 for 38 yards. The Indians had now scored 134 points in their first two playoff games and were gaining momentum with each round, firing on all cylinders as they advanced deeper into the postseason.

The Indians entered the third round of the playoffs playing their best football of the season, with confidence and momentum on their side. After two dominant playoff wins, they were focused, prepared, and determined not to back down as they faced a familiar and formidable opponent - the Refugio Bobcats. The two teams had met just three weeks earlier in the regular season finale, a game in which Ganado saw both positive moments and clear areas for improvement. The coaching staff and players worked hard in the weeks leading up to the rematch, making necessary adjustments and entering the game fired up and ready to compete. For the third consecutive year, the Indians and Bobcats faced off on the Friday after Thanksgiving, this time at Heroes Stadium in San Antonio. Unlike the past two meetings that ended in lopsided defeats for Ganado, the Indians were determined to change the narrative. Refugio had won eight straight games over Ganado dating back to 2014, all by wide margins. However, this game felt different, and Ganado's players came out with intensity and purpose. Despite cold, rainy, and windy conditions reminiscent of the 2020 playoff game, Ganado's defense came out strong, holding Refugio scoreless on their opening possessions. Although the Indians' offense struggled early, the defense continued to make plays. Refugio finally broke through late in the first quarter when Jordan King capitalized on a turnover and scored on a 28-yard run to give the Bobcats a 7–0 lead. Ganado responded with resilience. After a missed field goal attempt by the Indians, Refugio began to move the ball again, but Luke Bures made a huge play, intercepting a Kelan Brown pass and returning it 53 yards for a touchdown. Joe Rodriguez's extra point gave Ganado a 7–6 lead with just over four minutes remaining in the half, and the upset alert was very real. Unfortunately, the lead was short-lived. With just 27 seconds left in the second quarter, Brown connected with Isaiah Avery for a 32-yard touchdown pass to put Refugio ahead 12–7 going into halftime. Still, the Indians had executed an excellent first half, keeping one of the state's top-ranked teams on edge and out of rhythm. However, the second half told a different story. Refugio returned with urgency and erupted for 41 unanswered points, scoring on six straight possessions. The Bobcats' defense clamped down, holding the Indians to just 114 rushing yards and forcing two interceptions. Meanwhile, King had a career-best performance, rushing for 172 yards and two touchdowns. Refugio ultimately pulled away and ended Ganado's season with a 53–7 win. For the third straight season, the Indians' playoff run came to an end at the hands of Refugio, again in the same playoff round and again by a decisive margin. Despite the disappointment, the first half effort reflected the heart, preparation, and improvement of the Ganado team. Refugio would go on to defeat Shiner in the quarterfinals the following week before falling in the state championship game to Hawley, 54–28.

The Indians finished the season with a 9-4 record. Coach Ervin expressed pride in the team, especially considering the adversity they faced after the district loss to Three Rivers. He highlighted the significant improvement the team showed in the three weeks between their first loss of the season, which was the finale against Refugio, and their playoff rematch against the same opponent. In his final game of an outstanding four-year career, Kyle Bures-Guerrero passed for 152 yards and was able to finish the game - a milestone he had not achieved in the previous two playoff losses to Refugio due to early injuries. Coach Ervin praised Bures-Guerrero not only for his athletic abilities but also for his leadership and the positive influence he had behind the scenes, qualities that often go unnoticed. Bures-Guerrero finished his career as the school's all-time leading passer with 7,696 yards and, at that time, 86 touchdown passes. He also holds the school record for rushing touchdowns with 98 and ranks third all-time in career rushing yards with 4,867 as a quarterback, trailing only Josh Labay and Matthew Bures - both of whom played running back - a testament to his exceptional talent. Coach Ervin called him one of the best athletes he had ever seen play for the Indians. Following graduation, Bures-Guerrero signed with Texas Wesleyan University in Fort Worth. Other seniors who would be greatly missed included Clayton Webernick, Ashton Strauss, Fabien Almeda, Cole Blankenburg, Corbin Teague, Michael Bubela, Coltyn Chambless, Adam Tristan, and Angel Almeda. Coach Ervin was credited with doing an excellent job in his debut season as head coach, maintaining the team's winning tradition.

The program was far from finished, and what was about to unfold in the following two years promised to be memorable and exciting for the Indians.

Chapter 11

Haters Tour: Going Beyond Expectations

2023

To outsiders unfamiliar with Ganado, the football program appeared to be finished. The team faced the significant challenge of replacing a four-year starting quarterback who was a key athlete, and no one knew much about the other players. Additionally, depth was a concern as only 23 athletes showed up for football workouts on Monday, July 31, marking the earliest start to football practice in recent memory. The workouts took place in brutal conditions with a heat index exceeding 110 degrees during a very hot summer. Despite these challenges, these determined young men were committed to working hard, winning, and proving their doubters wrong. Before the season began, many predicted that Ganado could compete only for the first half of games but would tire out by the second half, particularly struggling in the fourth quarter. This assumption proved false as the team worked diligently to maintain their conditioning and compete effectively for four full quarters. Although many players played both offense and defense, they were physically ready to endure the entire game.

Junior Bryce Ullman took over as the starting quarterback following the departure of Kyle Bures-Guerrero. Football talent ran in Ullman's family; his uncle Clayton Hayden and grandfather Craig Hayden both had been Indians quarterbacks. Ullman had served as Bures-Guerrero's backup the previous season and had performed well in his playing time, including throwing two touchdown passes in playoff wins. He was noted for his quick release, accuracy, and ability to deliver the ball to his receivers. Additionally, Ullman served as the team's punter on special teams. The receiving corps was well-stocked with experienced players including junior Cain Hayden, Luke Bures, sophomore Landon Hicks, and Austen Pena. Junior Joe Rodriguez also contributed at receiver and was the team's kicker. Senior Dylan Holt, one of only three seniors on the team, returned as a running back. The other seniors were Vincent Barajas at guard and Martin Ramirez at tackle on the offensive line. The offensive line also featured junior Carter Kovar at center, with juniors Luke Green and Erick Guerrero playing tackle and guard, respectively. Defensively, expectations were high. A key change involved moving Holt from linebacker to defensive tackle, a move that proved highly effective. Guerrero played the other tackle position, while Green and sophomore John Utley played defensive end. At linebacker, Hicks returned alongside junior Vince Sablatura and Luke Bures, who transitioned from cornerback. Ullman switched from safety to cornerback, joining Pena at the position. Hayden returned at safety, and freshman Logan "Smoke" Bures started at the other safety spot. Logan, nicknamed "Smoke" by his friends, would have an outstanding freshman season and also contributed as a running back, sharing carries with Holt. One notable strength of this team was its speed, particularly in the defensive secondary and the receiving corps, which largely consisted of the same players. This speed was expected to be a significant advantage during the season.

Preseason predictions placed the Indians to finish fourth in their district, the final playoff seed, which was consistent with their finish the previous year. *Dave Campbell's Texas Football Magazine* ranked Ganado #21 in the state among Class 2A Division I schools. Refugio was favored to win the district with the #1 ranking, while Shiner was predicted to finish second and came in ranked #9, despite having a young team replacing a talented senior class that included Dalton Brooks, now playing at Texas A&M. Three Rivers was picked third in the district with a #17 ranking and retained nearly their entire roster from the previous year. With all of this in mind, the Indians were ready to buckle their chin straps and get to work. They steadily improved each week in practice, showed sharpness in scrimmages against Brazos and Tidehaven, and were prepared to prove the doubters wrong throughout the upcoming season.

The first doubt about Ganado's football team was silenced in the season opener, played at home on a hot Friday night against Van Vleck. Despite facing a talented program from a larger classification, the Indians never gave up and matched their opponent stride for stride. On Van Vleck's opening possession, the Indians' defense forced a punt on a long third down. On Ganado's first possession, quarterback Bryce Ullman quickly made an impact by connecting with Landon Hicks on a 78-yard touchdown pass, as Hicks outran the Van Vleck defenders to the end zone, giving the Indians a 7-0 lead. Van Vleck responded with a key 30-yard run by Corey Austin that set up their tying touchdown near the end of the first quarter, making the score 7-7. Hicks then set up Ganado's next scoring opportunity with a long kickoff return. Ullman followed with a big pass to Luke Bures that moved the Indians into the red zone, and Ullman finished the drive by finding Cain Hayden on a 6-yard touchdown pass to regain the lead, 14-7. Van Vleck answered back in the second quarter to tie the game at 14-14, and both teams' defenses tightened up, preventing any further scoring before halftime. Most of the second half was a defensive battle, with both teams attempting several fourth-down conversions to break the deadlock, but neither offense could find the end zone. The game appeared headed for overtime until the final two minutes when Van Vleck mounted a crucial drive and attempted a go-ahead field goal. Freshman Logan "Smoke" Bures came through in a big way by blocking the kick, recovering it, and nearly returning it all the way to the goal line. Using a "tush push" formation, Ullman then took the ball into the end zone as time expired, securing an exciting 20-14 victory for the Indians. Contrary to preseason doubts that the team would tire out in the second half - especially playing in extreme heat - Ganado showed no signs of fading. They played four solid quarters, battled hard throughout, and earned a well-deserved 1-0 start to the season. Ullman passed for 159 yards on just six completions and threw two touchdown passes, both caught by Hicks, who was the game's leading receiver with 118 yards on two receptions. Ullman also contributed 63 yards rushing, showcasing his dual-threat ability and leadership in his first game as the starting quarterback.

The Indians exploded offensively in their next game on the road at Palacios, securing a dominating 61-0 victory. The team's outburst began early with 34 first-quarter points and they led 54-0 at halftime. Defensively, the Indians were equally impressive, holding Palacios to just 62 total yards. Ullman led the offense with 191 yards passing and four touchdown passes to Hicks, Luke Bures, Logan Bures, and Austen Pena. Pena also contributed on special teams by blocking a punt and returning it for a touchdown, while Luke Bures returned a punt for a touchdown as well. The Indians dominated in all three phases of the game, proving that the team many had written off was now 2-0, and those wins came against two teams from larger classifications.

The true test came the following week on the road against East Bernard, who entered the game 0-2 but had shown improvement despite missing the playoffs for the first time since 2009. The Indians started strong, stopping East Bernard on their first possession with multiple tackles for loss, including a hard-hitting tackle by Dylan Holt.

Ganado's offense responded quickly as Ullman scrambled for a 54-yard touchdown, giving the Indians an early 7-0 lead. East Bernard answered back with a 54-yard touchdown pass from quarterback Clayton Fajkus to Maddox Crist, tying the game 7-7 in the first quarter. Ganado then regained the lead, aided by a strong kickoff return from Logan Bures, with Holt finishing the drive on a short two-yard touchdown run to make it 14-7 early in the second quarter. East Bernard tied the game again at 14-14 before beginning to stifle Ganado's offense, forcing mistakes including a safety and scoring another touchdown to take a 23-14 lead. However, the resilient Indians responded before halftime when Ullman connected with Hicks on a two-yard touchdown pass, closing the gap to 23-21 at the break. The third quarter turned into a defensive battle as both teams struggled to regain their offensive rhythm. Near the end of the quarter, East Bernard scored on a two-yard run by Alex Henriquez to extend their lead to 29-21. The Indians, plagued by mistakes and several high snaps that disrupted drives, found it difficult to generate offense in the second half. In the fourth quarter, however, Ganado mounted a drive that Ullman finished on a "tush push" at the goal line. The Indians attempted a two-point conversion to tie the game but failed, leaving them trailing 29-27 with about three minutes remaining. Ganado needed a defensive stop to get the ball back, but East Bernard's Henriquez dashed those hopes with a 50-yard touchdown run, sealing the game 35-27. Henriquez was the standout for East Bernard, rushing for 158 yards and scoring three touchdowns. Ullman was held under 100 yards passing, finishing with 88 yards, one touchdown, and his first interception of the season on the game's final play. He also rushed for 113 yards and scored two rushing touchdowns. Hicks led the receiving corps with 37 yards on four receptions and a touchdown. Despite the loss, the Indians battled hard through four full quarters and faced adversity head-on. Coach Ervin viewed the game as an opportunity for growth, emphasizing the need for increased focus and execution on every play. He credited the team for their resilience and expressed confidence that they would learn from their mistakes, rebound, and improve in the games ahead.

The Indians returned home for their homecoming game against Danbury, where they faced a tough challenge early on. Danbury came out strong on their opening drive, advancing the ball from their own 45-yard line all the way to Ganado's two-yard line. However, the

Indians' defense made a crucial goal-line stand, stopping Danbury on fourth down and forcing a turnover deep in their own end zone. This would be Danbury's only significant scoring threat of the night. Ganado quickly responded offensively when Ullman connected with Pena on a 42-yard touchdown pass to take a 7-0 lead. As the game progressed into the second quarter, the Indians' defense settled down. Holt made a key play by sacking a Danbury player in the end zone for a safety. Meanwhile, Ganado's offense continued to perform well, scoring two more touchdowns before halftime to lead 22-0. The Indians dominated the second half, pouring on 21 points in the third quarter alone. Freshman Logan Bures was a standout, scoring the final two touchdowns of the game - including a spectacular 51-yard touchdown run - and also intercepting a pass on defense. Ganado closed the game with a commanding 49-0 shutout victory. This was the team's first shutout of the season, and the offense put up impressive numbers. Ullman completed 12 of 15 passes for 179 yards and three touchdown passes, while rushing for 68 yards on just four carries. Logan Bures led the rushing attack with 105 yards on five carries and scored twice, including the 51-yard touchdown late in the game. Holt also contributed 78 rushing yards with two touchdowns. Pena was the leading receiver, hauling in four catches for 70 yards and two touchdowns, while Hayden caught two passes for 31 yards and a touchdown. The Indians responded strongly after their recent loss to East Bernard, finishing their non-district schedule with a solid 3-1 record. Their performance continued to defy doubters, showcasing the team's potential and readiness to compete in district play.

The Indians faced Shiner in their district opener, playing on Shiner's home field where Ganado had not won against them in ten years. Shiner came into the game as a young team struggling with a 0-4 record, making this a prime opportunity for the Indians to finally secure a victory. Early in the game, Ganado's defense forced Shiner to punt on their opening drive, giving the offense good field position. The Indians converted a crucial fourth down on their first possession, and shortly after, Ullman connected with Pena on a 25-yard touchdown pass to take a 7-0 lead in the first quarter. Ganado's defense continued to dominate, stopping Shiner again and setting up another scoring opportunity. Ullman again found Pena for a short three-yard touchdown pass, increasing the lead to 14-0 in the second quarter. Despite Ullman throwing an interception in the red zone later in the half, Shiner failed to capitalize offensively, and the Indians held a 14-0 lead at halftime. The Indians started the second half strongly, beginning their drive at midfield following a good punt return by Logan Bures. The running game, led by Logan Bures and Holt, advanced the ball inside the 10-yard line, where Ullman found Hayden for a 9-yard touchdown pass, extending the lead to 21-0 in the third quarter. Shiner finally mounted their first successful drive of the game, scoring their only touchdown on a short run by quarterback Carson Schuette, making it 21-6. In the fourth quarter, both teams traded possessions, but after Ganado stopped Shiner on a crucial fourth down, Logan Bures capped the scoring with a 13-yard touchdown run, sealing a 28-6 victory. Though the win was not perfect, it felt great for Ganado to finally defeat Shiner on their home field and start district play with a 1-0 record. Ullman passed for 154 yards and three touchdowns but was intercepted twice, which ended two potential scoring drives, keeping the final score closer than it might have been.

Following the win over Shiner, Ganado returned home and convincingly defeated Kenedy 48-16. Ullman had an outstanding game, passing for 253 yards and four touchdowns. Hayden was the leading receiver with 96 yards on two catches, including a 58-yard touchdown reception. Holt contributed with two touchdown receptions of 35 and 33 yards and added a rushing touchdown. Logan Bures had a big day rushing for 72 yards and scored two rushing touchdowns, along with catching a 62-yard touchdown on his only reception. Ganado built a commanding 41-0 lead by the third quarter before Kenedy scored twice late in the game. With the victory over Kenedy, Ganado improved to a 5-1 overall record and 2-0 in district play as they headed into their bye week, positioned exactly where they wanted to be in the season. Coming out of their bye week, Ganado traveled to Bloomington and delivered a dominant 62-6 victory. The win was a complete team effort, highlighted by Ullman's career-best performance, passing for 358 yards and throwing six touchdown passes while completing 21 of 23 attempts, nearly perfect accuracy. The offense spread the ball effectively, with nine different receivers catching passes. Logan Bures led the receiving corps with 114 yards on four receptions and two touchdowns, while also leading the team in rushing with 94 yards and scoring once on the ground. The defense contributed strongly as well, intercepting three passes and recovering a fumble, helping secure the comprehensive victory.

Around this time, Ganado welcomed a new superintendent, Dr. Jonathan Szymanski, who was living in East Bernard and serving as a city councilman there. Dr. Szymanski brought a wealth of experience, having previously worked as an assistant principal at Wharton High School, and as principal at Northwood High School in Rapides Parish, Louisiana, as well as at Port Allen Middle School in West Baton Rouge Parish, Louisiana. He was also familiar with the local area, being a graduate of Brazos High School in 1994, and had made his first varsity tackle in a football game at Ganado back in 1991. In addition to his educational career, Szymanski owned and operated his own insurance business for seven years. He and his family were a great fit for the Ganado community and were warmly welcomed.

With a 3-0 district record, the Indians were prepared to face Three Rivers, eager to avenge last season's loss. Three Rivers entered the game with a 5-3 record but had suffered tough defeats to Refugio and Shiner in district play. Despite high expectations - having lost only one senior and returning almost the entire team, including four-year starting quarterback Caden Soliz and standout receiver Derek Lancaster - Three Rivers was struggling. Like a "wounded animal," Three Rivers proved to be a dangerous opponent, and the Indians knew they were in for a tough battle. The first quarter was a defensive standoff as both teams exchanged possessions without scoring. Early in the second quarter, Luke Bures forced and recovered a fumble deep in Three Rivers territory, giving Ganado excellent field position. The Indians capitalized when Ullman connected with Hicks on a one-handed 9-yard touchdown catch, putting Ganado ahead 6-0 after a missed extra point by Joe Rodriguez. Following this, Three Rivers muffed the kickoff, again handing Ganado good field position, but the Indians could not capitalize on this opportunity. Both teams traded punts until Ullman found Hayden on a big gain deep into Three Rivers territory, then connected again with Hicks for a 30-yard touchdown, increasing Ganado's lead to 13-0. Three Rivers responded just before halftime with a late score, closing the half at 13-6 in favor of Ganado. The second half opened with Three Rivers scoring on their first possession, but a blocked extra point kept the game tied at 13-13. Ganado's offense stalled on the next drive, forcing a punt, and Three Rivers took advantage, scoring another touchdown to take their first lead of the game, 20-13, midway through the third quarter. Refusing to give up, Ganado answered as Hayden made a critical catch on a Ullman pass, setting up a short two-yard touchdown run by Ullman himself, tying the game 20-20 at the start of the fourth quarter. The contest continued as a classic, with both teams exchanging punts. The Indians made the decisive play when Holt broke free for a 50-yard touchdown run, giving Ganado a 27-20 lead with just minutes remaining. Three Rivers mounted a late drive and converted a crucial fourth-and-long, reaching inside the Ganado five-yard line with less than three minutes left. They scored and elected to attempt a two-point conversion to win the game outright. However, the Indians' defense held strong as Pena batted the conversion pass away, preserving Ganado's narrow 27-26 lead. Three Rivers attempted an onside kick, but Ganado recovered and secured the victory by picking up a first down to run out the clock. For Three Rivers, Soliz passed for 191 yards and a touchdown while rushing for 56 yards and scoring once. Kaiyden Thomas led their rushing attack with 90 yards and two touchdowns, and Lancaster recorded 111 yards receiving on seven catches. Ullman led Ganado with 210 passing yards and two touchdowns, both to Hicks, who had 53 yards on four receptions. Hayden was Ganado's leading receiver with 99 yards on four catches and made several critical plays that helped drive the offense. This hard-fought game tested the Indians' mental toughness, and they responded with composure and resilience. The win improved Ganado's district record to 4-0, putting them in a strong position to clinch the district championship. With only one district game left against Skidmore-Tynan, a victory there would secure a home district title game against Refugio in the season finale. The Indians traveled to Skidmore-Tynan and handled the game decisively with a 62-0 victory. Ullman threw for 325 yards and six touchdowns, distributing the ball to six different receivers, each scoring a touchdown. Luke Bures led the receiving corps with 101 yards on three catches and one touchdown. On the ground, Logan Bures dominated with 114 yards on only five carries and scored twice. With this win, the Indians improved to 8-1 overall and 5-0 in district play. Despite outside doubts, Ganado continued to prove their critics wrong week after week. Now, they had earned the opportunity to compete for the district title at home against the 8-1 Refugio team.

Refugio was the favorite to advance to state and potentially win the championship. They featured an explosive running back in Jordan King and boasted three all-state players: wide receiver Ernest Campbell, the fastest athlete in the state, linebacker Kaleb Brown, and defensive back

Isaiah Avery. For Ganado, this was the moment to prove they could compete with - and even beat - such a formidable opponent. In the previous year's regional playoff game, Ganado had given their all and only trailed 12-7 at halftime before falling apart in the second half and losing 53-7. This game represented their biggest challenge yet and an opportunity to silence doubters by showing that a team with limited depth could still belong at this level. The matchup was for the district championship, a scenario few outside Ganado had predicted back in August, but the team believed in themselves. The Indians started strong, forcing Refugio to punt on their first possession. Taking over at midfield, Ganado drove to the three-yard line but was set back by a penalty and missed a 24-yard field goal attempt by Rodriguez, which hit the right upright. Refugio capitalized on this miss as Campbell scored on a 51-yard touchdown run at the end of the first quarter, putting them up 7-0. Both teams then exchanged punts until Refugio faced a fourth-and-short at their own 30-yard line. The Indians' defense stuffed the attempt, giving Ganado possession with good field position, but the offense failed to score and turned the ball over on downs. Refugio took advantage, with King breaking loose for a 49-yard touchdown run to extend the lead to 14-0. The situation worsened when Ullman was intercepted on the next play, giving Refugio another opportunity which they converted as Kelan Brown connected with Chai Whitmire on a 38-yard touchdown pass, increasing the lead to 20-0. Despite another defensive stop by Ganado on a late first-half fourth down attempt, their offense struggled all half and they went into halftime trailing 20-0. The second half became a defensive battle, with both teams trading punts and stopping fourth-down attempts. Early in the fourth quarter, Refugio extended their lead with a 41-yard field goal by Brown, making it 23-0. Ganado fought hard and began to mount a promising drive inside Refugio territory, but Ullman was intercepted for the second time, allowing Refugio to capitalize again with a short touchdown run with just over three minutes left, pushing the score to 30-0. Despite the tough game, Ganado never quit and scored a late touchdown with six seconds remaining when Ullman connected with Hicks on a 15-yard pass, finalizing the score at 30-7. Refugio celebrated their district championship on Ganado's field. King had an impressive game, rushing for 233 yards and a touchdown, although a 75-yard touchdown run was negated by a penalty. Refugio was penalized nine times for 110 yards. Defensively, Refugio held Ganado's ground game to only 32 yards on 36 carries. Ullman passed for 194 yards and one touchdown, but his two interceptions proved costly. While Ganado had opportunities to score, execution and preventing big plays were crucial factors that didn't go their way. The team did not forget this game and knew that if they met Refugio again in the playoffs, they would be better prepared. Having faced them once, seen their speed and skill firsthand, Ganado was determined to return stronger next time.

The Indians finished the regular season with an 8-2 record, securing second place as the district runner-up - a respectable outcome for a team many had written off. This marked the beginning of a memorable playoff run. Ganado returned to Taft for the second consecutive year to face Santa Maria in the bi-district round on a Thursday night. The Indians dominated from the start, building a 41-0 halftime lead and ultimately winning 55-6 to advance to the area round. Ullman was nearly flawless in passing, completing 17 of 19 attempts for 218 yards and four touchdowns, each caught by a different receiver, showcasing a well-balanced offense.

Their next opponent was #9 ranked Mason, boasting an undefeated 11-0 record, and the game was held at Toyota Rattler Stadium in San Marcos. This matchup was the first meeting between Ganado and Mason since Mason defeated Ganado 7-0 in the 2011 regional playoffs and went on to win their first state title. Mason, which also won a state championship in 2018, was considered one of the premier programs in the region alongside Shiner and Refugio. Many outsiders predicted Mason would advance to face Refugio for the Region 4 championship, doubting Ganado's chances. However, Ganado was determined to prove those doubters wrong. The Indians opened the game with a strong drive, moving 61 yards over 14 plays and consuming seven minutes before Ullman connected with Luke Bures for a 15-yard touchdown, giving Ganado a 7-0 lead. Mason responded with a touchdown on their first possession, but their extra point attempt was blocked, and Pena returned the loose ball 85 yards for two points, pushing Ganado ahead 9-6. After this, Ganado's offense stalled briefly, gaining only five yards on their next two drives. However, before halftime, they mounted a successful drive capped by a two-yard touchdown run from Holt, extending their lead to 16-6 at the break. Mason scored on the opening drive of the second half, narrowing the gap to 16-12, but that would be as close as they got. On Ganado's next possession, Pena took a screen pass from Ullman, evaded several defenders, and raced 45 yards for a touchdown, increasing the lead to 23-12. The Indians then put the game away with a methodical 98-yard, 14-play drive, finished by Logan Bures' three-yard touchdown run, making the score 30-12 with nearly 12 minutes left. Ganado added one more score when Ullman ran 11 yards for a touchdown, sealing the final score at 37-12. Ullman finished the game with 222 passing yards, two touchdowns, and one interception. He also contributed 37 rushing yards and a touchdown. Defensively, aside from allowing Mason to score on the first possessions of each half, Ganado's defense performed strongly, shutting down Mason for the remainder of the game after their second-half touchdown. This victory sent a clear message and propelled the Indians into the regional round for the fifth consecutive year. Coach Ervin remarked after the game that within the Ganado community, the team believes they are very good and uses the lack of respect from media and outsiders as motivation. Despite being underappreciated outside their local area, the team remains focused on winning and lets the scoreboard speak for itself.

The following week, the Indians faced the undefeated 12-0 Holland team at Brenham's Cub Stadium the day after Thanksgiving. Both teams traded punts early in the game, but a muffed punt by Ganado gave Holland excellent field position just outside the red zone. Holland advanced to the Indian 10-yard line, but the Ganado defense stiffened and forced a missed field goal attempt. Ganado then found their offensive rhythm as Luke Bures made a spectacular one-handed catch from Ullman for the first score of the game. However, Rodriguez missed the extra point, making the score 6-0. The Indians continued to apply pressure by successfully executing an onside kick recovery deep in Holland territory. Ullman appeared to be on his way to the end zone on the next play but was tackled at the two-yard line, where Holt took the ball in for a touchdown, extending Ganado's lead to 13-0. The defense forced Holland to punt, and Ganado took over deep in their own territory with 97 yards to go. Logan Bures then broke loose for a 70-yard run to the Holland 12-yard line. Although the Holland defense held Ganado on fourth down, Rodriguez successfully kicked a 23-yard field goal, pushing the lead to 16-0. Holland managed to move the ball into the red zone before halftime but missed another field goal, allowing Ganado to maintain a 16-0 lead at the break. Ganado came out strong in the second half. On Holland's first possession, Logan Bures intercepted a pass and returned it 33 yards for a pick-six touchdown, increasing the lead to 23-0 and putting Ganado in a strong position to close out the game. However, Holland fought back with a touchdown on their next possession, cutting the score to 23-7. Ganado responded as Luke Bures caught a short pass from Ullman, and despite appearing to be tackled for minimal gain, he fell on top of a defender and continued to run for a 48-yard touchdown, pushing the lead to 30-7. Holland answered again with a touchdown drive, narrowing the score to 30-14 in a wild third-quarter shootout. Holland attempted an onside kick, but Ganado recovered and quickly answered with a 31-yard touchdown pass from Ullman to Pena, making the score 36-14. The Indians defense made crucial stops to prevent Holland from scoring further, while Ganado added two more fourth-quarter touchdowns - a run by Ullman and a 17-yard pass from Ullman to Hayden - extending the lead to 50-14. Holland scored the final points of the game late, resulting in a final score of 50-22. Ullman finished with 288 passing yards, four touchdowns, and one interception. He also ran for 57 yards, scoring one touchdown. Luke Bures led the receivers with 113 yards on four receptions and two touchdowns, while Holt led the rushing attack with 82 yards and one touchdown. Overall, the Indians rushed for a total of 262 yards on 28 attempts, showcasing perfect offensive balance. For the second consecutive week, Ganado defeated another undefeated team and advanced to the quarterfinals for the first time since 2019. This achievement was a testament to the hard work and dedication of the team. Awaiting them next was their old rival, #2 ranked Refugio.

Four weeks earlier, on November 3, Refugio had defeated Ganado 30-7 to claim the district championship. Although Ganado performed well in some areas during that game, there were still improvements to be made. However, all week leading up to their next meeting, Ganado maintained a strong mindset that they could be the more physical team and win. Nothing was going to stop the Indians. At this point in the season, Ganado was playing the best football of the year and had stepped up their game once the playoffs began. Quarterback Ullman was emerging as a confident leader on the field. For context, Refugio had won the last ten meetings against Ganado dating back to 2014 and had ended Ganado's season the previous three years in the regional round with lopsided scores. This losing streak had to end, and the Indians were determined to put a stop to it. The day before the game, Chris Thomasson from *KIII 3News* in Corpus Christi responded to Refugio fans on Facebook, mistakenly stating the semifinal matchup between Refugio and Timpson, would be played in the Houston area, which was a disrespect to Ganado. This echoed similar disrespect from 1996 when Refugio prematurely prepared for their next opponent (Groveton), assuming Ganado was an easy win. Ganado embraced this doubt and disrespect, adopting the nickname "Haters Tour" and using it as motivation to prove the doubters wrong.

On Thursday, November 30, only Ganado knew what was about to unfold as fans filled Victoria's Memorial Stadium. The Indians delivered one of the most dominant performances ever seen. Starting on offense, Ganado executed trick plays early, with Ullman connecting to Luke Bures on a flea-flicker for a big gain that energized the crowd. Despite an interception inside the red zone on the next play, Ganado forced Refugio to punt and then scored again when Ullman found Hicks for a 32-yard touchdown, giving Ganado a 7-0 lead late in the first quarter. Refugio converted a fourth down on their next drive and moved into Ganado's red zone, facing another fourth and short. However, Ganado's defense held strong and took over inside their own 20-yard line. Both teams exchanged punts throughout the second quarter, with Ganado's drives occasionally stalled by missed snaps. Near halftime, Refugio quarterback Kelan Brown was pressured and sacked by John Utley, who forced a fumble recovered by Holt at the three-yard line. Holt ran it in for a touchdown, extending Ganado's lead to 14-0 at halftime. Refugio opened the second half with a 63-yard, 12-play drive capped by an 18-yard touchdown run from Jordan King, narrowing the score to 14-6. It seemed like history might repeat itself, but Ganado responded by scoring on three of their next four possessions to put the game out of reach. Ullman connected with Logan Bures on a 15-yard touchdown pass to make it 21-6 at the end of the third quarter. The Indians continued to dominate defensively, forcing Refugio to punt again. One of the game's most memorable plays came when Holt, playing the game of his career, rambled 57 yards for a touchdown early in the fourth quarter to extend the lead to 28-6. After another Refugio punt, Ullman threw a short pass to Hayden, who broke tackles and sprinted 37 yards for a touchdown, pushing the score to 34-6. Refugio managed to score once more, bringing the score to 34-12, but the game was far from close. On the final play, Utley sacked Brown again, forcing a fumble that Holt recovered and returned 10 yards for a touchdown, sealing a commanding 41-12 victory for Ganado.

Ganado had finally overcome the Refugio obstacle that had haunted them for years, silencing all critics. The team believed in themselves and learned from their 30-7 loss four weeks prior. Ganado's defense was dominant, holding Refugio to only 93 rushing yards and limiting Jordan King to 46 yards after he had rushed for 233 yards in the previous matchup. The Indians also contained a high-powered offense that averaged 46.8 points per game. Defensive back Austen Pena excelled in coverage against Refugio's Ernest Campbell, holding him to just one catch for seven yards and intercepting a pass. Defensive coordinator Jason Chambless and assistant Trey Thedford designed a strong game plan that the players executed flawlessly. Holt was outstanding, playing the best game of his career. He dominated the line of scrimmage from his defensive tackle position, making plays alongside Utley and scoring two defensive touchdowns. He also had a strong offensive game, rushing for 126 yards and a touchdown. Ullman completed 12 of 18 passes for 192 yards and three touchdowns. The entire team dominated the game, much to the shock of news reporters from Victoria and Corpus Christi, including Greg Tepper, chief editor of *Dave Campbell's Texas Football Magazine*, who is known for favoring winning programs and often shows little respect for others. This game was also the final one for Refugio head coach Jason Herring, who resigned after the season but remained the school's athletic director. His defensive coordinator, Drew Cox, was promoted to head coach.

Ganado was on a mission, playing in the semifinals for the first time since 2009, with a chance to earn a berth at the state championship. Despite their recent successes, the Indians still felt they were not receiving the respect they deserved. Their next opponent was the top-ranked Timpson team, led by their 5-star recruit quarterback Terry Bussey, who was committed to Texas A&M. Bussey also played safety on defense, and Timpson's roster was filled with talented athletes. Timpson was making their fourth consecutive semifinal appearance but had been denied a trip to the state championship the previous three years - twice by Shiner, who won state titles in 2020 and 2021, and last season by Refugio on a last-second field goal. Most state polls favored Timpson heavily, seemingly overlooking the teams Ganado had just defeated. It appeared that Ganado would need to win the state championship to finally earn widespread respect. Despite the odds, Ganado was undeterred and prepared to compete just as fiercely as they had against Refugio. One notable challenge for the Indians was that several players had been battling the flu during the week, so the team was not at full strength. However, the illness would not stop them from giving their best effort on the field. On Thursday, December 7, Ganado traveled to Woodforest Bank Stadium in Shenandoah - the same venue where they had last played a semifinal game in 2009, which resulted in a loss to Cayuga. As the Indians took the field, a cheerleader-run sign drew attention; it read: "Hey Dave Campbell, you picked us 4th in our District… You meant Top 4 in the State, Right? #haterstours23 #underdogs."

Ganado came out strong, scoring on their opening possession when Ullman connected with Pena for a 37-yard touchdown pass, taking a 7-0 lead. Timpson quickly responded as Bussey capped their drive with a 6-yard touchdown run, tying the game at 7-7. Ganado answered back with Ullman scoring on a one-yard run, ending the first quarter ahead 14-7. The Indians extended their lead in the second quarter on a five-yard touchdown pass from Ullman to Hayden, making it 21-7. Timpson managed to score later in the quarter, narrowing the score to 21-14, which held through halftime. In the second half, Ganado's offense continued well in the first half, but the momentum shifted to Timpson. Midway through the third quarter, after Timpson tied the game 21-21, Ganado faced a second-and-goal from the two-yard line and seemed poised to regain the lead. However, Timpson's defense broke through for the first time all night, tackling Holt for a three-yard loss - the only negative rushing play of this game. Two plays later, Rodriguez missed a field goal attempt, keeping the score tied and shifting momentum fully to Timpson. Timpson then took over and Bussey scored on a 12-yard touchdown run to give Timpson a 28-21 lead at the end of the third quarter. Bussey sealed the scoring in the fourth quarter with a seven-yard touchdown run, extending the lead to 35-21 and ending Ganado's remarkable season. Bussey finished the game with 194 passing yards, two passing touchdowns, 141 rushing yards, and three rushing touchdowns. Coach Ervin acknowledged that Bussey was "as he is advertised and really, really good." The game plan had focused on limiting Bussey's big plays, and the Indians succeeded in that effort, as Timpson only had two plays longer than 20 yards all game. Ullman was held under 100 yards passing for only the second time all season, completing 80 yards and two touchdowns. Holt rushed for 101 yards in his final game, concluding his football career.

Coming into the season, the seniors were determined to leave a lasting legacy for the future of the football program, according to Coach Ervin. Only three seniors - Holt, Martin Ramirez, and Vincent Barajas - would graduate, leaving behind their legacy but also paving the way for a very experienced team to return in 2024. Holt signed with Howard Payne University to continue his football career at the next level. Ullman had an outstanding season, setting single-season school records with 3,111 passing yards and 47 touchdown passes. This team was the first Ganado squad in 14 years to reach the semifinals, which was a special achievement that had been a long time coming. Considering the program had been doubted by many who claimed it was finished or lacked the ability to compete, this team proved those critics wrong throughout the season. They finished with an impressive 12-3 record, marking Ganado's first 12-win season in 20 years since 2003. Even though several players battled the flu late in the season, the team fought hard against a very talented Timpson squad and gave them a strong challenge. By the end of the year, Ganado had gained statewide respect for their accomplishments, although some doubters still remained. The following week, Timpson dominated Tolar with a 49-7 victory in the Class 2A Division I state championship game. This decisive win further fueled Ganado's motivation and raised expectations for what the team could achieve in 2024.

Chapter 12

Champions at Last

2024

On February 1, during the biannual UIL realignment, Ganado remained in District 15-2A Division I, although the district itself underwent significant changes. Refugio moved to District 16, and Shiner dropped to Class 2A Division II, leaving Ganado as the clear favorite to win their first football district championship since 2013. Only Bloomington and Kenedy stayed in the district from the previous lineup, while old district rivals Schulenburg, Flatonia, and Weimar were added, all of whom Ganado had faced in the 2020 and 2021 seasons. Additionally, Danbury joined the district after moving down from 3A. In the spring, the Indians' baseball team, which included many football players, made a historic run to the regional final before losing to a strong Flatonia team, signaling a promising future. Summer then arrived and passed quickly, setting the stage for what was to come.

On June 22, the preseason rankings by *Dave Campbell's Texas Football Magazine* were released, and Ganado was picked as the number one team in Class 2A Division I. This recognition was well-deserved, considering the team had only lost three seniors and still had a very talented senior class returning. The magazine may have been influenced by the cheerleader's run-through sign at the Timpson game, but the respect was earned, and now it was time for the team to back it up on the field. A week later, on June 28, Ganado's athletes participated in the 7 on 7 state tournament and fell just one game short of advancing to the semifinal round after a loss to Tidehaven. Ganado finished 5-1 in state tournament play, marking their best performance since they began competing in 7 on 7. However, they did not forget that Tidehaven's fans mocked them after the game by shouting "Week 4! Week 4!" - a reference to their upcoming non-district football matchup on September 20, which Ganado was determined to win.

As football season approached, excitement was high. On July 8, Ganado narrowly avoided disaster when Hurricane Beryl, a Category 2 storm, landed just east of Palacios. While neighboring counties and Houston suffered more damage, Ganado and Jackson County were ready to help those affected. Later that month, troubling news emerged: Bryce Ullman, one of Ganado's gifted athletes, was diagnosed with a stress fracture in his lower back. He began physical therapy and was scheduled to see a doctor on September 19 - the day before the final non-district game against Tidehaven - in hopes of receiving clearance to play. This injury was kept private within the team and the Ganado community due to its sensitive nature. Ullman's injury was attributed to overuse, as he had not had any rest while competing in multiple sports, putting his senior season in jeopardy. About a month later, it was reported that Logan "Smoke" Bures also appeared to have a similar stress fracture in his lower back and was expected to be sidelined for an extended period. This news cast a negative cloud over the start of the season, raising questions about why such setbacks were occurring just when everything seemed aligned for Ganado to compete for a state championship. Fortunately, a couple of weeks later, it was confirmed that Bures did not have a fracture and was expected to return around the same time as Ullman, provided all went well. Despite the early challenges, there was still hope for the team as the season drew closer.

To start the season, freshman Landyn Arriaga took the snaps at quarterback and performed well early on. The entire receiving corps, consisting of Landon Hicks, Austen Pena, Cain Hayden, and Luke Bures, returned after combining for an impressive 2,603 yards and 36 touchdowns the previous season. This group was a highly dangerous offensive threat and was widely regarded as the best receiving corps in the state. Logan Bures, who was named the district's newcomer of the year as a freshman last season after rushing for 675 yards and 10 touchdowns, was expected to provide a significant boost to the offense once he recovered from his injury. In the meantime, senior Vince Sablatura filled the running back position, bringing experience from multiple years in the backfield. The offensive line was composed of strong and experienced players, including seniors Luke Green at tackle, Erick Guerrero at guard, and Carter Kovar at center. Senior David Almeda joined as a guard, while junior Ayden Tudyk took the other tackle spot. Senior Joe Rodriguez returned as the team's kicker for his third year. On defense, the lineup was solid across the board, with Green and junior John Utley at defensive ends, Guerrero at tackle, and Tudyk filling the position left vacant by graduate Dylan Holt. The linebacker group included Sablatura, Hicks, and Logan Bures, while the secondary, known for its speed, featured Pena and Luke Bures at cornerback and Hayden and Ullman at safety. While Logan Bures and Ullman were sidelined with injuries, Rodriguez and senior Callen Hajovsky - both of whom also played receiver - stepped in at defensive back positions. This team had tremendous potential but was also united as one cohesive unit, which made them special. The players put in the necessary work and were ready to compete. After strong performances in scrimmages against Brazos and Shiner, the team was prepared and eager for the season to begin, with expectations running high.

The Indians opened the football season with three consecutive home games, beginning with a matchup against Van Vleck. Originally scheduled as an away game, the venue was moved to Ganado due to delays in the installation of Van Vleck's new artificial turf field. The Indians came out strong, scoring on their opening possession after converting a fourth down, with senior Vince Sablatura capping the drive with a 7-yard touchdown run to give Ganado a 6-0 lead. On the ensuing kickoff, Ganado executed a successful onside kick, quickly regaining possession. Freshman quarterback Landyn Arriaga then connected with Luke Bures for a 32-yard touchdown, extending the lead to 12-0 in the first quarter. Van Vleck's offense got its first chance but immediately fumbled on their first snap, and the Indians recovered. Sablatura capitalized again with a 3-yard touchdown run, making it 19-0 and giving the impression that a blowout might be underway. However, Van Vleck responded quickly as their standout running back, Cory Austin, broke free for a 75-yard touchdown, cutting the lead to 19-6. The teams then traded possessions, with Ganado turning the ball over on downs and later intercepting a Van Vleck pass to end a drive, leaving the halftime score at 19-6. Van Vleck came out strong in the second half, with Austin scoring again on their second play from scrimmage with a 66-yard run to make it 19-13. The Indians' once-effective ground game was shut down in the second half as Van Vleck's defense adjusted, forcing Ganado to punt. Van Vleck continued to ride Austin's hot hand, as he scored his third touchdown on a 69-yard run, giving his team a 20-19 lead in the third quarter. Ganado quickly answered, with Austen Pena returning the ensuing kickoff 91 yards for a touchdown to retake the lead at 26-20. The third quarter was full of fireworks, as Van Vleck's Steve Moore responded with a 74-yard touchdown run to tie the game at 26-26 after a missed extra point. In the fourth quarter, both defenses tightened up, but Ganado gained an edge by blocking a Van Vleck punt, setting up good field position. The Indians converted a crucial fourth down, and Luke Bures finished the drive with a 6-yard touchdown run to reclaim the lead, 33-26. Van Vleck attempted a late comeback, but Ganado sealed the win with their second interception of the game, securing a hard-fought 33-26 victory to start the season 1-0. Sablatura led the ground game with 151 rushing yards and two touchdowns, while freshman quarterback Arriaga managed the offense efficiently, throwing for a touchdown and maintaining composure in his varsity debut. Despite some concern over giving up several explosive plays - particularly to Austin, who rushed for 254 yards and three scores - the defense held strong when it mattered most. Given that Austin was likely the best running back Ganado would face all season, the performance was viewed as a learning opportunity. Overall, it was a solid and encouraging win against a talented Van Vleck team that would go on to reach the regional round of the playoffs. The victory provided momentum and confidence for the season ahead.

In the second game of the season, the Indians hosted Boling and overcame a shaky start to earn a 21-7 victory and improve to 2-0. The game began with the Indian offense being stopped on their opening series, followed by a blocked punt that gave Boling possession inside Ganado's 10-yard line. However, the Indian defense stepped up in a big way, with Sablatura making a key tackle for a loss and Callen Hajovsky intercepting a pass near the goal line to halt the scoring threat. Following the turnover, Arriaga launched a deep pass down the sideline to Pena, who made the catch, cut inside, and outran the defense for a thrilling 93-yard touchdown, giving Ganado an early 7-0 lead. Boling responded with their only sustained drive and score of the game to tie it at 7-7. Ganado's offense moved the ball again but missed a field goal attempt by Joe Rodriguez as the first quarter ended. Early in the second quarter, Luke Bures came up with an interception on Boling's next possession, setting the Indians up in the red zone. The offense converted a short fourth down, and Arriaga connected with Cain Hayden for a 7-yard touchdown pass, giving Ganado a 14-7 lead at halftime. To open the second half, Boling mishandled the kickoff due to a miscommunication, leaving the ball untouched and allowing Ganado to recover it. The Indians quickly capitalized, with Arriaga running in an 8-yard touchdown to extend the lead to 21-7. The rest of the game became a defensive battle, with both teams struggling to generate offensive momentum. After giving up big plays the previous week,

Ganado's defense rebounded with a strong performance, showcasing the dominance and discipline they were expected to bring all season. Coach Ervin praised Arriaga for his impressive play, noting his 213 passing yards and composure as a freshman. He also highlighted the defense's much-improved performance. With the win, Ganado moved to 2-0 on the season, demonstrating growth on both sides of the ball.

In their third consecutive home game, the Ganado Indians faced off against traditional powerhouse East Bernard. The matchup carried extra weight after last season's close contest, where Ganado jumped out early before ultimately falling 35-27. This time, East Bernard came in with a new head coach and a major offensive shift, abandoning their trademark slot-T in favor of a spread system. Ganado, ranked #1 in the state, understood they had a target on their back, and East Bernard was ready to challenge them. The Indians were already dealing with adversity, missing key starters Logan Bures and Bryce Ullman. Additionally, their offensive line was depleted, forcing two freshmen into starting roles - an unfortunate situation against East Bernard's dominant defensive tackles, Tamarcus Sanders and Ty Domel. These two controlled the line of scrimmage, and as a result, Ganado's offense struggled to gain traction, going into halftime trailing 13-0. Early in the second half, Ganado appeared to have East Bernard backed up deep in their own territory, setting up a potential momentum shift. Instead, Malik Thomas found a crease and broke free for a 93-yard touchdown, putting East Bernard up 20-0. Thomas had a stellar night, rushing for 152 yards and scoring three total touchdowns - two on the ground and one receiving from quarterback Dan Bartlett. Despite the deficit, Ganado showed resilience. Arriaga connected with Luke Bures for a 25-yard touchdown in the third quarter, and then with Pena for a 5-yard score early in the fourth, narrowing the gap to 20-12 with just over 10 minutes left to play. The comeback seemed within reach. However, East Bernard responded with a decisive scoring drive to extend their lead to 26-12. Arriaga then threw his first interception of the season, which was nearly returned for a touchdown, with the Indians making the stop at their own two-yard line. With the outcome decided and only seconds remaining, East Bernard had the opportunity to kneel and end the game, but instead called a timeout and ran in another touchdown. This unnecessary score sparked frustration and outrage from the Ganado crowd, who saw it as unsportsmanlike. East Bernard walked away with a 33-12 win, handing Ganado its first loss of the season. The defeat dropped Ganado to 2-1 and from #1 to #3 in the state rankings. The team left the field feeling deflated and disappointed. However, in the postgame aftermath, someone made a bold statement: "We will see who gets the last laugh when we're holding up that trophy in December." That comment proved prophetic, as this loss would be Ganado's only one of the season. Despite the outcome, Arriaga had a strong showing, throwing for 189 yards and two touchdowns while managing the game effectively under pressure. The offense was limited to just 44 rushing yards on 21 attempts due to East Bernard's defensive front. Luke Bures recorded 74 receiving yards and a touchdown on three catches, Pena added 39 yards and a touchdown on five receptions, and Hayden contributed 60 yards on seven catches. The game was a tough lesson for the Indians, but one that would fuel their determination the rest of the season.

On September 19, Bryce Ullman was officially cleared to return to action - initially on offense only - with plans to gradually ease him back into defensive duties. Although his clearance came that day, Ullman had already been practicing for two weeks in preparation, fully expecting to play against Tidehaven. In a moment that seemed almost prophetic, he received a fortune cookie that read, "An exciting sporting event is in your near future," perfectly foreshadowing what would unfold the following night. Notably, his return came exactly three months before the Class 2A Division I state championship, scheduled for December 19 at AT&T Stadium - a date that would become significant later in the season.

The atmosphere was electric as Ganado traveled to Delvin Taska Stadium in El Maton to face the defending 3A Division II state finalist Tidehaven Tigers in their final non-district game. When Ullman took the field for warmups, the energy shifted. The team looked rejuvenated, determined, and entirely different from the one that had lost to East Bernard just a week earlier. Tidehaven, having prepared for freshman quarterback Landyn Arriaga, was caught off guard. Tidehaven received the opening kickoff, but their possession was quickly cut short by an acrobatic interception from Hajovsky, giving Ganado great field position. The Indians capitalized, with Luke Bures punching in a one-yard touchdown to give Ganado an early 7-0 lead. Tidehaven responded with a promising drive, but the Ganado defense held strong on fourth down. After a few exchanged possessions, Ganado struck again in the second quarter with two effective screen passes to Hicks and Pena, setting up Ullman's first touchdown pass of the season - a 3-yard connection to Pena, extending the lead to 14-0. The Indians' defense continued to shine, forcing another turnover on downs. On the ensuing drive, a batted pass miraculously landed in the hands of offensive lineman Luke Green, who rumbled for 9 yards to keep the momentum alive. Ullman then connected with Luke Bures for a 9-yard touchdown, sending Ganado into halftime with a commanding 21-0 lead. In the second half, Tidehaven attempted to mount a comeback but was again denied on fourth down by Ganado's defense. Ullman responded with a short pass to Hayden, who broke loose for a 77-yard touchdown, making it 28-0. On the next possession, Rodriguez intercepted a Tidehaven pass, and Ullman soon found Hicks for an 11-yard touchdown, increasing the lead to 35-0. Luke Bures added a third interception for Ganado on Tidehaven's next drive. After a strong punt return set the Indians up at midfield, Ullman hit Pena on a short route that turned into a 51-yard touchdown, pushing the lead to 42-0. Tidehaven finally scored in the fourth quarter, but it was too little, too late, as Ganado sealed an emphatic 42-6 win. As the final seconds ticked off, the Ganado crowd echoed chants of "Week 4! Week 4!" - a response to Tidehaven's taunting back in June during the 7-on-7 tournament. The game was a complete statement of dominance by the Indians. Ullman's return gave the team a massive boost in confidence, and he delivered a career-best performance, throwing for 402 yards and five touchdowns. Pena led the receivers with 11 catches for 166 yards and two scores. Coach Ervin praised the team's overall execution, with special emphasis on the suffocating defense that forced three interceptions and multiple fourth-down stops. This performance solidified Ganado's identity as a top contender and marked the turning point in their season. From that point forward, as district play began, the Indians would go on a dominant run - winning every game in convincing fashion over the next two months.

The Indians returned home for their district opener against Flatonia with a full-strength roster, as both Ullman and Logan Bures were back in action. Bures made an immediate impact on his first carry, nearly scoring on a 47-yard run. On the very next play, Ullman connected with Hicks for a touchdown, giving the Indians a 7-0 lead and setting the tone for what would become a historic night. Ganado dominated in every phase of the game, routing Flatonia 84-3 in a record-breaking performance. The 84 points set a new school record, surpassing the previous mark of 78 set in 1941. The Indians also set records for most touchdowns in a game with 12 and most extra points, as Rodriguez went a perfect 12-for-12 on PATs. Ullman was nearly flawless, throwing for 221 yards and a career-high seven touchdown passes, tying the school's single-game record previously set by Kyle Bures-Guerrero in 2021. Logan Bures had a strong season debut, rushing for 155 yards and a touchdown, while Hayden led the receivers with 104 yards and four touchdowns on five catches. The defense was equally dominant, holding Flatonia to just 50 total yards and three first downs. Lone Star Gridiron's Chris Doelle was in attendance and in his weekly Gulf Coast Huddle football show stated, "I have been involved in Texas high school football for over 40 years and I have never seen team speed like this Ganado squad at the 2A level - they WILL win state!"

Coach Ervin praised his team's execution, discipline, and pride but reminded them not to grow complacent. The Indians then traveled to Kenedy for their second district matchup and won 35-0, despite running only 17 offensive plays. On the game's first snap, Ullman found Hayden for a 60-yard touchdown, and later connected with Pena on a 43-yard score in the third quarter, finishing with 159 passing yards. Although Kenedy's slot-T offense controlled time of possession, Ganado's defense stood firm, earning their first shutout of the season. Key contributions included 12 tackles, two tackles for loss, and a forced fumble by Hicks. While defensive penalties extended some Kenedy drives, the unit held firm when it mattered most. Back at home the following week, Ganado faced Weimar in what many anticipated to be a de facto district championship game. Like Kenedy, Weimar ran a slot-T offense and entered the game with momentum after a big win over Schulenburg. Ganado answered the challenge by setting the tone early, forcing a three-and-out on Weimar's first possession and scoring on their own opening drive as Ullman connected with Hayden for a 24-yard touchdown. The Indians built a commanding 27-0 lead by halftime and went on to win 41-0. Ullman threw four touchdown passes and totaled 210 yards through the air, while also throwing his first interception of the season. Hayden had 32 receiving yards and two touchdowns, while Hicks contributed a 75-yard touchdown catch in the second quarter. The rushing attack was highly efficient, with Logan Bures gaining 124 yards and scoring on a 41-yard run in the fourth quarter. Sablatura added 65 yards and a 35-yard touchdown run in the first quarter. Defensively, the Indians collected their second consecutive shutout, showcasing improved play against the slot-T and silencing any lingering doubts about their ability to defend against run-heavy teams. At 3-0 in district play and sitting atop the standings, Ganado had clearly established itself as the team to beat. With momentum on their side and both the offense and defense firing on all cylinders, the Indians were inching closer to securing their first district title since 2013.

In the following week of district play, the Indians traveled to Schulenburg in what was considered their toughest challenge within the district. A win would all but guarantee Ganado the district championship, and the Indians were clearly up to the task from the opening whistle. The defense immediately set the tone by stopping Schulenburg on their first possession. Ganado then struck quickly on offense, as Ullman connected with Logan Bures for a 21-yard touchdown pass, giving the Indians a 6-0 lead after a missed extra point. Schulenburg fumbled on its next possession, setting up Ganado with excellent field position. Logan Bures capitalized again, this time on a 15-yard touchdown run to extend the lead to 13-0. Although Schulenburg returned the ensuing kickoff to the Ganado 11-yard line, the Indian defense held firm, forcing a turnover on downs at their own 5-yard line. On the very next play, Ullman connected with Hicks in stride down the sideline for a stunning 95-yard touchdown, pushing the lead to 20-0 by the end of the first quarter. Ganado continued their dominance early in the second quarter by blocking a Schulenburg punt, which set up a short field. Ullman then found Logan Bures again for a 4-yard touchdown pass to extend the lead to 27-0. Schulenburg finally mounted a response, aided by a Ganado pass interference penalty, but the Indians held once more as Luke Bures intercepted a pass near the red zone. However, on the ensuing possession, Ullman was pressured in his own end zone and forced to throw the ball away, resulting in a safety. Schulenburg followed with a touchdown on their next drive, cutting the lead to 27-10. Ganado answered immediately before halftime, with Ullman connecting with Hicks again on a screen pass that the senior receiver turned into a touchdown, giving the Indians a 34-10 lead at the break. In the second half, both teams traded scores, but Schulenburg was never able to close the gap, and Ganado cruised to a 61-31 victory. Although there were some defensive concerns, particularly with Schulenburg's talented quarterback Aaron Janecek and receiver Jayse Janda making plays, the game was never truly in doubt. The Indians built a commanding 27-0 lead before giving up any points and consistently stayed ahead because Schulenburg's defense simply could not stop Ganado's explosive offense. Ullman had a career night, throwing for a season-high and school-record 467 passing yards and seven touchdowns - his second seven-touchdown game of the season. Hicks also had a career-best performance, finishing with 161 receiving yards and four touchdowns on six catches. Logan Bures added to the offensive explosion with 53 receiving yards and three touchdowns, while also rushing for 99 yards and another score. Coach Ervin emphasized that facing a team like Schulenburg and their potent passing attack was an important test that would help prepare the Indians for postseason challenges. Despite surrendering 31 points, he credited the defense for making timely plays and praised the offense for being completely unstoppable and executing at an elite level. With the win, Ganado remained undefeated in district play and in full control of the district title race.

Heading into a well-earned bye week after playing eight consecutive games, the Ganado Indians stood at an impressive 7-1 overall and 4-0 in district play. With just one district game remaining, a win over Bloomington would clinch the Indians' first district title since 2013. The matchup also marked a special occasion - Senior Night - for 16 Ganado seniors in their final regular season home game. From the opening whistle, the Indians dominated. Facing a Bloomington team that, despite showing improvement this season and seeking its first playoff berth since 1999, was no match for the top-ranked Ganado squad. Ganado exploded out of the gate, scoring touchdowns on their first five possessions to take a commanding 35-0 lead by the end of the first quarter. By the end of the game, the Indians had rewritten the record books with an 86-0 victory, breaking their previous school record for points in a game. Ullman once again demonstrated elite form, throwing for 202 yards and seven touchdown passes for the third time this season, connecting with five different receivers. Luke Bures led the receiving corps with 80 yards and two touchdowns.
Defensively, Ganado was relentless, limiting Bloomington to just 52 total yards and forcing six turnovers - five fumble recoveries and one interception. Defensive scores included fumble returns by Logan Bures and Hajovsky, while Luke Reid added a safety. Coach Ervin praised the team's execution and effort, calling it a proud moment to clinch the district title after an 11-year drought. The Indians closed the regular

season on the road at Danbury, opening up a 28-0 lead by the end of the first quarter. With the game quickly out of reach, officials ran a continuous clock the rest of the way, and Ganado cruised to a 49-0 win to finish the regular season with a 9-1 record. Ullman was again efficient, completing all five of his passes for 94 yards and two touchdowns - one each to Hajovsky and Hayden. Logan Bures added 109 rushing yards and two touchdowns on just three carries, while Hicks contributed a defensive score with a fumble return for a touchdown. With the victory, the Indians secured their sixth consecutive playoff appearance dating back to 2019. The team remained focused on its season-long goal: to win a state championship - though they would take it one game at a time.

During the week leading up to Ganado's first playoff game, a historic achievement brought pride to the entire community. On November 12, the *Pride of the Tribe* Marching Band advanced to the UIL State Finals for the first time in school history, performing at the Alamodome in San Antonio. The band not only reached the finals but earned silver medals, finishing as the Class 2A State Runner-Up. This marked their ninth state appearance since 2009 and fifth consecutive trip since 2020, but it was the first time the band advanced to the final round - an incredible accomplishment that set the tone for what would become a historic playoff run for the football team. With momentum riding high in Ganado, the Indians began their journey through the Class 2A Division I football playoffs that Thursday night with a bi-district matchup against familiar foe Skidmore-Tynan at Memorial Stadium in Victoria. The two teams had met in each of the past two seasons in district competition, with Ganado winning decisively 70-0 in 2022 and 62-0 in 2023. This year proved no different, as the Indians dominated from the opening whistle, racing out to a 68-0 halftime lead and ultimately cruising to a 75-15 victory. Ullman accounted for six total touchdowns - throwing for 218 yards and four scores and adding two rushing touchdowns, including a 56-yard run that made it 75-0 in the third quarter. After that, the backups entered the game with a running clock. Logan Bures had another standout performance, scoring four touchdowns by rushing for 86 yards and two scores, catching a touchdown pass, and returning an interception for a defensive score. The defense also tallied four sacks in a completely one-sided win, advancing Ganado to the Area round.

In Area, the Indians faced a stiffer test in perennial playoff contender Crawford. This marked only the second time the two programs had met, the last being a heartbreaking 29-28 overtime loss for Ganado in the 1997 playoffs. However, the Indians showed no signs of letting history repeat itself. On a Friday night in Rockdale, Ganado delivered another dominant performance, overwhelming Crawford 59-0. The Indians were strong in all three phases of the game. Ullman threw for 229 yards and three touchdowns, while Logan Bures put on a show, rushing for 107 yards and three touchdowns and returning a punt 79 yards for another score. Rodriguez was perfect on special teams, going 8-for-8 on extra points and adding a 23-yard field goal. The defense contributed two fumble recoveries and consistently shut down Crawford's offense. Despite the commanding win, one concern emerged - Ganado was flagged for numerous penalties, which could become costly as the level of competition continued to rise. Still, the team had now won nine straight games, improving to 11-1 on the season, with each of those victories coming by 30 points or more. Since their lone loss to East Bernard in Week 3, the Indians had been virtually untouchable, and the postseason was just heating up. The community's pride extended from the band to the gridiron, and the excitement was building with every step toward a potential state championship.

For nearly a year and throughout the entire offseason, the talk around Ganado football centered on a highly anticipated rematch with Refugio. Many fans, analysts, and players believed that the winner of this playoff clash would be the favorite to advance to the state championship - and possibly win it all. The buildup was reminiscent of the 2011 playoff matchup between Ganado and Mason, which Mason won 7-0 en route to its first state title. Both Ganado and Refugio had been ranked in the top four of the Class 2A Division I state poll all season long, setting the stage for what was expected to be a monumental showdown. The tension leading up to the game was amplified by last year's stunning result, when Ganado dominated Refugio 41-12 in the quarterfinals, sending shockwaves throughout Texas. Many detractors claimed Ganado was simply lucky or that Refugio had overlooked them. However, the Indians used that as motivation and were determined to prove that last year's result was no fluke. It was time to silence the doubters and ignore the "outside noise." This game was expected to be an offensive shootout, with both teams showcasing some of the most explosive playmakers in the state.

Ganado entered the game averaging 49.8 points per game while allowing just 10.1, including four shutouts. Led by quarterback Ullman and a dangerous receiving corps featuring Hicks, Luke Bures, Pena, and Hayden, the Indians were considered nearly impossible to stop through the air. Meanwhile, Refugio brought in a potent offense of their own, averaging 61.8 points per game while giving up only 8.0 points per contest. Their star player, running back Jordan King, had already racked up 2,200 rushing yards and 39 touchdowns - an average of 16.2 yards per carry. The game was played at Sandcrab Stadium in Port Lavaca, the site of two previous playoff meetings between the schools, with the series tied 1-1. Ganado had defeated Refugio 7-6 in bi-district play in 2005, while Refugio had won 54-7 in the regional round in 2021. History seemed to favor Ganado, who had never lost to Refugio in the playoffs when serving as the designated home team, with wins in 1996, 2001, and 2005. A massive crowd filled the stands, including fans from nearby schools who came to witness the marquee matchup. Both teams entered with identical 11-1 records, and neither was expected to back down. It was clear that this game would come down to execution, composure, and - above all - the ability to make key defensive stops. With so much at stake and emotions running high, the regional playoff battle between Ganado and Refugio was finally ready to unfold.

The much-anticipated game between Ganado and Refugio finally began, with Ganado deferring the opening kickoff to the second half. This gave Refugio the first opportunity on offense, and a strong kickoff return put them in Ganado territory early. On the very first snap, Refugio's Jordan King broke off a first down run, moving the team just outside the red zone. However, Ganado's defense made a crucial stand, forcing Refugio to face a fourth down, which they failed to convert, handing possession back to Ganado. This defensive stop set the tone for the rest of the night. On their first possession, Ganado started at their 25-yard line and efficiently drove down the field using a balanced mix of runs and passes. The drive culminated in a five-yard touchdown run by Logan Bures, giving Ganado a 7-0 lead with just over three minutes left in the first quarter. Refugio returned to offense with good field position but was forced to punt by the resilient Ganado defense. Ganado seemed poised to extend their lead as they moved deep into Refugio territory with key passes from Ullman to Pena and Hayden. However, on a short fourth down inside the 10-yard line, Refugio's defense made a critical stop. Refugio then looked ready to respond, with quarterback Kelan Brown breaking free for a big gain before a hard hit by Luke Bures, who jarred the ball loose, which Ganado recovered at their own 31-yard line. Shortly after, Refugio intercepted Ullman near the Ganado 40-yard line, but as the first half expired, Ganado maintained their 7-0 lead after a defensive pass breakup by Sablatura in the end zone. In the second half, Ganado received the kickoff but was stopped by Refugio's defense. Refugio capitalized with a strong drive, highlighted by a 19-yard touchdown run by King; however, the extra point was blocked, leaving the score 7-6 with just over four minutes left in the third quarter. Ganado responded quickly when Logan Bures made a significant run to the Refugio 22-yard line. A short time later, Ullman connected with Pena for a 12-yard touchdown pass, extending Ganado's lead to 14-6 with less than a minute remaining in the third quarter. Despite being down, Refugio pushed into Ganado's red zone once again but were denied by another huge fourth-down defensive stop by the Indians. Ganado then took control of the ball with under seven minutes remaining. Logan Bures continued to carry the offense, moving the chains and using up valuable clock in an effort to secure the victory. However, Ganado struggled with some uncharacteristic dropped passes, leading to a turnover on downs and giving Refugio one last chance to tie the game. With 3:25 remaining, Refugio took over at Ganado's 23-yard line needing 77 yards to score. They converted a critical fourth down near midfield but were ultimately stopped by Ganado's defense, which played a bend-but-don't-break style throughout the game. The Indians offense then took over with less than a minute left and ran out the clock, kneeling in victory formation to secure a 14-6 win.

This hard-fought victory silenced all doubters questioning Ganado's ability to beat Refugio again. The win marked back-to-back playoff victories over Refugio and prevented them from advancing to the quarterfinals for the first time in 17 years. King rushed for 148 yards and a touchdown, but Refugio's passing attack was limited, with Brown held to just 27 yards. Refugio's offense failed to score despite reaching inside Ganado's 28, 11, and 16-yard lines. Ganado's defense played a pivotal role in making crucial stops throughout the game. Ganado faced a rare low-scoring contest but responded well under pressure. Logan Bures had an outstanding performance on the ground, rushing for 182 yards on 22 carries and scoring a touchdown. Coach Ervin praised the team's physical and mental toughness, noting that their game plan to run the ball and control the clock was essential to winning against an explosive Refugio offense. The team's resilience was evident as they battled adversity throughout the game and continued fighting until the final whistle. With this victory, the Indians answered the call and now needed to take care of business in two more games to reach their ultimate goal.

A very athletic Marlin team awaited the Indians in the quarterfinals. Marlin had just defeated Mason in a high-scoring shootout, 40-37, the previous week. Marlin featured speed across the board and a dominant, powerful offensive line, including three-star athlete Brysen Maxwell-Steele, who weighed 300 pounds. Coming into the game, Marlin's defense had recorded 30 sacks. The quarterfinal matchup was held at Toyota Rattler Stadium in San Marcos, the same venue where Ganado had defeated Mason in the Area round last season. The game started off rough for both teams, as each lost two fumbles in the first quarter. Despite this, Ganado's defense remained strong, holding Marlin out of the end zone even as they penetrated deep into Ganado territory, reaching the 4 and 13-yard lines. In the second quarter, Ganado began to find their rhythm and scored first when Ullman connected with Pena on a 28-yard touchdown pass. Logan Bures followed with a 13-yard touchdown run, giving Ganado a 14-0 lead with less than three minutes left in the half. Marlin quickly responded with an 11-yard touchdown run by their quarterback, Roderick Sutters, narrowing the score to 14-7 with just over a minute left in the second quarter. However, momentum shifted dramatically before halftime when Marlin was pinned near their own end zone. Ullman blocked a Marlin punt and recovered it for a touchdown with only four seconds remaining in the half, sending Ganado into the locker room leading 21-7. The second half began with both teams exchanging possessions. Then, Ganado mounted a drive capped by a three-yard touchdown run from Luke Bures, extending their lead to 28-7 with just over a minute and a half left in the third quarter. Marlin fought back with a determined 13-play, 83-yard drive, ending with a 4-yard touchdown run by DeAngelo Wright, bringing the score to 28-14 with just over nine minutes left in the game. Any hopes of a Marlin comeback were dashed on the very next kickoff, when Logan Bures returned it 80 yards for a touchdown, increasing Ganado's lead to 34-14. The Indians put the finishing touches on the game when Sablatura scored on a short 2-yard touchdown run, making the final score 41-14 in favor of Ganado. With this victory, Ganado advanced to the semifinals for the second consecutive year - a feat they had not achieved since the 2008 and 2009 seasons, and marking only the sixth time in school history. Additionally, Ganado made more history by breaking a pattern: in previous years, after defeating Refugio in the playoffs, the team would lose the following week. This time, however, Ganado proved it was their time to shine. Ullman had an outstanding all-around performance, blocking a punt and recovering it for a touchdown, passing for 188 yards and a touchdown, rushing for 53 yards, and intercepting a pass. Logan Bures also had a strong game, rushing for 142 yards and scoring a touchdown. This comprehensive team effort ensured the Indians continued their playoff run with confidence and momentum.

The Indians faced Joaquin in the semifinals, a team that had recently upset Honey Grove 46-22. Joaquin had a run-first team, running a slot-T offense, which was familiar territory for Ganado since they had faced similar styles against Kenedy and Weimar during district play. The semifinal game took place at Woodforest Bank Stadium in Shenandoah, the same venue where Ganado had lost to Timpson the previous year. This time, however, the Indians were determined to make history and finally break through to the state championship game for the first time in school history. Unlike their previous five semifinal appearances, Ganado entered the game as the favorite to win. The key, as it had been all season, was to play sound football and execute their game plan. Midway through the first quarter, Ganado's defense made the game's first big play when two defenders held up Joaquin's fullback and Hayden stripped the ball, recovering it and returning it 58 yards for a touchdown. This gave Ganado an early 7-0 lead. After stopping Joaquin and forcing a punt, the Indians' offense responded swiftly, with Ullman scoring on a 9-yard run to extend the lead to 14-0 by the end of the first quarter. The Indians knew their defense would be challenged and held up well for most of the game. However, Joaquin running back Elijah Hardinson broke free for a 79-yard touchdown run, cutting the lead to 14-8 with 6:12 remaining in the first half. Aside from that long run, Ganado's defense limited Joaquin to just 3.5 yards per carry overall and only 2.5 yards per carry in the second half. Joaquin rushed for 232 yards on 46 attempts but completed only five of 12 passes for 51 yards. Ganado responded quickly to Hardinson's touchdown as Ullman connected with Hayden on a 13-yard touchdown pass, pushing the lead to 21-8 at halftime. With just one half remaining, the Indians were on the cusp of fulfilling their destiny. Last year, Ganado was in a similar position at halftime but ultimately fell short. This year, the team was determined to finish the job. Early in the third quarter, Ganado moved the ball efficiently on their first possession, highlighted by big runs from Logan Bures of 35 and 22 yards. Ullman capped the drive by connecting with Hayden again on an 8-yard touchdown pass, extending the lead to 28-8. Joaquin's offense struggled to gain momentum and quickly punted the ball back. Although Joaquin's defense managed to stop Ganado on a fourth down, the Indians continued to dominate. Later, Logan Bures scored on a 6-yard run with 4:42 left in the game, increasing Ganado's lead to 35-8. With the outcome firmly in their favor, Joaquin scored a late touchdown with only 12 seconds remaining. Ganado's defense held strong, limiting Joaquin to just 104 total yards in the second half, with 57 of those yards coming after the Indians had taken the 35-8 lead. Ullman had an impressive game, passing for 120 yards and two touchdowns while rushing for another. Hayden played a crucial role with a fumble recovery touchdown and two receiving touchdowns on just two catches for 21 yards. Pena led the team in receiving yards with 83 on six receptions, and Logan Bures dominated the ground game with 192 yards and a touchdown. As the final seconds ticked off the clock, excitement erupted for Ganado as they secured their first-ever trip to the state championship game. Tabbed as the preseason #1 team, the hard work had finally paid off. Coach Ervin expressed immense pride in the team for reaching this historic milestone but reminded everyone that their journey was not over. Ullman recalled walking off the field after the previous year's loss to Timpson, when former player Terry Bussey, now at Texas A&M, encouraged him to "go win state next year." That motivation stayed with Ullman, and now the Indians were just one win away from achieving their ultimate goal. A large crowd welcomed the team home past midnight congratulating them on their first state championship berth.

As the Indians set their sights on AT&T Stadium in Arlington for the state championship, they knew there was still one game to be played and won. Their opponent was Stamford, the team standing in the way of Ganado's ultimate goal. Throughout the season, it seemed likely that Stamford would be the final hurdle, as they were consistently ranked in the top 10 and entered the championship game with a perfect 15-0 record. Stamford's senior class was especially dominant, boasting 20 seniors who contributed heavily to their success. Offensively, Stamford was explosive, averaging 47.1 points per game and only being held under 30 points once during the season - a 28-13 semifinal win over Hamilton. This marked Stamford's eighth state appearance, with back-to-back titles in 2012 and 2013. Stamford's offense was led by quarterback Christian Duran, who had thrown for 2,251 yards with 21 touchdowns and only four interceptions entering the game. He was also a strong threat on the ground, rushing for 845 yards and 23 touchdowns. Fullback Kaston Vega was another key player, rushing for 1,728 yards and 31 touchdowns with an impressive 11.7 yards per carry average. Additionally, Cle' Whitfield contributed both rushing (831 yards and 12 touchdowns) and receiving (24 catches for 501 yards and 7 touchdowns) when lined up as a slot receiver. Defensively, Stamford was strong and closely matched with Ganado, as both teams entered the game yielding just over 10 points per game - Stamford with three shutouts and Ganado with five. Ganado came into the contest averaging 45 points scored and 9 points allowed per game.

The excitement and anticipation for the game were palpable. This was Ganado's first-ever appearance in the state championship, and the entire town showed its pride, decorating in maroon and white. The occasion held special meaning for Ed Kacer, an 87-year-old barber who had been a fixture in Ganado since opening his shop in 1957 and had been a loyal Ganado Indian fan for decades. Before the team's departure to Arlington, a window outside his barbershop was painted with an image of Santa Claus and a Christmas list reading, "All I want for Christmas is a State Championship!" The night before the team left, the town gathered at the stadium, where Mr. Kacer gave an inspiring pep talk. He expressed how proud he was of the team for reaching the state championship for the first time in school history and urged them to stay focused and not get overwhelmed by the atmosphere of the big game. "Just go out and play football," he advised. After the game, they could celebrate. Mr. Kacer was also interviewed by *Dave Campbell's Texas Football* during the championship event, capturing his heartfelt pride for the team. For fans unable to attend or watch the game on television, the game was broadcasted live on *96 Country, 96.1 FM* out of El Campo. The broadcast team featured Roland Orsak, known as the voice of the East Bernard Brahmas and a 1983 Ganado alumnus, alongside Ike Kuehn, a 2008 Ganado alumnus and former player who has been the voice of the Ganado Indians, calling games from the press box, since 2019. Kuehn had also called two playoff games from the press box during the team's journey, including the matches against Crawford and Refugio. On the morning of Wednesday, December 18, the final people out of town were reminded to "turn out the light" as they departed for Arlington. That evening, as fans arrived at their hotels, the skies were clear with a beautiful orange sunset, a poignant reminder of LaMarquis Lee, a player who would have been part of the team but tragically lost his life in an auto accident while returning from youth football practice in 2019. Lee's favorite color was orange, and many believed his spirit was watching over the team throughout their entire journey. The Indians honored Lee all season by carrying his #89 jersey to every game. Alongside Lee, many other departed Ganado fans and supporters would have been proud of this historic moment, and it was clear that a higher power had been guiding the team every step of the way.

The moment had finally arrived! On the morning of Thursday, December 19, a crowd of 7,858 gathered for the Class 2A Division I state championship game at AT&T Stadium, with kickoff scheduled for 11:00 a.m. It was the first of three games to be played that day. As fans lined up outside the stadium, I found myself standing among Stamford supporters, and one of them expressed how unfortunate it was that someone had to lose this game. He showed great respect for Ganado, and I shared his sentiments, wishing for a good, fair contest and luck for both teams. Entering the stadium felt surreal - the Ganado Indians had finally made it here after many years of waiting, now just 48 minutes away from winning the school's very first state title. From the start, the Indians were focused and did not let the grandeur of the stadium overwhelm them. Ganado won the coin toss and chose to defer, kicking off to Stamford. The kickoff resulted in a touchback, and Stamford began their first drive at the Ganado 20-yard line. On Stamford's initial possession, Hayden read the receiver's route perfectly, intercepted the pass, and returned it to the Stamford 14-yard line. Taking advantage, Ganado moved the ball downfield with a completion from Ullman to Pena, and Ullman finished the drive with a 6-yard touchdown run. Rodriquez's extra point put Ganado ahead 7-0. Stamford quickly showed why they were worthy opponents by answering with a touchdown of their own. They converted a short fourth down and then scored on a third-and-14 play, with quarterback

Duran connecting with Brayden Jimenez on a 36-yard pass to tie the game 7-7 in the first quarter. Stamford would never lead after this point, although Ganado never held more than a seven-point lead throughout the game. The Indians attempted to respond as Hayden made a crucial third-down catch, followed by another key reception by Pena to reach the red zone. Ullman then scored again on a keeper, but the touchdown was nullified by a Ganado penalty. On fourth-and-21 at Stamford's 24-yard line, Ullman's pass fell incomplete, and Stamford took over on downs. The defense stepped up and forced a Stamford punt, which set the stage for Logan Bures' huge punt return to the Stamford 19-yard line. With excellent field position, Ullman connected with Hayden on a 13-yard touchdown pass, putting Ganado ahead 14-7 midway through the second quarter. Once again, Ganado's defense forced a punt, and the offense advanced to the red zone but was stopped on fourth-and-two at the Stamford 18-yard line, turning the ball over on downs. As the first half ended, Stamford threw a desperate Hail Mary, but Hayden intercepted the pass at the goal line to preserve Ganado's 14-7 halftime lead.

The intensity increased in the second half. Ganado received the kickoff, but on their first offensive snap, Ullman was intercepted by Whitfield, giving Stamford the ball at Ganado's 18-yard line. Stamford capitalized quickly as Vega scored on a fourth-and-goal run from the one-yard line to tie the game 14-14. The Indians showed remarkable resilience on the ensuing possession, driving 98 yards downfield with Ullman throwing a 15-yard touchdown pass to Hayden, regaining the lead at 21-14 late in the third quarter. Once again, the Indians' defense forced a punt, and Logan Bures delivered another impressive punt return, this time to the Stamford 37-yard line. However, Ganado's drive stalled, and they attempted a 33-yard field goal by Rodriquez that sailed wide left. Stamford took over and sustained their drive by converting two crucial fourth downs, including a fourth-and-14 catch by a receiver to the Ganado 6-yard line. Vega scored on the next play from five yards out to tie the game at 21-21 early in the fourth quarter. Ganado then mounted what they hoped would be the game-winning drive. The Indians moved the ball to the Stamford 4-yard line with just two seconds remaining. Rodriquez's field goal attempt narrowly missed, sending the game into overtime tied at 21-21.

In overtime, it was crucial to remain focused and treat the score as if it were 0-0. Ganado began the first overtime from their own 25-yard line.

Ullman made a strong run to the goal line but was ruled down just inches short after a review. Two plays later, Logan Bures powered into the end zone, and Rodriquez's extra point gave Ganado a 28-21 lead. Stamford quickly answered with a 19-yard touchdown pass from Duran to Whitfield, tying the score 28-28 and forcing a second overtime. Neither team scored in the second overtime, and Ganado missed a long field goal attempt, so the game proceeded to a third overtime. In this format, each team would have just one play from the two-yard line, essentially a two-point conversion attempt. Ganado had the first attempt in the third overtime. Ullman threw to Pena in the corner of the end zone; the pass was high, but Pena used his athleticism to leap and make the clutch catch, putting Ganado ahead 30-28. Interestingly, the play was originally designed for Hayden, but Ullman made an excellent throw to Pena. Now Stamford had their chance. They tried to catch Ganado off guard with a trick play, but it failed. Duran handed the ball to Vega, who was unable to find running room and instead lateralled to a receiver. Sablatura disrupted the play, and Ullman leapt to intercept the pass. FINALLY! After 97 years of school history and an intense triple-overtime battle, the Ganado Indians had finally won their first-ever football state championship.

The Ganado crowd and sideline erupted with excitement as the celebration of their hard-fought victory began. The state championship game showcased numerous heroes, with Hayden earning the defensive MVP honors for his two interceptions, while also contributing 103 yards on six receptions and scoring two touchdowns. Hayden set impressive school records during the 2024 season, including 17 touchdowns in a single season and 37 receiving touchdowns over his career. Additionally, he played in 57 consecutive games since his freshman year in 2021 and signed to play at Mary Hardin-Baylor at the next level. Ullman earned the offensive MVP honors by passing for 167 yards and two touchdowns, as well as rushing for 48 yards and one touchdown. He set school records with 48 touchdown passes in the 2024 season and 98 total touchdown passes over his career. It was especially meaningful to see cousins Ullman and Hayden finish their football careers together, both winning MVP honors and leading their team to victory in their senior year - there was no better way to conclude their time as Indians. This win also marked Ganado's 50th playoff victory in school history. The team had entered the 2024 season with a determined goal to win the state championship. Many of the players, especially the seniors, had been working hard since their youth football days, where most had won four or five youth Super Bowl titles. Their dedication finally paid off, and this achievement can never be taken away from them. Early concerns about injuries to Ullman and Logan Bures were alleviated as the team remained healthy when it mattered most, a blessing they credited to divine intervention. This victory was especially meaningful for former Ganado players who had come close but never won a state title, and it brought immense pride to the entire community and fans. It was particularly special for Mr. Kacer, who was present to witness the moment and see his Christmas wish fulfilled. The 2024 state championship game also featured two historic milestones: it was the longest game ever played in Texas high school football history, and Coach Josh Ervin, at just 30 years old, became the youngest coach ever to win a Texas high school football state championship at any level. The Ganado community welcomed home their state champion Indians late that Thursday night, making December 19, 2024, a day that will always be remembered as a "Great Day to be an Indian."

On February 9, 2025 - Super Bowl Sunday - the Ganado Indians football team was honored with a parade through downtown and a ceremony at the stadium to celebrate their historic state championship win. Several dignitaries participated in the ceremony, including Ganado Mayor Clinton Tegeler, Jackson County Commissioner Wayne Bubela, Jackson County Judge Jill Sklar, State Representative and former county sheriff Andy Louderback, 2017 Ganado graduate and former football player Christian Palacios, who now works for U.S. Congressman Michael Cloud, and Superintendent Dr. Jonathan Szymanski. Each delivered speeches recognizing the team's achievement. Judge Sklar officially declared February 9, 2025, as "Ganado Indians Day" on behalf of Jackson County to honor the county's first-ever state football champions. Former sheriff Kelly Janica presented each player with a challenge coin, and a new sign was unveiled inside the stadium that read, "Indian Football State Champions 2024." Coach Ervin expressed gratitude to the community, emphasizing their vital role in the team's success through constant support and assistance.

On April 29, the team received their state championship rings during a well-attended ring ceremony at the Inez Community Center, continuing the celebration. Just one month later, on May 29, the Ganado Maidens softball team added to the town's success by winning their first-ever state title with a dramatic 5-4 victory over Riesel at Red & Charline McCombs Stadium in Austin, claiming the Class 2A Division I state softball championship. These achievements marked the 2024–2025 school year as the most successful in the school's history. A long-held dream had finally come true, and the Ganado school gym now proudly holds two new trophies - one for football and one for softball state championships. The town of Ganado had truly earned its celebration. Finally, the achievement was realized, and it was truly well deserved.

AFTERWORD

In the fall of 2024, leading up to the state championship, 2007 Ganado alumnus Zachary Petrash, also known as Zachary Grant, released a song titled "Ganado" that talks about his roots. The song's opening lyrics, "Where Sundays are Holy, Fridays are too," perfectly capture the spirit of life in Ganado. The town is home to wonderful people and is rooted in a Christian community, but what truly makes Ganado special is the strong support from the community for all kinds of events. It is not just about football - whether it is the band, other sports, church activities, or community functions, everyone in Ganado comes together to help. When someone is in need or when a tragedy or catastrophic event occurs, the community unites to provide support. The football program itself has experienced both highs and lows. There were many years when the program was average and did not achieve much success. However, when the program began to flourish in 1995, the excitement and community support grew, bringing Ganado closer together. Over the last 30 years, there have been lean periods, which are common in a small school like Ganado where talent levels can fluctuate, but the program has always managed to rise again. To all Ganado alumni and those who have played for the Ganado Indians in the past, this state championship is dedicated to you. Winning the first championship is always the hardest, but with the talent and promise evident for the future, it is very likely that more state championships will come. Best wishes and good luck to the future generations of Ganado football!

INDEX

GANADO INDIANS FOOTBALL HISTORY

The Ganado Indians' first football season was in 1928

Undefeated 10-0 seasons (3): 1996, 2010, 2011

Winless seasons (7): 1929, 1930, 1931, 1933, 1953, 1988, 1989

District Championships (17): 1939, 1942, 1943, 1959, 1967, 1969 (Tri), 1978 (Co), 1995 (Tri), 1996, 1999 (Co), 2000, 2001, 2003, 2010, 2011, 2013 and 2024

First playoff team was in 1939 Ganado has advanced to the playoffs 27 times with a 50-24-1 playoff record

Playoff Appearances: 1939, 1942, 1943, 1959, 1967, 1982, 1996, 1997, 1998, 1999, 2000, 2001, 2002, 2003, 2005, 2008, 2009, 2010, 2011, 2012, 2013, 2019, 2020, 2021, 2022, 2023 and 2024

Bi-District Finalist: 1939, 1942, 1943, 1959, 1967, 1982

Area Finalist: 1997, 2000, 2002, 2005, 2012

Regional Finalist: 1999, 2010, 2011, 2013, 2020, 2021, 2022

Quarterfinalist: 1998, 2003, 2019

Semifinalist: 1996, 2001, 2008, 2009, 2023

State Finals: 2024

State Champions: 2024

GANADO INDIANS FOOTBALL CHRONOLOGICAL HISTORY

Year	Record	Head Coach	Season Outcome
1928	1-4	W.B. Connell	No Playoffs
1929	0-4	W.B. Connell	No Playoffs
1930	0-7	Mac McFarland	No Playoffs
1931	0-8	Mac McFarland	No Playoffs
1932	1-7-1	J.C. Tomlinson	No Playoffs
1933	0-1	Fred Walker	No Playoffs
1934	2-4-3	Fred Walker	No Playoffs
1935	8-1	Fred Walker	No Playoffs
1936	8-2	John Ledbetter	No Playoffs
1937	4-5	W.T. Varnell	No Playoffs
1938	2-5-1	W.T. Varnell	No Playoffs
1939	8-3-1	W.T. Varnell	District Champion/Bi-District Finalist
1940	3-6	W.T. Varnell	No Playoffs
1941	3-5-2	W.T. Varnell	No Playoffs
1942	7-1-2	Jack Compton	District Champion/Bi-District Finalist
1943	3-6	Jack Compton	District Champion/Bi-District Finalist
1944	4-3-3	C.D. Winstead	No Playoffs
1945	3-5	C.D. Winstead	No Playoffs
1946	1-7	A.H. Cheek	No Playoffs
1947	6-3-1	Tom Talley	No Playoffs
1948	5-4-1	Tom Talley	No Playoffs
1949	3-6-1	Tom Talley	No Playoffs
1950	7-3	Tom Talley	No Playoffs
1951	6-4	Tom Talley	No Playoffs
1952	3-7	Tom Talley	No Playoffs
1953	0-10	Tom Talley	No Playoffs
1954	4-4-2	Paul Stewart	No Playoffs
1955	5-4-1	Frank Hafernick	No Playoffs
1956	6-4	Frank Hafernick	No Playoffs
1957	4-5-1	Frank Hafernick	No Playoffs
1958	3-6-1	Frank Hafernick	No Playoffs
1959	6-3-2	Leo Chafin	District Champion/Bi-District Finalist
1960	3-7	Leo Chafin	No Playoffs
1961	8-2	Leo Chafin	No Playoffs
1962	1-9	Gene Smith	No Playoffs
1963	2-8	Gene Smith	No Playoffs
1964	3-7	Gene Smith	No Playoffs
1965	1-9	Paul Hatem	No Playoffs

Year	Record	Coach	Playoffs
1966	6-4	Paul Hatem	No Playoffs
1967	8-3	Bob Caskey	District Champion/Bi-District Finalist
1968	6-2-2	Bob Caskey	No Playoffs
1969	9-1	Bob Caskey	Tri-District Champion/No Playoffs
1970	7-3	Jim Allen	No Playoffs
1971	4-5-1	Jim Allen	No Playoffs
1972	3-6	Jim Allen	No Playoffs
1973	0-8-2	Buddy Kellar	No Playoffs
1974	3-7	Buddy Kellar	No Playoffs
1975	1-9	Bill Kyle	No Playoffs
1976	5-5	Bill Kyle	No Playoffs
1977	6-4	Bill Kyle	No Playoffs
1978	6-4	Bill Kyle	Co-District Champion/ No Playoffs
1979	5-5	Bill Kyle	No Playoffs
1980	6-4	Rusty Herridge	No Playoffs
1981	7-3	Rusty Herridge	No Playoffs
1982	7-4	Tom Jones	Bi-District Finalist
1983	7-2-1	Tom Jones	No Playoffs
1984	7-3	Tom Jones	No Playoffs
1985	1-8-1	Tom Jones	No Playoffs
1986	3-7	Tom Jones	No Playoffs
1987	1-9	Tom Jones	No Playoffs
1988	0-9	Ralph Diaz	No Playoffs
1989	0-10	Ralph Diaz	No Playoffs
1990	5-5	Tucker Rackley	No Playoffs
1991	3-6-1	Tucker Rackley	No Playoffs
1992	5-5	Tucker Rackley	No Playoffs
1993	4-6	Tucker Rackley	No Playoffs
1994	4-6	Tucker Rackley	No Playoffs
1995	9-1	Monte Althaus	Tri-District Champion/No Playoffs
1996	14-1	Monte Althaus	District Champion/Semifinalist
1997	10-2	Monte Althaus	Area Finalist
1998	11-3	Monte Althaus	Quarterfinalist
1999	8-5	Monte Althaus	District Co-Champion/Regional Finalist
2000	9-3	Monte Althaus	District Champion/Area Finalist
2001	11-3	Keith Wright	District Champion/Semifinalist
2002	9-3	Keith Wright	Area Finalist
2003	12-2	Keith Wright	District Champion/Quarterfinalist
2004	5-5	Mark Byrd	No Playoffs
2005	6-5	Mark Byrd	Area Finalist
2006	1-9	Mike Rabe	No Playoffs

Year	Record	Coach	Playoffs
2007	3-7	Mike Rabe	No Playoffs
2008	9-4	Mike Rabe	Semifinalist
2009	9-5	Mike Rabe	Semifinalist
2010	11-1	Jimmy Thompson	District Champion/Regional Finalist
2011	11-1	Jimmy Thompson	District Champion/Regional Finalist
2012	8-4	Jimmy Thompson	Area Finalist
2013	9-3	Jimmy Thompson	District Champion/Regional Finalist
2014	3-7	Jim Bird	No Playoffs
2015	3-7	Keith Wright	No Playoffs
2016	5-5	Keith Wright	No Playoffs
2017	2-7	Keith Wright (0-2), Johny Lesak (2-5)	No Playoffs
2018	4-6	Brent Bennett	No Playoffs
2019	10-4	Brent Bennett	Quarterfinalist
2020	6-5	Brent Bennett	Regional Finalist
2021	7-6	Brent Bennett	Regional Finalist
2022	9-4	Josh Ervin	Regional Finalist
2023	12-3	Josh Ervin	Semifinalist
2024	15-1	Josh Ervin	District Champion/State Champions

GANADO INDIANS FOOTBALL PLAYOFF HISTORY

1939
Bi-District, Schulenburg, 13-13, Tie

1942
Bi-District, Sugar Land, 12-7, Won

1943
Bi-District, Bastrop, 13-31, Loss

1959
Bi-District, Katy, 14-38, Loss

1967
Bi-District, Sweeny, 6-28, Loss

1982
Bi-District, Shiner, 24-27, Loss

1996
Bi-District, Weimar, 34-19, Won
Area, Rogers, 35-7, Won
Regional, Freer, 21-3, Won
Quarterfinal, Refugio, 6-0, Won
Semifinal, Groveton, 6-14, Lost

1997
Bi-District, Schulenburg, 28-21, Won
Area, Crawford, 28-29, Lost

1998
Bi-District, Yorktown, 38-13, Won
Area, Winters, 31-6, Won
Regional, Poth, 14-7, Won
Quarterfinal, Goldthwaite, 19-22, Lost

1999

Bi-District, Weimar, 49-14, Won
Area, Little River Academy, 15-10, Won
Regional, Refugio, 7-54, Lost

2000
Bi-District, East Bernard, 7-0, Won
Area, Rogers, 6-20, Lost

2001
Bi-District, Brazos, 35-28, Won
Area, Comfort, 49-17, Won
Regional, Stockdale, 48-6, Won
Quarterfinal, Refugio, 7-0, Won
Semifinal, Garrison, 9-21, Lost

2002
Bi-District, East Bernard, 20-7, Won
Area, Rogers, 12-16, Lost

2003
Bi-District, Hitchcock, 23-20, Won
Area, Junction, 16-3, Won
Regional, Poth, 48-6, Won
Quarterfinal, Rogers, 17-29, Lost

2005
Bi-District, Refugio, 7-6, Won
Area, Skidmore-Tynan, 13-28, Lost

2008
Bi-District, BYE
Area, Chilton, 21-6, Won
Regional, Mason, 23-14, Won
Quarterfinal, Falls City, 14-7, Won
Semifinal, Cayuga, 7-42, Lost

2009
Bi-District, BYE
Area, Bartlett, 36-12, Won
Regional, La Pryor, 29-28, Won

Quarterfinal, Falls City, 24-21, Won
Semifinal, Cayuga, 19-41, Lost

2010
Bi-District, BYE
Area, Winters, 41-6, Won
Regional, Goldthwaite, 14-21, Lost

2011
Bi-District, BYE
Area, Goldthwaite, 28-0, Won
Regional, Mason, 0-7, Lost

2012
Bi-District, Ben Bolt, 55-35, Won
Area, Weimar, 21-34, Lost

2013
Bi-District, BYE
Area, Brackettville, 37-14, Won
Regional, Thorndale, 17-21, Lost

2019
Bi-District, Brady, 49-25, Won
Area, Corpus Christi London, 23-16, Won
Regional, Poth, 28-14, Won
Quarterfinal, East Bernard, 10-30, Lost

2020
Bi-District, Johnson City, 55-14, Won
Area, Three Rivers, 55-0, Won
Regional, Refugio, 2-54, Lost

2021
Bi-District, Ozona, 68-18, Won
Area, La Villa, 60-23, Won
Regional, Refugio, 7-54, Lost

2022

Bi-District, La Villa, 68-6, Won
Area, Thorndale, 66-12, Won
Regional, Refugio, 7-53, Lost

2023
Bi-District, Santa Maria, 55-6, Won
Area, Mason, 37-12, Won
Regional, Holland, 50-22, Won
Quarterfinal, Refugio, 41-12, Won
Semifinal, Timpson, 21-35, Lost

2024
Bi-District, Skidmore-Tynan, 75-15, Won
Area, Crawford, 59-0, Won
Regional, Refugio, 14-6, Won
Quarterfinal, Marlin, 41-14, Won
Semifinal, Joaquin, 35-14, Won
State, Stamford, 30-28 (3OT), Won

GANADO INDIANS FOOTBALL STAT LEADERS

Passing

Most Passing Yards in a Season: Bryce Ullman; 3,111 yards; 2023
Most Passing Touchdowns in a Season: Bryce Ullman, 48 touchdowns, 2024
Most Passing Yards in a Game: Bryce Ullman, 467 yards, 2024 vs. Schulenburg
Most Passing Touchdowns in a Game: (Tied) 7, Bryce Ullman, 2024 vs. Flatonia, Schulenburg and Bloomington; Kyle Bures-Guerrero, 2021 vs. Ozona
Most Passing Yards in a Career: Kyle Bures-Guerrero; 7,696 yards; 2019-2022
Most Passing Touchdowns in a Career: Bryce Ullman, 98 touchdowns, 2022-2024

Rushing

Most Rushing Yards in a Season: Matthew Bures; 2,395 yards; 2001
Most Rushing Touchdowns in a Season: Matthew Bures, 37 touchdowns, 2001
Most Rushing Yards in a Career: Josh Labay; 5,799 yards; 2008-2011
Most Rushing Touchdowns in a Career: Kyle Bures-Guerrero, 98 touchdowns, 2019-2022

Receiving

Most Receiving Yards in a Season: Riley Hurt; 1,015 yards; 2021
Most Receiving Touchdowns in a Season: Cain Hayden, 17 touchdowns, 2024
Most Receiving Yards in a Career: Riley Hurt; 3,038 yards; 2018-2021
Most Receiving Touchdowns in a Career: Cain Hayden, 37 touchdowns, 2021-2024

RESOURCES

The Victoria Advocate

Jackson County Herald Tribune

Lone Star Gridiron

texashighschoolfootballhistory.com

pigskinprep.com

MaxPreps

Dave Campbell's Texas Football

Book Cover: Chris Doelle

Photos

1959 District Champion/Bi-District Finalist

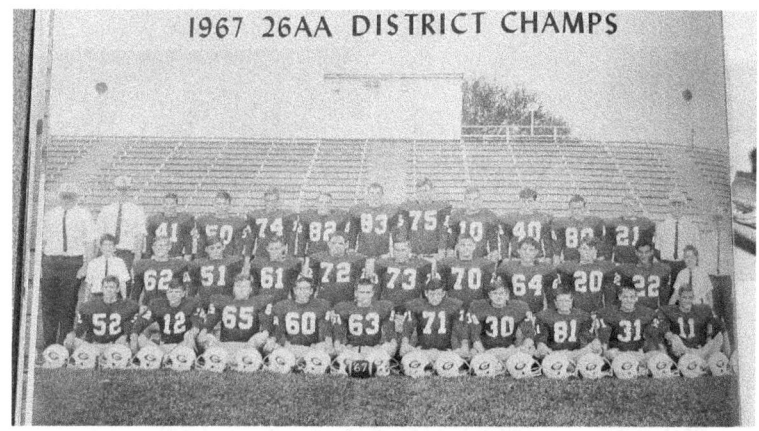

1967 District Champion/Bi-District Finalist

1969 Tri-District Champion/No Playoffs

THE MIGHTY INDIANS

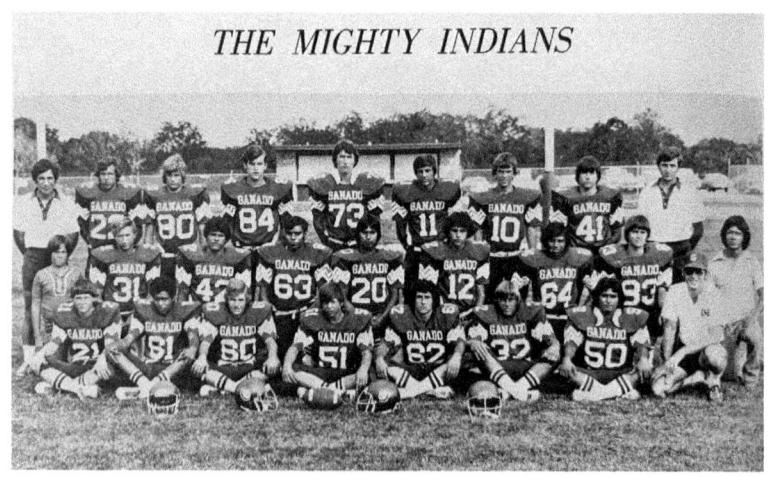

1978 Co-District Champion/ No Playoffs

1982 Bi-District Finalist

1995 Tri-District Champion/No Playoffs

1996 District Champion/Semifinalist

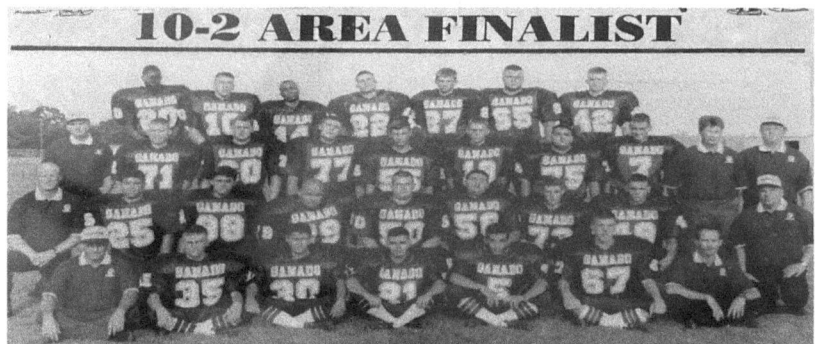

1997 Area Finalist

1998 Quarterfinalist

1999 District Co-Champion/Regional Finalist

2000 District Champion/Area Finalist

2001 District Champion/Semifinalist

2002 Area Finalist

2003 District Champion/Quarterfinalist

2005 Area Finalist

2008 Semifinalist

2009 Semifinalist

2010 District Champion/Regional Finalist

2011 District Champion/Regional Finalist

2012 Area Finalist

2013 District Champion/Regional Finalist

2019 Quarterfinalist

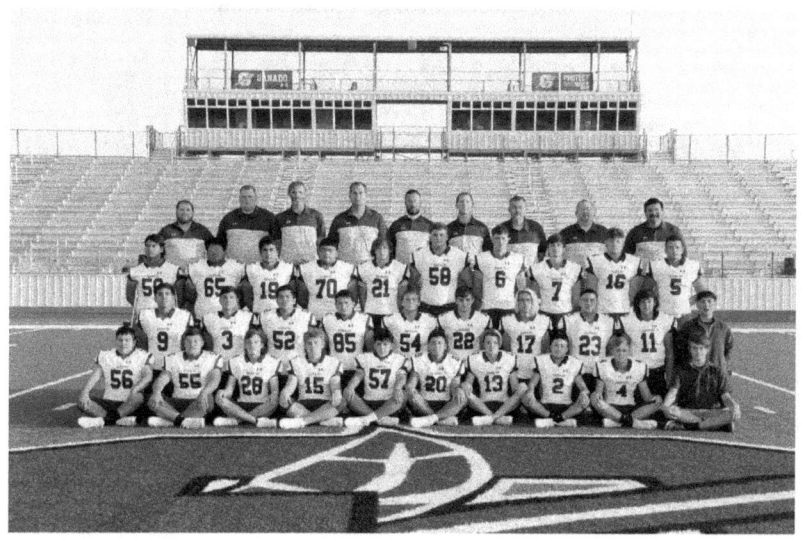

2020 Regional Finalist

2021 Regional Finalist

2022 Regional Finalist

2023 Semifinalist

2024 District Champion/State Champions

Authors Page

Clint Hensley has been a devoted historian and supporter of Ganado High School athletics since attending his first Indians football game in 1993. A 2001 Ganado graduate, Clint has spent decades compiling team histories, statistics, and archives, preserving the legacy of his alma mater's sports programs. His passion for the game and dedication to documenting its stories helped bring this book to life, capturing the journey from the program's humble beginnings to its first-ever state football championship. When he's not chronicling Ganado's athletic history, Clint works in the Environmental department at Formosa Plastics and enjoys life with his wife, Laura, in Morales, Texas.

Chris Doelle is founder and Managing Partner of Lone Star Gridiron (http://www.lonestargridiron.com), regarded by many as the statewide leader in news and information about Texas High School Football. For the past 21 years, under his guidance, LSG has prided itself on providing only positive stories about "the greatest sport in the greatest state." Throughout that entire run, Chris has hosted and produced coach interview shows, amassing thousands of episodes that capture the voices, strategies, and spirit of Texas high school football. His relationships with the UIL, THSCA, and THSADA have grown because of the shared belief in the power and importance of this game and these coaches. From his days playing 2A Texas football, officiating, coaching, founding LSG, and authoring numerous books, Chris has been on the frontlines of sharing these stories. In addition to his passion for this sport, he is Director of Fresh Media Works, a marketing and publishing company.

Also by Clint Hensley

This, his passion project, is his first publication.

Also by Chris Doelle

Rocket Man: The Story of D.W. Rutledge and the Judson High School Football Dynasty

Valley Ball: The Heart & History of Rio Grande Valley Football

All I Need to Know I Learned from My High School Football Coach

Student-Athlete Social Media Playbook: What Every Coach & Athletic Director Needs to Know About Social Media

Escaping a Manipulative Relationship: A step-by-step guide to leaving a controlling sociopath and becoming who you are destined to be.

Lame Jokes Rule - Volume 1: 500 eye-rolling jokes, puns, guffaws, gut-busters and groaners

Lame Jokes Rule - Volume 2: 500 eye-rolling jokes, puns, guffaws, gut-busters and groaners

Football Legends - a football board game that allows you to play real high school, college and professional football teams against each other based on their real stats. Any team, any year

Basketball Legends - a basketball board game that allows you to play real high school, college and professional football teams against each other based on their real stats. Men's & Women's

www.ingramcontent.com/pod-product-compliance
Lightning Source LLC
Chambersburg PA
CBHW070635160426
43194CB00009B/1473